WRITING THE CLASSICAL WAY I: ANCIENT

STUDENT BOOK

3rd Edition

EILEEN CUNNINGHAM

Cover image photographer: Nicola Belopitov
Date created: August 16, 2015

Text Copyright © 2020 Eileen Cunningham
All Rights Reserved
ISBN-13: 979-8663727662

To the community of the

Classical School of Wichita

Table of Contents

Fable 1
Narrative 13
Description 51
Writing a Good Paragraph 71
Outlining 103
Proverb 113
Chreia 131
Refutation 147
Confirmation 173
Commonplace 201
Encomium 213
Invective 233
Comparison 247
Speech-in-Character 265
Thesis 281
Legislation 301

Image Attribution I-1
Endnotes E-1

INTRODUCTION

Pronunciation of *progymnasmata*

Sometimes people pronounce *progymnasmata* as if the syllable *-gym-* were pronounced as the name *Jim*. However, the word *progymnasmata* originated in ancient Greece, and Greek does not have the sound *j* [dʒ]. Further, in Greek, the vowel spelled with the letter *y* was pronounced as *oo*, as in our word *doom*. Thus, the best English rendering would be /prō-gūm-NÄZ- mə-tə /.

History of the Progymnasmata

Writing the Classical Way introduces learners to the various elements of the progymnasmata, which are the preliminary exercises that prepare learners for full-blown rhetoric classes. The origins of the progymnasmata are unknown, although the earliest mention of them can be found in a rhetorical handbook dated to the fourth century BC. By the first century AD, separate handbooks for the progymnasmata were being written and circulated. Perhaps the most famous handbooks were written by the rhetorician Hermogenes of Tarsus in the second century AD, the great orator Aphthonius the Sophist in the fourth century AD, and the teacher Nicolaus the Sophist in the fifth century AD.[1] They generally included the following fourteen exercises:

Fable (*Mythos*)	Commonplace (*Koinos topos*)
Narrative (*Diêgêma*)	Encomium (*Enkōmion*)
Description (*Ekphrasis*)	Invective (*Psogos*)
Proverb (*Gnōmê*)	Comparison (*Synkrisis*)
Anecdote (*Chreia*)	Speech in Character (*Prosōpopoeia*)
Refutation (*Anaskeuê*)	Thesis (*Thesis*)
Confirmation (*Kataskeuê*)	Legislation (*Nomos*)

A Note to Teachers

Writing the Classical Way has three volumes. Book I, which is recommended for seventh graders, covers the Ancient period (classical Greece and Rome, plus the periods comprising the Old and New Testaments). Book II, recommended for eighth graders, covers the Medieval period with some selections as well from the Early Modern period. Book III, still in production, is recommended for 9th graders and covers the Modern period. Although the books do become incrementally more difficult, one may safely begin with any of the books in order to coordinate with the historical period the student is studying.

The books also include sections on standard paragraph organization and outlining. Although the progymnasmata should be taught in order, these bonus chapters may be taught at the teacher's discretion.

Each chapter that introduces a progymnasmata exercise is designed to accommodate the three stages of the *trivium*: grammar stage, logic stage, and rhetoric stage. At the beginning of each chapter (and in other segments within each chapter), there are *grammar stage* materials in which the students learn the basic approaches to the topic at hand, such as "Approaches to Encomium." *Logic stage* exercises are those labeled as THINK IT THROUGH as well as analyses of model paragraphs and numbered exercises on which students can cut their teeth before writing the major essay(s) in the chapter. Each chapter culminates in a *rhetoric stage* composition in which students can employ their new skills in creative and, it is hoped, thought-provoking essays. These are labeled with the heading *Now You Try It*. Of course, teachers are always free to provide their own essay topics.

Please note that when public domain translations from earlier centuries are used, we have on occasion modified punctuation and spelling to accord with today's standards. In addition to the ancient models, we have included eloquent writings and speeches from more recent authors so that students can see exemplary discourse created in their own language. All quotations from the Bible are from the English Standard Version unless otherwise indicated.

Acknowledgements

I wish to thank the Classical School of Wichita's board, administration, faculty, parents, and students for supporting this project. Their feedback has improved the materials greatly. I also wish to acknowledge the invaluable help of A. Crist and E. Burd for their assistance in the production of the manuscript and offer a special thank you as well to Amy Alexander Carmichael, whose writing, translating, and editing were foundational to Lochinvar Press. I further wish to express my deepest appreciation for the patience, encouragement, and support (as well as ice cream) from my husband, Patric. One goal of this book is to ensure that the quality of the materials honors our Lord and Savior, Jesus Christ: "Whatever you do, work heartily, as for the Lord and not for men, knowing that from the Lord you will receive the inheritance as your reward. You are serving the Lord Christ" (Colossians 3:23–24).

FABLE

Chapter 1

Introduction

> One day, the Hare was boasting that he was faster than any other animal. To prove his point, he challenged all the other animals to a race, but only the Tortoise accepted. Thinking that he would beat the Tortoise easily, the Hare lay down for a nap. However, the Hare slept too long and woke up to find that the Tortoise had already crossed the finish line.
>
> *Moral:* Slow and steady wins the race.

A tale like that of the tortoise and the hare is what we call a *fable*. A fable is a short story with a moral. The world's most famous author of fables is Aesop, a Greek slave, though many other peoples and cultures have also told fables. Aesop's fables show the value of true friendship ("The Travelers and the Bear"), the importance of hard work ("The Ant and the Grasshopper"), and the foolishness of wanting what you do not have ("The Dog and the Shadow").

Aesop
c. 620 – 564 BC

In ancient Greece and Rome, parents and nurses told these fables to their children, much like we read bedtime stories today. By the time children entered school, they were very familiar with the tales of Aesop. Because children knew the fables so well, their first writing exercise often was retelling these fables. As the students grew up, they learned to use fables to be persuasive as an adult.

Since a fable is a humorous and memorable way of making a point, Greek and Roman orators used fables most frequently in legislative speeches, when they wished to give advice about some contemplated action. For example, the Roman senator Menenius Agrippa (sixth century B.C.) once had to persuade the plebeians to stop demanding grain from the patricians. Menenius told a fable about the human body, saying that the parts of the body began to resent the stomach, because it ate all the food and seemed to have no practical use. The parts of the body decided to starve the stomach into submission, but they found that they, too, were starving. They then realized that the stomach was an important part of the body. The moral, said Menenius, was that the plebeians were the parts of the body, and they could not live without the patricians (the stomach). Won over by his fable, the plebeians agreed to stop their rebellion.

Fables, however, were not just used by the Greeks and Romans. Hebrew writers often used fables, too. For example, in Judges 9, Gideon's son Jotham uses the fable of the bramble to prove that Abimelech should not be made king. Jesus used many fables as well, though his fables are normally called *parables*. Some examples are the parables of the wedding feast, the lost sheep, and the persistent widow.

Nor are fables confined to the ancient world. In the twelfth century AD, Geoffrey Chaucer wrote the *Canterbury Tales*. One of these, the "Nun's Priest's Tale," is a fable that covers over 600 lines of poetry. In this tale, the proud rooster Chanticleer dreams of his death by a fox. Chanticleer is frightened by his dreams, but his wife flatters him into believing that the dream will not come true. However, Chanticleer *is* later captured by a fox, who prevents Chanticleer's retreat by flattering him, then capturing him when his guard is down. But the rooster, having learned his lesson, uses flattery of the fox to his own advantage. Besides teaching that flattery should never be trusted, the "Nun's Priest's Tale" is an entertaining and humorous story in its own right and has been retold many times.

Today, a speaker might use a fable as a humorous way of making a point without being overbearing. Children's stories sometimes use the format of a fable to teach lessons to the very young. One example is Beatrix Potter's illustrated fable, "The Tale of Peter Rabbit," written in 1902. In whatever form the fable appears, it is an imaginative and fun way to teach the importance of right behavior.

Definition and Purpose of a Fable

The fable is a short story with a moral. Fables are used to teach a moral lesson or to give advice on ethical or advantageous behavior. A fable might be used by:

- the poet or creative writer: to make his story more interesting.
- the educator: to teach a moral lesson to children.
- the policy maker: to convince people to behave a certain way.

- the pastor and ethicist: to make a point gently.

The fable is usually followed by a simple statement of the lesson to be learned, which is called its *moral*. Though commonly placed at the end of the story, it can also be placed before the story, which makes the moral very clear. In rare cases, the moral is omitted entirely and must be grasped intuitively.

THINK IT THROUGH: *Green Eggs and Ham* is a popular children's story by Dr. Seuss. In this story, Sam-I-Am tries to get the main character to eat green eggs and ham, but he refuses for most of the book. What happens when he finally eats the food? What is the lesson to be learned?

Parables in the Bible

Both the Old and the New Testament contain fable-like narratives which are called *parables*. The word *parable* is derived from the Greek word *parabolē* (pä-RÄ-bə-lē), which means "comparison," "illustration," or "analogy." As Christianity spread throughout Europe, the word took on the Latin sense of *allegory*, which is a narrative with a "hidden" meaning, usually about morality, religion, or politics.

In Proverbs 1:5-6, Solomon wrote:

> Let the wise hear and increase in learning,
>   and the one who understands obtain guidance,
> to understand a proverb and a saying,
>   the words of the wise and their riddles.

In Proverbs 25:2, he wrote:

> It is the glory of God to conceal things,
>   but the glory of kings is to search things out.

Indeed, the Bible does present some teachings concealed, or hidden, in such literary styles as proverbs, riddles, and parables. Parables do not always include an explicit moral stated at the beginning or end of the narrative, but they do, nevertheless, have a lesson.

THINK IT THROUGH: What is the lesson (or moral) of the Parable of the Prodigal Son in Luke 15:11-32?

Characters in a Fable

Characters in a fable may be (a) humans, (b) animals, (c) elements of nature, (d) manufactured objects, (e) gods/goddesses, or (f) a mixture of these. Instead of having names such as *Julius* or *Hank*, the characters in a fable have names like "the Hare," "the Crow, or "the Farmer." Notice, however, that these normally common nouns are capitalized so that the word has the effect of a proper noun.

Writers of fables use a technique called *personification*, which means that they give characteristics of a person to animals, elements of nature, and manufactured objects. That is to say, they have personality traits (such as the boastfulness of the Hare), and they speak.

Expanding a Fable

In the ancient world, since students normally entered school already familiar with many fables, the educators would often ask them to expand a fable to make it more interesting. To expand a fable, one adds dialogue and description, especially that which adds to the personality of a character.

For example, the opening sentence of "The Tortoise and the Hare" in its original form is, "One day, the Hare was boasting that he was faster than any other animal." One could expand this with dialogue and description that show the personality of the Hare, thus:

> One fine afternoon, the Hare was feeling particularly self-satisfied and began speaking to the other animals nearby. "I am the fastest animal anywhere. I can beat *you*," he said, pointing to the Squirrel, "and *you*," he said, pointing to the Groundhog, "and I can certainly beat *you*," he said, pointing to the Tortoise with a laugh.

EXERCISE 1.1: Analyzing an Expanded Fable

Directions: Answer each question regarding the expansion of "The Tortoise and the Hare."

1. How does the phrase *one day* in the original change in the expansion?

2. How does the dialogue show the Hare's boastfulness?

3. What details are added?

4. How do the new details enhance the story?

EXERCISE 1.2: Analyzing a Fable

Directions: Read the fables below and answer the questions that follow.

The Crow and the Pitcher

In a spell of dry weather, when the Birds could find very little to drink, a thirsty Crow found a pitcher with a little water in it. But the pitcher was high and had a narrow neck, and no matter how he tried, the Crow could not reach the water. The poor thing felt as if he must die of thirst.

Then an idea came to him. Picking up some small pebbles, he dropped them into the pitcher one by one. With each pebble the water rose a little higher until at last it was near enough so he could drink.

Moral: In a pinch a good use of our wits may help us out.[2]

Questions:

1. In one or two sentences, summarize the story of "The Crow and the Pitcher."

2. What kind of characters are in this story?

3. What is the moral of this fable? Where is it located?

EXERCISE 1.3: Analyzing a Parable of Jesus

The Good Samaritan

But he [a lawyer], desiring to justify himself, said to Jesus, "And who is my neighbor?" Jesus replied, "A man was going down from Jerusalem to Jericho, and he fell among robbers, who stripped him and beat him and departed, leaving him half dead. Now by chance a priest was going down that road, and when he saw him he passed by on the other side. So likewise a Levite, when he came to the place and saw him, passed by on the other side. But a Samaritan, as he journeyed, came to where he was, and when he saw him, he had compassion. He went to him and bound up his wounds, pouring on oil and wine. Then he set him on his own animal and brought him to an inn and took care of him. And the next day he took out two denarii and gave them to the innkeeper, saying, 'Take care of him, and whatever more you spend, I will repay you when I come back.' Which of these three, do you think, proved to be a neighbor to the man who fell among the robbers?" He said,

"The one who showed him mercy." And Jesus said to him, "You go, and do likewise" (Luke 10:29-37).

1. In one or two sentences, summarize the parable of "The Good Samaritan."

2. At the inn, what does the dialogue of the Samaritan show about his character?

3. What is the moral of this parable? Where is it located?

EXERCISE 1.4: Analyzing an Expanded Fable

Directions: Read the following two versions of the same fable. The second version has been expanded with dialogue and description. After reading, answer the questions.

Dirt Cheap

Hermes wanted to find out how highly men valued him, and taking the shape of a human being, he went to a sculptor's workshop. On seeing a statue of Zeus he inquired its price. "A drachma," the man said. With a laugh Hermes went on to ask the same question about one representing Hera and was told that it was more expensive than the other. At length he noticed a statue of himself. Thinking that his dual character as the messenger of Zeus and the God of Gain must cause him to be held in high esteem by mankind, he asked: "And how much is the Hermes?" "Oh," replied the sculptor, "if you buy the other two, I'll throw him in for nothing."[3]

Hermes

Moral: Do not be conceited, for the truth about you will be revealed.

Hermes and the Sculptor

One fine summer's day, the god Hermes decided to see how highly men valued him. Disguising himself as a handsome young man, he strolled into the workshop of the most famous sculptor in Athens. After carelessly examining a statue of Zeus, Hermes asked the sculptor, "How much do you want for Zeus?"

"A drachma," said the man.

Chuckling to himself, Hermes picked up a statuette of Hera. "And how much does this little statue cost?" he inquired.

"Two drachmas," the sculptor answered.

After looking through the entire shop, Hermes finally spotted a statue of himself tucked away in a dusty corner. The statue was twice as big as the statue of Zeus! Thinking that men must value him greatly because he was the messenger of both Zeus and the God of Gain, Hermes confidently asserted, "That fine statue of Hermes must be worth a great deal of money."

"Oh," replied the sculptor, "if you buy the other two, I'll throw him in for nothing."

Moral: Do not be conceited, for the truth about you will be revealed.

1. In one or two sentences, summarize the fable "Dirt Cheap."

2. What is the moral of "Dirt Cheap"?

3. How was the phrase "taking the shape of a human being" made more descriptive in the expanded version?

4. What dialogue was added in the expanded version?

5. How does the expansion make the fable more interesting?

EXERCISE 1.5: Expanding a Fable (Class Exercise)

<u>Directions</u>: Project the following fable on the board. As a class, indicate places where dialogue and description could be added. Then, have one class member serve as a scribe to write on the board an expanded fable dictated by the class members.

The Wind and the Sun

A dispute once arose between the Wind and the Sun, which was the stronger of the two, and they agreed to put the point upon this issue, that whichever soonest made a traveler take off his cloak, should be accounted the more powerful. The Wind began and blew with all his might and main a blast, cold and fierce as a Thracian storm; but the stronger he blew, the closer the traveler wrapped his cloak around him and the tighter he grasped it with his hands. Then broke out the Sun: with his welcome beams he dispersed the vapor and the cold; the traveler felt the genial warmth, and as the Sun shone brighter and brighter, he sat down, overcome with the heat, and cast his cloak on the ground.

Thus, the Sun was declared the conqueror; and it has ever been deemed that persuasion is better than force; and that the sunshine of a kind and gentle manner will sooner lay open a poor man's heart than all the threatenings and force of blustering authority.[4]

Now You Try It

Chapter 1 Essay
Expanding a Fable

Specifications

1. The purpose of this assignment is to demonstrate that you can expand a fable with dialogue and descriptive detail in order to entertain and edify the young.

2. Begin by reading "The Fox and the Crow," which appears below. As you read, pay attention to the personality of each character.

3. Expand the fable by adding dialogue and descriptive detail, being sure to remain consistent with the personality established in the original.

4. Follow your teacher's instructions regarding preparation of the manuscript.

The Fox and the Crow

A Crow was sitting on a branch of a tree with a piece of cheese in her beak when a Fox observed her and set his wits to work to discover a way of getting the cheese. Coming and standing under the tree, he looked up and made some lovely compliments about the Crow as if to himself, but all the while knowing she would hear and be flattered. Lastly, he wondered aloud if she could also sing beautifully. And, just as the Fox had planned, the Crow was hugely flattered by what she heard, and just to show the Fox that she could sing beautifully, she gave a loud caw. Down came the cheese, of course, and the Fox, snatching it up, told the Crow she had beauty, but not wits.[5]

Expanding a Fable
Pre-Writing Activity

What details can you add to show what kind of day it was when this happened?	
What adjectives might you use to describe the Crow?	
What adjectives might you use to describe the Fox?	
What kind of tree is it?	
What is a better noun than *piece* in the phrase "*piece* of cheese"?	
What compliment(s) might you imagine the Fox saying under his breath?	
How will the reader know the Crow feels flattered? What gestures might she make?	
What dialogue could you write that shows the Fox's attitude when he talks to the Crow at the end?	

NARRATIVE

Chapter 2

Introduction

Have you ever been on the verge of dozing off in a class or a church service when, through the fog, you hear the speaker say something like, "It was a little bit like the third game in the World Series last week"? All of a sudden, you perk up and listen to what the speaker has to say. Everyone loves a good story, and the Greeks knew that stories were primary to the communication of ideas.

Indeed, the very first works of literature on record in western civilization, Homer's *Iliad* and *Odyssey*, were first and foremost great stories, and the narrative tradition of the Hebrew writers also has spellbinding power as men are cast into the sea, thrown among lions, and beheaded for the satisfaction of a dancing girl. In short, narrative has a strong appeal to listeners and readers.

Definition and Purposes of Narrative

Aphthonius the Sophist, a Greek scholar of the fourth century AD, defined Narrative as "an exposition of an action that has happened or [is] as though it had happened,"[6] the former being history, the latter fiction (or drama, the primary genre of fictional writing of the period).

The early writers also distinguished between *narrative (diêgêma)* and narration *(diêgêsis)*. As Hermogenes explained, a *narrative (diêgêma)* is "concerned with one thing" and narration *(diêgêsis)* "with many."[7] To be specific, the entire *History* of Thucydides as an example of narrative *(diêgêma)* while one episode in the *History*, such as that of the boar of Mysia, which appears below, would be deemed narration *(diêgêsis)*.

The purposes of narrative, as indicated by the early teachers of rhetoric, included the following:

- As proof of an argument in an oration
- As the summary of a crime in a trial in a court of law

- As the summary of claims to be refuted or confirmed
- As proof of a person's character
- As the conveyance of truth regarding historical events
- As entertainment, as in epic poetry or drama (and, by inference, in subsequent time periods in short stories and novels)

Six Elements of the Narrative

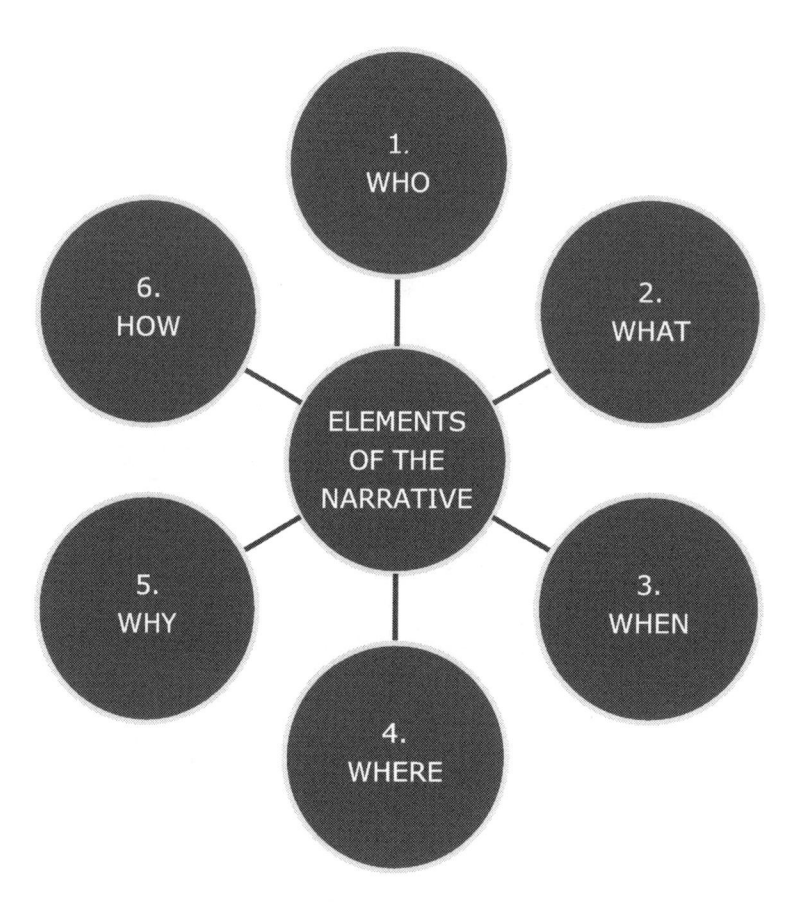

```
        1. WHO
6. HOW          2. WHAT
    ELEMENTS OF THE NARRATIVE
5. WHY          3. WHEN
        4. WHERE
```

A narrative has six elements, each of which is explained in the chart on the next page.

Element	Considerations
Agent (Who)	Who is the protagonist (the "good guy")? Who is the antagonist (the "bad guy")? Possibilities: a person (e.g., Odysseus), an animal (e.g., Black Beauty), an allegorical figure (e.g., Mr. Worldly Wise), a spiritual being (e.g., Apollyon), or a vivified object (e.g., Gandalf's sword). The acronym NAGNAME can help you remember these aspects of Agent. <u>N</u>ame? <u>A</u>ge? <u>G</u>ender? <u>N</u>ationality (or variants involving ethnic or religious group in multi-cultural countries)? <u>A</u>ppearance? <u>M</u>ental state? <u>E</u>motional state? NOTE: Not every approach may be needed.
Action (What)	What conflict does the character face? What does he/she do to solve the conflict? What is the climax (high point of the action)? How do things turn out in the end?
Time (When)	How long does the event take? What is the time of day (morning, afternoon, night)? What is the historical era (ancient Greece, medieval France, etc.)?
Place (Where)	What is the location of the action? Is distance a factor? What is the terrain (e.g., rocky, boggy)? Is the climate (or weather) involved?
Cause (Why)	What is the cause of the action? What is the motive of the character(s)?
Manner (How)	What is the way in which the action is carried out (e.g., brute force, heavenly intervention, magic, deception)? What is the moral manner (e.g., lying, murder, cowardice, good/bad attitude)? What is the comportment of the characters (e.g., behavior, demeanor)?

EXERCISE 2.1: Elements of Narrative

Directions: Please begin by reading the excerpt from the second chapter of Luke and then analyze the elements of narrative by completing the chart that follows. (NOTE: Some elements are directly stated; others are implied.)

The Boy Jesus in the Temple
(Luke 2:41-51)

[41] Now his parents went to Jerusalem every year at the Feast of the Passover. [42] And when he was twelve years old, they went up according to custom. [43] And when the feast was ended, as they were returning, the boy Jesus stayed behind in Jerusalem. His parents did not know it, [44] but supposing him to be in the group they went a day's journey, but then they began to search for him among their relatives and acquaintances, [45] and when they did not find him, they returned to Jerusalem, searching for him. [46] After three days they found him in the temple, sitting among the teachers, listening to them and asking them questions. [47] And all who heard him were amazed at his understanding and his answers. [48] And when his parents saw him, they were astonished. And his mother said to him, "Son, why have you treated us so? Behold, your father and I have been searching for you in great distress." [49] And he said to them, "Why were you looking for me? Did you not know that I must be in my Father's house?" [50] And they did not understand the saying that he spoke to them. [51] And he went down with them and came to Nazareth and was submissive to them. And his mother treasured up all these things in her heart.

Elements of the Narrative
1. WHO was involved in this narrative?
a. Names

b. Age of Jesus	
c. Gender	
d. Nationality	
e. Mental/emotional state i. Parents when they discovered Jesus was missing (implied vv. 44-46) ii. Parents when they discovered Jesus in the temple (v.48) iii. All involved (v. 47)	

2. WHAT happened in this narrative?

In one or two sentences, summarize what happened in the narrative:

3. WHEN did this event happen?

a. Holy day of the Jewish calendar	

b. Year (based on age of Jesus)	
4. WHERE did this event happen?	
a. City	
b. Building	
5. WHY does Jesus seem to have stayed behind?	
Despite his age . . .	
6. HOW did the persons in the narrative comport themselves?	
a. Mary and Joseph (v. 48-49)	
b. Mary and Joseph (v. 50)	
c. Jesus at the time (v. 49)	
d. Jesus after arriving home (v. 51a)	
e. Mary in the aftermath (v. 51b)	

Now You Try It

Chapter 2, Essay 1
Elements of Narrative

Specifications

1. The purpose of this assignment is to compose a short narrative with all six elements: agent (who), action (what), time (when), place (where), cause (why), and manner (how).

2. Choose one of these topics or, if your teacher approves, another that can be expressed with all six approaches:

    - a scary incident at camp (or elsewhere)
    - a time you (or a character) fell into or out of something
    - an incident involving the neighbor's dog (cat, pet snake, etc.)
    - a memorable Christmas morning
    - a natural disaster (tornado, fire, hurricane, earthquake, thunderstorm)

3. Use your imagination as you complete the pre-writing activity.

4. Follow your teacher's instructions regarding preparation of the manuscript.

Elements of Narrative: Pre-Writing Activity

My narrative will be about _____.

Element	Considerations
Agent (Who)	Name: Age: Gender: Nationality/Ethnic group: Appearance: Mental/Emotional state:
Action (What)	
Time (When)	
Place (Where)	
Cause (Why)	
Manner (How)	

Narrative Modes

There are three narrative modes: indicative (statements), interrogative (questions), and comparative (contrasts), each with its own techniques. Take, for example, the narrative of the Sirens from Book XII of Homer's *Odyssey*. A person summarizing the tale could express the same idea in all three modes:

a. **Indicative:** Odysseus was a curious adventurer who wished to understand the world.

b. **Interrogative:** Warned of the dangers of the Sirens' song, what kind of man would leave his ears unsealed to its power?

c. **Comparative:** Unlike some leaders, who would have plugged their own ears as well, Odysseus considered this challenge a way to broaden his understanding of the world and its ways.

Below are summaries of the story written in the various modes.

The Story of the Sirens
By Homer

I. Indicative Mode

While on the island of Aeaea, Odysseus was warned by the goddess Circe that as he continued his journey, he and his men would be tempted to destruction by the Sirens, beautiful creatures who enchanted sailors with singing, tempted them ashore, and then destroyed them. To prevent this from happening, Circe advised Odysseus to plug the men's ears as they passed the Sirens, adding that if he wanted to hear the voices for himself, he should have his men restrain him so that he could not break away and go to them. Accordingly, Odysseus had his men plug their ears with beeswax and tie him to the mast, commanding them not to release him, no matter how much he begged them to do so. Indeed, when they reached the Sirens, Odysseus heard their enchanting song and, longing to go ashore, frowned at his men, signaling them to release him. However, Eurylochus and Perimedes remembered what Odysseus had said in advance of the adventure and bound him even tighter. When they were finally safely past the Sirens, the men removed the wax from their ears and unbound Odysseus.

II. Interrogative Mode

What does Odysseus' decision to listen to the Sirens tell us about him? What kind of man would trust the goddess who had ensnared him? Warned of the power of the Sirens' song, why would he not have taken a different route to avoid the lure of their singing? So warned, what kind of man would have sealed the ears of his crew but left his own unsealed? Did he trust his crew not to release him, even if he begged for release? Was it their respect for him that enabled Eurylochus and Perimedes to resist his demands for release? Who else, but Odysseus, could prepare for and endure the ordeal of the Sirens?

III. Comparative Mode

Although Odysseus had been warned that the song of the Sirens could lure him to destruction, he still decided he wanted to hear them. Instead of plugging his ears with wax, as he had told his men to do, he kept his ears open so that he could hear them. However, in order to restrain himself from responding, he had his men bind him to the mast so that he would not be able to move toward the Sirens. Unlike some leaders, who would have plugged their own ears as well, Odysseus considered this challenge a way to broaden his understanding of the world and its ways. In one sense, Odysseus could be contrasted with Solomon in the book of I Kings. Despite God's clear commandment not to worship other gods, Solomon succumbed to the "song" of his foreign wives and began to worship Ashoreth, a chief goddess of the Sidonians, and Milcum, the god of the Ammonites. For this, he was punished, losing ten of the twelve tribes of Israel. Now here's the difference: Whereas Solomon listened to his wives and succumbed, Odysseus found a way to gain knowledge without giving in or suffering loss.

EXERCISE 2.2: Analyzing Narrative Modes

Directions: After reading "The Story of the Sirens" in all three modes, analyze narrative modes by locating specific features.

1. What punctuation mark is used at the end of a sentence in Indicative Mode?

2. What punctuation mark is used at the end of a sentence in Interrogative Mode?

3. In Comparative Mode, underline structure words that help create contrast. (There are eight.) The first one is underlined as an example.

EXERCISE 2.3: Analyzing Interrogative Mode

Directions: The narrative below comes from *The Histories* of Herodotus, a Greek historian of the fifth century BC. Translated into English by George Rawlinson in 1910, it has been paraphrased here in Modern English. After reading the excerpt, please answer the questions that follow.

The Mysian Boar
By Herodotus

[1] Croesus, king of Lydia, was the father of two sons. One of whom was deaf and mute, leaving Croesus to put all his hopes in the other son. However, he once had a dream that this second son would die young, pierced by an iron weapon. Now it happened that the Mysians, neighbors of Croesus, had for a long time endured the wasting of their country by a huge monster of a boar that ate their crops and killed their people. They, therefore, sought help from Croesus, begging him to send his son to aid the Mysian youths. But Croesus remembered his dream and answered: "Say no more of my son going with you;

there is no way that can happen. He has just gotten married and is busy with his new life. However, I will send you a band of Lydians along with all my huntsmen and hounds to help you rid yourselves of this brute."

[2] Though the Mysians were satisfied with this offer, the king's son was upset: "Father, in the past you considered it the noblest and most appropriate thing for me to take part in your wars and hunting parties, and you encouraged me to win glory for myself. But now you are keeping me away from both, though you have never seen me guilty of cowardice or lack of spirit. How am I to hold my head up as I walk to and from the forum? What will the citizens think of me? Even worse, what will my bride think? What sort of man will she suppose her husband to be? Either let me go to chase the boar or give me a reason why I should not."

[3] Croesus reminded his son of his dream and his fear that he would die young, killed by the blow of an iron weapon. "Oh, father," the youth replied, "I don't blame you for trying to keep me safe after such a terrible dream, but, as you say yourself, the dream indicated death by an iron weapon. But with what hands can a boar kill me? What iron weapon can he bear? If the dream had said I would die pierced by a tusk, then I would understand your decision, but it said an iron weapon. Therefore, please reconsider and let me go with the Mysians."

[4] And Croesus relented, saying, "There you've got me, my son. Your interpretation is better than mine. I yield and change my mind. You can go with the Mysians."[8]

1. Is Paragraph 1 written in indicative or interrogative mode?

2. How many interrogatives did Herodotus employ in Paragraph 2?

3. How many in Paragraph 3?

4. Is the conclusion (Paragraph 4) in the indicative or interrogative mode?

5. Who uses the interrogative—the father or the son? Why do you think Herodotus decided to place this character's complaints in interrogative form?

THINK IT THROUGH: In small groups or with the class as a whole, convert the indicative narrative of Luke 2:41-51 ("The Boy Jesus in the Temple") into an interrogative narrative, focusing on the reason Luke probably included this incident in his gospel.

Types of Narrative

This chapter will focus on three types of narrative: mythical, historical, and fictive. The late fifth-century scholar Nicolaus the Sophist explained the difference between the first two by saying, "Mythical are those not worthy of unquestioned belief and having a suspicion of falsehood, like stories about the Cyclopses and Centaurs; historical narratives are concerned with ancient events that are admitted to have happened." Even with this important distinction, Nicolaus states that mythical narratives can still be used in persuasive writing and speaking. Regarding fictive narratives, Nicolaus said, "Fictive narratives share with fables the fact that both have been made up, but they differ from each other in that fictive narratives, even if they did not happen, could happen in nature, while fables neither happened nor could happen naturally." [9]

The Mythical Narrative

The mythical narrative had its origins in ancient Greece and Rome. These narratives were primarily stories about gods and heroes and were intended to teach a moral or provide insight into human behavior. This purpose is what makes them suitable for use in persuasive writing.

IMPORTANT: There are two ways to define *myth*. One usage of the word relates to imaginary stories such as the "The Legend of Atalanta," which appears below. However, another usage of the word relates to true stories of an actual heroic figure. These are often used to teach us life lessons. Though they may have happened in the past, they have the power to influence behavior today. This is sometimes referred to as the "power of myth."

Model Mythical Narrative

The Legend of Atalanta

Long long ago in faraway Greece, King Iasos was sadly disappointed when a daughter, Atalanta, was born to him. He had so wanted a son that he took the baby girl out into the wilderness and left her to be killed by wild animals. However, a mother boar took the girl in and raised her in the wild. Atalanta learned to run fast on a hunt so that she could get meat to sustain herself, and over the years she became very fleet of foot. One day she was reunited with her father, who said he would like her to be married. (Perhaps he thought he could get something for her beauty!) Atalanta said she would never marry unless her father could find a man who could outrun her, so the father sent word about to bring in contestants for his daughter's hand. Because of the girl's great beauty, many men were willing to take up the challenge, but time after time Atalanta proved that she was the master of the race. Now one day a handsome young prince appeared and, believing that Atalanta was both beautiful and strong, greatly desired her hand in marriage. He spoke to the goddess Aphrodite, who gave him several golden apples and a strategy for success in the foot race with the princess. When the day of the race came, young Melanian (for that was his name) managed to sneak the three apples onto the racing path. At first, the young man had the advantage and sprinted out in front of Atalanta. Ahead a number of strides, he stealthily dropped one of the golden apples on the path so that when Atalanta came along, she would be tempted by the luscious fruit and lose valuable seconds when she stooped to gather it up. The plan worked, and Atalanta continued to run behind Melanian. Then Melanian dropped the second and eventually the third of the golden apples, and each time Atalanta stooped to pick up an apple, she lost more and more time and fell farther and farther behind. As a result, Melanian beat her to the finish line and Atalanta was forced to keep her end of the bargain. However, though she realized the guile in which Melanian had engaged, she realized he had played his trick out of love for her and was willing to accept the hand the young prince offered her in marriage.[10]

EXERCISE 2.4: Analyzing Mythical Narrative

Directions: After reading the narrative about Atalanta, analyze Mythical Narrative by answering these questions.

1. Certainly this Mythical Narrative is applicable to real life in that it considers three human traits: vanity, trickery, and love. Analyze each below.

   a. In what way does the legend show human vanity?

   b. In what way does the legend show human trickery?

   c. In what way is the legend about love?

   d. Do you think "The Legend of Atalanta" is more about vanity, trickery, or love? Explain your answer.

2. Write a moral to the story that reflects your answer to Question #1d.

The Mythical Legend in America: The Tall Tale

The popularity of mythical legends has survived through the centuries. In the United States, they appeared on the frontier in the form of tall tales such as those about Paul Bunyan. An actual Tennessee frontiersman who collected and/or wrote many tall tales was Davy Crockett, who cleverly enhanced their appeal by making himself the hero of the tales.

EXERCISE 2.5: Analyzing an American Tall Tale

Directions: Read "The Tale of Sally Crockett" below and then answer the questions that follow.

The Tale of Sally Crockett
By Davy Crockett

(1) Now, I met my wife, Sally Ann Thunder Ann Whirlwind Crockett, at a barn dance. (2) She had said that she would marry any feller what could out-dance her, and she had already danced 8 of them to the ground and was still as fresh as a daisy. (3) Well, sir, when I saw her, I thought she was the most beautiful thing I'd ever laid eyes on, so I decided to go for her hand myself. (4) So we danced and we danced and we danced all night long and into the next day, we did reels and quadrilles and whatchamacallits, until we wore out a dozen fiddlers, and we kept on a-dancing until finally she fell down exhausted. (5) She had met her match. (6) So we got ourselves hitched and moved out to the wild frontier.[11]

1. **Literary technique: hyperbole**

   Hyperbole can be defined as exaggeration for effect—in this case, humorous effect. What parts of Davy's story employ hyperbole?

2. What features of language are used to create a conversational tone?

   a. **Conversational transitions:** In Sentences #3, 4, and 6, what conversational transitions are used to move the narrative from point to point? (Copy the first word of each sentence in the space provided.)

   b. **Pronunciation spelling:** In the following sentences, how are certain words spelled to render Davy's Tennessee accent?

Sentence #2, *fellows*:

Sentence #4, *dancing*:

   c. **"Folksy" language:**

In Sentence #4, when Davy can't remember the names of all the dances, what folksy catch-all word does he use for them?

In Sentence #6, what slang synonym does Davy use for *got married?*

   d. **Nonstandard grammar:**

In Sentence #2, the usual "any feller *who* could out-dance her" is changed to what nonstandard form?

3. What do this tale and the tale of Atalanta reveal about those we might consider a worthy husband or wife? Do you agree or disagree with the idea? Why or why not?

The Historical Narrative

Historical narratives create a record of past events that have shaped a culture. They can be found in textbooks as a record of human accomplishments and failures. In a positive vein, they can be used at patriotic events to honor the nation's heroes. In a negative vein, they can teach us how to avoid the mistakes of the past. They can also be employed by religious leaders to show the faith or foolishness of Bible characters in order to align human conduct with Biblical teachings about what is right and true.

THINK IT THROUGH: What does the story of Valley Forge teach us?

THINK IT THROUGH: What does the Biblical story of the Fall teach us?

Model Historical Narrative

INTRODUCTION: *Julius Caesar (100 BC- 44 BC) was a Roman general and political leader who is considered one of the greatest military figures of all time. His conquest of Gaul was legendary. Plutarch claimed that by the time Caesar had been in Gaul for ten years, he had taken 800 towns, subdued 300 states, and engaged 3 million men, 1 million of whom he had killed and another million taken captive. In the passage below, Plutarch examines his effect on the men whom he led.*

Julius Caesar's Leadership
By Plutarch

[Julius Caesar] was so much master of the good-will and hearty service of his soldiers that those who in other expeditions were but ordinary men displayed a courage past defeating or withstanding when they went upon any danger where Caesar's glory was concerned. Such a one was Acilius, who, in the sea-fight before Marseilles [49 BC], had his right hand struck off with a sword, yet did not quit his buckler out of his left, but struck the enemies in the face with it, till he drove them off and made himself master of the vessel. Such another was Cassius Scaeva, who, in a battle near Dyrrhachium [48 BC], had one of his eyes shot out with an arrow, his shoulder pierced with one javelin, and his thigh with another; and having received one hundred and thirty darts upon his target, called to the enemy, as though he would surrender himself. But when two of them came up to him, he cut off the shoulder of one with a sword, and by a blow over the face forced the other to retire, and so with the assistance of his friends, who now came up, made his escape. Again, in Britain [55 BC], when some of the foremost officers had accidentally got into a morass full of water, and there were assaulted by the enemy, a common soldier, whilst Caesar stood and looked on, threw himself in the midst of them, and after many signal demonstrations of his valor, rescued the officers and beat off the barbarians. He himself, in the end, took to the water, and with much difficulty, partly by swimming, partly by wading, passed it, but in the passage lost his shield. Caesar and his officers saw it and admired, and went to meet him with joy and acclamation. But the soldier, much dejected and in tears, threw himself down at Caesar's feet and begged his pardon for having let go his buckler. Another time in Africa [47 BC], Scipio, having taken a ship of Caesar's in which Granius Petro, lately appointed *quaestor*, was sailing, gave the other passengers as free prize to his soldiers, but thought fit to offer the quaestor his life. But he [Granius] said it was not usual for Caesar's soldiers to take but give mercy, and having said so, fell upon his sword and killed himself.[12]

EXERCISE 2.6: Analyzing Historical Narrative

Directions: After reading the narrative about the leadership of Julius Caesar, please analyze Historical Narrative by answering these questions.

1. **Agent (Who):** Who is the main subject of this narrative?

2. **Action (What):** What did Caesar's men do?

3. **Time (When):** When did the events in this narrative occur?

4. **Place (Where):** Where did each of these four events occur?

5. **Cause (Why):** In the opening sentence, what reason is given to explain why Caesar's men would go to such extraordinary lengths? Please answer in your own words.

6. **Manner (How):** Explain how each of these deeds was accomplished.

    a. How did Acilius fight even after his right hand was severed from his body?

b. How did Cassius Scaeva manage to escape from two of the enemy despite his many injuries?

c. How did a common soldier rescue officers in Britain?

d. How did Granius Petro display his devotion to Caesar and his ethic?

Writing the Classical Way I

Now You Try It

Chapter 2, Essay 2
Historical Narrative

Specifications

1. The purpose of this assignment is to demonstrate your ability to write a historical narrative.

2. Choose one of these topics or, if your teacher approves, another related to your reading of Scripture or history:

   a. Can dreams come from God?
   b. Can one person change the world?
   c. What does the Battle of Jericho teach us about God (Joshua 6)?
   d. Other: _____?

3. Complete the pre-writing activity on the next page.

4. The answer to the question you chose in #2 above will become your first sentence. Then support the truth of the statement by writing a narrative that proves it.

5. Follow your teacher's instructions regarding preparation of the manuscript.

Historical Narrative: Pre-Writing Activity

I will write about _____.

Element	Details
Agent (Who)	
Action (What)	
Time (When)	
Place (Where)	
Cause (Why)	
Manner (How)	

The Fictive Narrative

The fictive narrative is an account of imaginary events. In our time period, it is most commonly referred to as fiction. As indicated above, Nicolaus the Sophist noted that fictive narratives were like fables in that both are imaginary, but they differ in that fables could never actually happen. Animals and trees, of course, do not talk.

Still, Nicolaus' distinction does not account for fiction with fantasy elements such as C. S. Lewis's *Lord of the Rings* trilogy, which emerged centuries after the time of Nicolaus.

Genres

The term *genre* (ZHÄN-rə) refers to the various forms of literature. In addition to Greek mythology and the fables of Aesop, the genres of the classical Greek authors were primarily epic poetry, such as Homer's *Iliad*, and plays, such as Sophocles' *Oedipus Rex*, forms which continued through the Roman period. In the medieval period, another genre emerged—heroic tales such as the Arthurian legends. The genres of the modern short story and the novel emerged after the invention of the printing press. After the Industrial Revolution, both fantasy novels, which may be considered to have developed from mythology and epic poetry, and science fiction came on the scene.

Aristotle's *Poetics*

In the fourth century BC, the philosopher Plato actually called for the banning of dramatic literature (i.e., plays) because the misbehavior of the gods, as shown in the plays, was damaging to the moral development of young people. His student Aristotle, however, wrote *Poetics* in order to lay out the principles of quality fictive narratives. Since epics and plays were presented orally to an audience, Aristotle's principles applied to both, and they are still applicable in some ways to the newer genres such as short stories and novels.

Aristotle identified six elements of fictive, or dramatic, literature and listed them in order of importance: plot, character, thought, diction, song, and spectacle. In this chapter, we will focus on plot and diction.

Plot

Plot structure, as Aristotle conceived it, is often represented by a diagram such as the following:

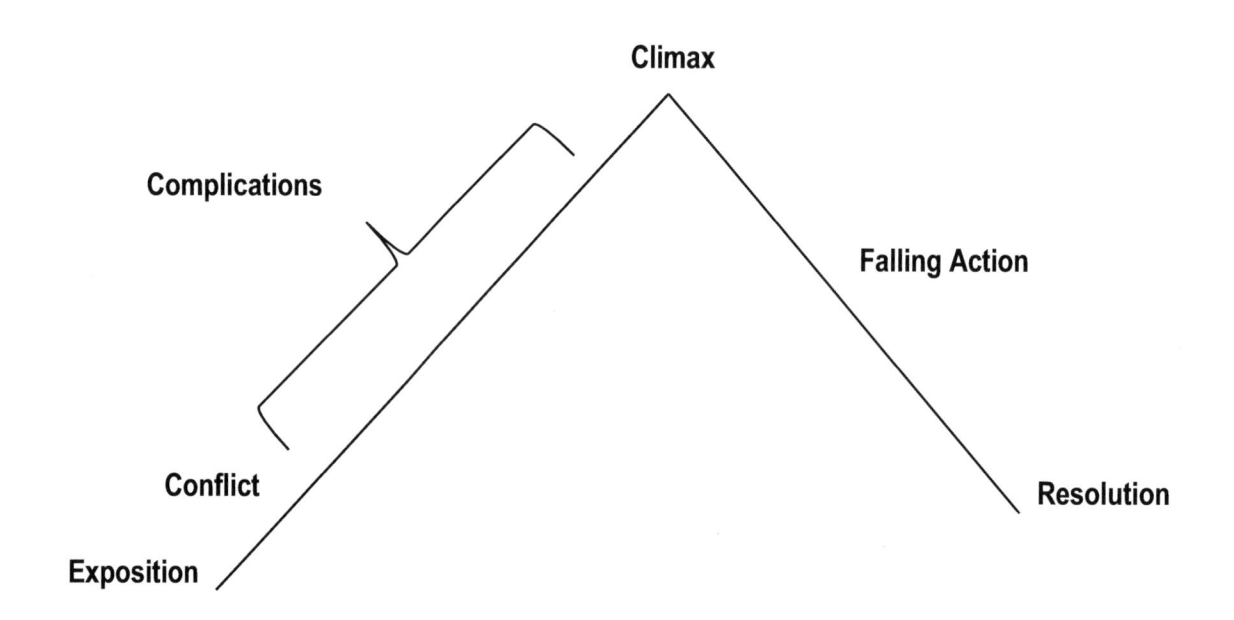

```
                            Climax
                             /\
                            /  \
           Complications   /    \
                          /      \  Falling Action
                         /        \
                        /          \
              Conflict /            \  Resolution
                      /              \
           Exposition
```

The first step in plot structure is *exposition*, which identifies the setting (place and time) and the main character. Setting is what George Lucas had in mind when he began the opening crawl of *Star Wars* with the words, "A long time ago in a galaxy far, far away. . . ." This opening, of course, is far more vague than that of the typical story, which normally provides an era and a spot on the globe, as time and place greatly influence the action. Some examples are Boston in the Revolutionary War era in *Johnny Tremain,* England in the medieval period in the legends of King Arthur, and New England in the seventeenth century in *The Witch of Blackbird Pond.*

The second step in plot structure is *conflict*. Here the reader finds out what problem the character is facing.

The third step in a plot sequence is actually a series of events, called *complications*. When people remark, "The plot thickens," they are referring to this part of the story. The complications could be either attempts the character makes to resolve the conflict or additional obstacles that are introduced to make the resolution even more difficult.

When composing this part of the story, it is important to remember that each step of the plot emerges from what has gone before. Chance, or "coincidence," has no part in a quality plot.

More than halfway through the story comes the fourth step, the *climax*, or high point, of the action. This is the natural outcome of all the steps that have come before. In an old western, this would be where the final fistfight occurs, the one which will determine whether the good guy or the bad guy will win, whether the character will resolve the conflict or fail, perhaps even die.

Next comes *falling action*. This is the portion of the story where loose ends are tied up. In the fairy tale "Cinderella," for example, once the prince has placed the glass slipper on Cinderella's foot, the falling action of the tale is the wedding and the forgiveness of the step-mother and the ugly step-sisters.

Last is the *resolution*. This is the final part of the narrative—the part where the hero rides out of town into the sunset on his beautiful steed.

Types of Conflict

Conflict can be defined as the problem the character must solve in the story. Though some types of conflict in literature have come to prominence only in the Age of

Science and Industry, all have roots in ancient mythology. Below is a chart showing seven types of conflict with examples from both ancient and modern writings.

Type of Conflict	Ancient Example	Modern Example
Man vs. Man[a]	The Greeks and Trojans fight over Helen in Homer's *Iliad*.	The French and English fight for control of North America in *The Last of the Mohicans*.
Man vs. God (or Fate)	Oedipus struggles against an evil prophecy in Sophocles' *Oedipus Rex*.	Pinocchio, though a "wooden boy," strays from the narrow way in Carlo Collodi's *Pinocchio*
Man vs. Nature	Jason must defeat the bulls of Colchis before he can take the fleece in the *Argonautica* by Apollonius of Rhodes.	A plantation owner must stave off an invasion of soldier ants in Carl Stephenson's "Leiningen Versus the Ants."
Man vs. Self	Icarus is destroyed by conceit in the myth "Daedalus and Icarus."	The evil inner self takes over the good Dr. Jekyll in Robert Louis Stevenson's *Dr. Jekyll and Mr. Hyde*.
Man vs. Machine/Technology	Talos, the giant automaton, protected Crete in the *Argonautica* and other tales.	Dr. Frankenstein's creation runs amok in Mary Shelley's *Frankenstein: Or, the Modern Prometheus*.
Man vs. Society/Government	Antigone defies the king in Sophocles' *Antigone*.	Winston struggles against a totalitarian state ("Big Brother") in George Orwell's *1984*.
Man vs. the Unknown	Odysseus is tempted by the Sirens in Homer's *Odyssey*.	Earth is invaded by Martians in H. G. Wells' *War of the Worlds*.

[a] Though some today note these conflicts as, say, "Person vs. Person," "Human vs. Human," or even "Character vs. Character," I have chosen to retain the traditional term *Man* for *Person* not only because in its singular form without an article such as *a*, *an*, or *the* , the term includes both men and women, but also because it is more euphonic.

THINK IT THROUGH: With your classmates, brainstorm a list of books or short stories that fit each of these types of conflict.

Example of Modern Fictive Narrative

Excerpt from *Boy Life on the Prairie*
By Hamlin Garland

One afternoon in the autumn of 1868 Duncan Stewart, leading his little fleet of "prairie schooners," entered upon "The Big Prairie" of northern Iowa, and pushed resolutely on into the west. His four-horse canvas-covered wagon was followed by two other lighter vehicles, one of which was driven by his wife, and the other by a hired freighter. At the rear of all the wagons, and urging forward a dozen or sixteen cattle, trotted a gaunt youth and a small boy.

The boy had tears upon his face, and was limping with a stone-bruise. He could hardly look over the wild oats, which tossed their gleaming bayonets in the wind, and when he dashed out into the blue joint and wild sunflowers, to bring the cattle into the road, he could be traced only by the ripple he made, like a trout in a pool. He was a small edition of his father. He wore the same color and check in his hickory shirt and his long pantaloons of blue denim had suspenders precisely like those of the men. Indeed, he considered himself a man, notwithstanding the tear-stains on his brown cheeks.

It seemed a long time since leaving his native Wisconsin coolly[b] behind, with only a momentary sadness, but now, after nearly a week of travel, it seemed his father must be leading them all to the edge of the world, and Lincoln was very sad and weary.

"Company, halt!" called the Captain. One by one the teams stopped, and the cattle began to feed (they were always ready to eat), and Mr. Stewart, coming back where his wife sat, said cheerily: —

---

[b] Coullee: A landform, a valley created by erosion.

"Well, Kate, here's the big prairie I told you of, and beyond that blue line of timber you see is Sun Prairie, and home." Mrs. Stewart did not smile. She was too weary, and the wailing of little Mary in her arms was dispiriting.

"Come here, Lincoln," said Mr. Stewart. "Here we are, out of sight of the works of man. Not a house in sight — climb up here and see."

Lincoln rustled along through the tall grass, and, clambering up the wagon wheel, stood silently beside his mother. Tired as he was, the scene made an indelible impression on him. It was as though he had suddenly been transported into another world, a world where time did not exist; where snow never fell, and the grass waved forever under a cloudless sky. A great awe fell upon him as he looked, and he could not utter a word.

At last Mr. Stewart cheerily called: "Attention, battalion! We must reach Sun Prairie to-night. Forward, march!" Again the little wagon train took up its slow way through the tall ranks of the wild oats, and the drooping, flaming sunflowers. Slowly the sun sank. The crickets began to cry, the night-hawks whizzed and boomed, and long before the prairie was crossed the night had come.

Being too tired to foot it any longer behind the cracking heels of the cows, Lincoln climbed into the wagon beside his little brother, who was already asleep, and, resting his head against his mother's knee, lay for a long time, listening to the chuck-chuckle of the wheels, watching the light go out of the sky, and counting the stars as they appeared.

At last they entered the wood, which seemed a very threatening place indeed, and his alert ears caught every sound, — the hoot of owls, the quavering cry of coons, the twitter of night birds. But at last his weariness overcame him, and he dozed off, hearing the clank of the whippletrees, the creak of the horses' harness, the vibrant voice of his father, and the occasional cry of the hired hand, urging the cattle forward through the dark.

He was roused once by the ripple of a stream, wherein the horses thrust their hot nozzles, he heard the grind of wheels on the pebbly bottom, and the wild shouts of the resolute men as they scrambled up the opposite bank, and entered once more the dark aisles of the forest. Here the road was smoother, and to the soft rumble of the wheels the boy slept. At last, deep in the night, so it seemed to Lincoln, his father shouted: "Wake up, everybody. We're almost home." Then, facing the darkness, he cried, in western fashion, "Hello! the house!"

Dazed and stupid, Lincoln stepped down the wheel to the ground, his legs numb with sleep. Owen followed, querulous as a sick puppy, and together they stood in the darkness, waiting further command.

From a small frame house, nearby, a man with a lantern appeared.

"Hello!" he said, yawning with sleep. "Is that you, Stewart? I'd jest about give you up."

While the men unhitched the teams, Stewart helped his wife and children to the house, where Mrs. Hutchinson, a tall, thin woman, with a pleasant smile, made them welcome. She helped Mrs. Stewart remove her things, and then set out some bread and milk for the boys, which they ate in silence, their heavy eyelids drooping.

When Mr. Stewart came in, he said: "Now, Lincoln, you and Will are to sleep in the other shack. Run right along, before you go to sleep. Owen will stay here."

Without in the least knowing the why or wherefore, Lincoln set forth beside the hired man, out into the unknown. They walked rapidly for a long time, and, as his blood began to stir again, Lincoln awoke to the wonder and mystery of the hour. The strange grasses under his feet, the unknown stars over his head, the dim objects on the horizon, were all the fashioning of a mind in the world of dreams. His soul ached with the passion of his remembered visions and his forebodings.

At last they came to a small cabin on the banks of a deep ravine. Opening the door, the men lit a candle, and spread their burden of blankets on the floor. Lincoln crept between them like a sleepy puppy, and in a few minutes this unknown actual world merged itself in the mystery of dreams.

When he woke, the sun was shining, hot and red, through the open windows, and the men were smoking their pipes by the rough fence before the door. Lincoln hurried out to see what kind of a world this was to which his night's journey had hurried him. It was, for the most part, a level land, covered with short grass intermixed with tall weeds, and with many purple and yellow flowers. A little way off, to the right, stood a small house, and about as far to the right was another, before which stood the wagons belonging to his father. Directly in front was a wide expanse of rolling prairie, cut by a deep ravine, while to the north, beyond the small farm which was fenced, a still wider region rolled away into unexplored and marvelous distance. Altogether it was a land to exalt a boy who had lived all his life in a thickly settled Wisconsin coolly, where the horizon line was high and small of circuit.

In less than two hours the wagons were unloaded, the stove was set up in the kitchen, the family clock was ticking on its shelf, and the bureau set against the wall. It was amazing to see how these familiar things and his mother's bustling presence changed the looks of the cabin. Little Mary was quite happy crawling about the floor, and Owen, who had explored the barn and found a lizard to play with, was entirely at home. Lincoln had climbed to the roof of the house, and was still trying to comprehend this mighty stretch of grasses. Sitting astride the roof board, he gazed away into the north west, where no house broke the horizon line, wondering what lay beyond that high ridge.

While seated thus, he heard a distant roar and trample, and saw a cloud of dust rising along the fence which bounded the farm to the west. It was like the rush of a whirlwind, and, before he could call to his father, out on the smooth sod to the south burst a platoon of wild horses, led by a beautiful roan[c] mare. The boy's heart leaped with excitement as the shaggy colts swept round to the east, racing like wolves at play. Their long tails and abundant manes streamed in the wind like banners, and their imperious bugling voiced their contempt for man.

Lincoln clapped his hands with joy, and all of the family ran to the fence to enjoy the sight. A boy, splendidly mounted on a fleet roan, the mate of the

---

[c] Having a coat of one color mixed with hairs of other colors

leader, was riding at a slashing pace, with intent to turn the troop to the south. He was a superb rider, and the little Morgan strove gallantly without need of whip or spur. He laid out like a hare. He seemed to float like a hawk, skimming the weeds, and her rider sat him like one born to the saddle, erect and supple, and of little hindrance to the beast.

On swept the herd, circling to the left, heading for the wild lands to the east. Gallantly strove the roan with his resolute rider, disdaining to be beaten by his own mate, his breath roaring like a furnace, his nostrils blown like trumpets, his hoofs pounding the resounding sod.

All in vain; even with the inside track he was no match for his wild, free mate. The herd drew ahead, and, plunging through a short lane, vanished over a big swell to the east, and their drumming rush died rapidly away into silence.

This was a glorious introduction to the life of the prairies, and Lincoln's heart filled with boundless joy, and longing to know it — all of it, east, west, north, and south. He had no further wish to return to his coolly home. The horseman had become his ideal, the prairie his domain.[13]

EXERCISE 2.7: Analyzing Fictive Narrative

<u>Directions</u>: After reading the excerpt from *Boy Life on the Prairie,* analyze the plot structure by answering the questions below.

1. **Exposition:**

    a. Where and when is the story set?

    b. Who is the main character?

2. **Conflict:** Which of the seven types of conflict is at play here? Explain your answer.

3. **Complications:**

a. *Lincoln crawls up into the wagon and is awed by the prairie.*

b.

c.

d.

4. **Climax:**

5. **Falling action:**

6. **Resolution:**

EXERCISE 2.8: Practicing Exposition and Conflict

Directions: Choose three of the narrative conflicts from the list below. Then for each one you choose, brainstorm a time, place, and character, and provide a one-sentence statement of a plot line. The first one serves as an example.

A. Man vs. Nature
B. Man vs. Man
C. Man vs. Self
D. Man vs. God (or Fate)
E. Man vs. Society
F. Man vs. Technology
G. Man vs. the Unknown

1. **Conflict:** *Man vs. Nature*

   Time: *1868*

   Place: *Kansas*

Character: *Polly, a 12-year-old girl*

Plot line: *After her father dies from a snakebite at his trading post, Polly must find a way to survive on the prairie.*

2. **Conflict:**

   Time:

   Place:

   Character:

   Plot line:

3. **Conflict:**

   Time:

   Place:

   Character:

   Plot line:

4. **Conflict:**

   Time:

   Place:

   Character:

   Plot line:

Diction

The word *diction,* which is derived from the Latin word *dicere,* "to say," refers to word usage in speech or writing. In fictive writing, the issue of diction appears in the well-known advisory for creative writers: "Show. Don't tell."

Let's say you are introducing a character with sandy blonde hair. At first, you might think it is sensible simply to tell your reader, "Tessa had sandy-blonde hair." After all, this is the way you might tell your friend in a phone conversation. However, fictive narrative differs from daily conversation in that it can be made to do more than one thing at a time. That is to say, physical attributes can be introduced along with other details. For example, one could write:

> Hanging upside down on the branch of the old oak, Tessa could not see much through the sandy hair that now hung over her face like a drying tea towel on her mother's clothesline.

In this case, we learn quite a bit more about Tessa than her hair color. We learn that (a) she is something of a tomboy, who likes to hang upside down on tree branches; (b) she is young enough to want to hang upside down on a tree branch; (c) she lives in a time period when families dried their laundry outdoors on a clothesline rather than in a drier; (d) she lives with her mother; and (e) she lives in an area that has stately trees.

THINK IT THROUGH: On a piece of paper, write a short statement that tells a fact about a character (such as "Ned had a scab on his knee"). Exchange papers with a classmate. Then develop a description that shows rather than tells something about the person your classmate created. What can you add that creates a more complete picture in the reader's mind? Read your more developed description to the class.

Another way a writer can show the idea in his or her mind is to select words carefully. If a character is going to walk down the street, the good writer will select the verb which not only conveys the action but also reveals the character's mental or emotional state. For example, did the character amble, stroll, bounce, dash, crawl, skulk, or jog?

THINK IT THROUGH: Below are the first two paragraphs from *Boy Life on the Prairie*, which appeared above. What synonyms are used to show the movement of the family, the horses, and the wagon?

> One afternoon in the autumn of 1868 Duncan Stewart, <u>leading</u> his little fleet of "prairie schooners," <u>entered</u> upon "The Big Prairie" of northern Iowa, and <u>pushed</u> resolutely on into the west. His four-horse canvas-covered wagon was <u>followed</u> by two other lighter vehicles, one of which <u>was driven</u> by his wife, and the other by a hired freighter. At the rear of all the wagons, and urging <u>forward</u> a dozen or sixteen cattle, <u>trotted</u> a gaunt youth and a small boy.
>
> The boy had tears upon his face, and <u>was limping</u> with a stone-bruise. He could hardly look over the wild oats, which tossed their gleaming bayonets in the wind, and when he <u>dashed</u> out into the blue joint and wild sunflowers, to bring the cattle into the road, he could be traced only by the <u>ripple</u> he made, like a trout in a pool.

EXERCISE 2.9: "Show. Don't Tell."

<u>Directions</u>: In each sentence, change the italicized verb to show, rather than simply tell, what image is evoked in your mind. The first one serves as an example.

1. Dora *sat* on the sofa.
    Dora <u>slumped</u> on the sofa.

2. Sam *ate* his sandwich.

3. Anna *saw* a canoe.

4. Andrew *lay* by the fireside.

5. Kate *drank* her tea.

6. The car *moved forward*.

Now You Try It

Chapter 2, Essay 3
Fictive Narrative

Specifications

1. The purpose of this assignment is to demonstrate your ability to write a fictive narrative.

2. Choose one of these topics or, with the approval of your teacher, another that interests you:

   a. a narrative involving super powers
   b. a narrative about a creepy (or kind, or clever) neighbor
   c. a narrative about boys/girls in the summertime
   d. a narrative set at Christmastime

3. Complete the pre-writing activity on the next page.

4. Compose a narrative, being sure to *show* rather than tell.

5. Follow your teacher's instructions regarding preparation of the manuscript.

Fictive Narrative: Pre-Writing Activity

My fictive narrative will be about ._____.

Element	Details
Agent (Who)	
Action (What)	
Time (When)	
Place (Where)	
Cause (Why)	
Manner (How)	

DESCRIPTION

Chapter 3

Introduction

Imagine yourself one day in one of the following situations—a crime victim, a witness in a court of law, an advertiser, a news reporter, a teller of tales around a campfire, a soldier writing a letter home, a teenager explaining how it was you came to wreck the family car! What do all these situations have in common? They all require description of an important—or sometimes entertaining—situation. When such a situation arises, writers can establish clarity in two ways: (a) the mental image the readers create in their minds and (b) the emotion that surrounds the event under discussion. That is where your skills as a descriptive writer will help you make an impact not just for a teacher or a publisher, but for the society as a whole.

Definition and Purpose

Description is the art of conveying an image in one person's mind into that of another person's by the use of words. In fictive writing, the purpose is not only to convey an image but to create a feeling about the object of the description. To that end, it employs appeals to the senses of sight, sound, taste, smell, and touch. In nonfictive writing, as, for example, in a court of law, its purpose is to convey detailed and accurate information for a purpose beyond entertainment.

Notes on Descriptive Writing

All elements of narrative can be described: agent, action, time, place, cause, and manner. One author well known for his ability to describe all aspects of narrative was Stephen Crane. Look at the various examples from Crane's classic novel of the American Civil War, *The Red Badge of Courage*.[14]

Stephen Crane (1871-1900)

a. **Agent (Who):** In Chapter One, Crane introduces us to the young private *who* will be the main character in the story:

> When [Henry] had stood in the doorway with his soldier's clothes on his back, and with the light of excitement and expectancy in his eyes almost defeating the glow of regret for the home bonds, he had seen two tears leaving their trails on his mother's scarred cheeks.

b. **Action (What):** We also learn in Chapter One that Henry has been dreaming of *what* he needs to do.

> He had, of course, dreamed of battles all his life—of vague and bloody conflicts that had thrilled him with their sweep and fire. In visions he had seen himself in many struggles. He had imagined peoples secure in the shadow of his eagle-eyed prowess. But awake he had regarded battles as crimson blotches on the pages of the past. He had put them as things of the bygone with his thought-images of heavy crowns and high castles. There was a portion of the world's history which he had regarded as the time of wars, but it, he thought, had been long gone over the horizon and had disappeared forever.

c. **Time (When):** In Chapter Two, Crane describes the pre-dawn morning *when* the soldiers are given their marching orders.

> One morning, however, he found himself in the ranks of his prepared regiment. The men were whispering speculations and recounting the old rumors. In the gloom before the break of the day their uniforms glowed a deep purple hue. From across the river the red eyes were still peering. In the eastern sky there was a yellow patch like a rug laid for the feet of the coming sun; and against it, black and patternlike, loomed the gigantic figure of the colonel on a gigantic horse.

d. **Place (Where):** In Chapter One, Crane describes *where* the private is quartered, thus:

> He lay down on a wide bunk that stretched across the end of the room. In the other end, cracker boxes were made to serve as furniture. They were grouped about the fireplace. A picture from an illustrated weekly was upon the log walls, and three rifles were paralleled on pegs. Equipments [*sic*] hung on handy

projections, and some tin dishes lay upon a small pile of firewood. A folded tent was serving as a roof.

e. **Cause (Why):** In Chapter Two, Crane descriptively explains *why* it is that Henry is longing for home:

> He wished, without reserve, that he was at home again making the endless rounds from the house to the barn, from the barn to the fields, from the fields to the barn, from the barn to the house. He remembered he had so often cursed the brindle cow and her mates, and had sometimes flung milking stools. But, from his present point of view, there was a halo of happiness about each of their heads, and he would have sacrificed all the brass buttons on the continent to have been enabled to return to them. He told himself that he was not formed for a soldier. And he mused seriously upon the radical differences between himself and those men who were dodging implike around the fires.

f. **Manner (How):** In Chapter Three, Crane describes *how* Henry moved as his regiment moved toward their first skirmish with the enemy:

> The youth tried to observe everything. He did not use care to avoid trees and branches, and his forgotten feet were constantly knocking against stones or getting entangled in briers [*sic*]. He was aware that these battalions with their commotions were woven red and startling into the gentle fabric of softened greens and browns. It looked to be a wrong place for a battle field [*sic*].

In short, we see that good writing describes all elements: agent, action, time, place, cause, and manner. In the next section, we will examine the techniques that writers use for each of the elements.

Approaches to Description of a Person

As indicated in Chapter 2, "Narrative," there are basically seven approaches to the description of a person, which can be called to mind by the mnemonic device: NAGNAME. Each approach is explained in the chart below with examples from *Red Badge of Courage* following.

Approach	Details
Name	The name can sometimes reflect attributes of the character: Solomon (suggesting wisdom); Oliver Twist (suggesting the twists and turns of the character's life), etc. Non-human characters are also named: e.g., HAL (Heuristically Programmed ALgorithmic_Computer) in *2001: A Space Odyssey*.
Age	Key considerations can involve the exact age or life stage (young, middle-aged, old). Action sometimes depends on age (e.g., the helpless grandmother in "Little Red Riding Hood").
Gender	One's gender often affects society's expectations for a person and, hence, becomes a factor in the action of a story. The Biblical narrative of Queen Esther, the Greek myth of the Amazons, the culture of the Spartan warrior are examples.
Nationality	The classical concept of nationality, in multi-cultural times, includes all identities that could form a character's ideas and actions: nation, region, ethnicity, creed, etc.
Appearance	Appearance includes hair, skin, facial features, body form, facial expression, voice, posture, physical abilities, disabilities, infirmities, clothing, and mannerisms.
Mental state	Mental state refers to the mind of the character: sane or insane, logical or illogical, aware or unaware, confused, drugged, brainwashed, composed, etc.
Emotional state	A character's emotional state can be described as content, upset, jubilant, depressed, outraged, morose, excited, sarcastic, egotistical, kind, fearful, etc.

All of these approaches appear in *The Red Badge of Courage*. When Crane created his character, Henry Fleming, his idea was to explore how a young soldier, full of dreams of heroism but gripped with the fear that is a natural part of battle, would react in battle. To set all of this up for the reader, Crane employed all the approaches for describing persons:

a. **Name**

In Chapter One, Crane lets his reader know his character's first name when the fellow's mother says, "*Henry*, don't you be a fool." It isn't until Chapter Eleven that Crane reveals Henry's last name when he shows us Henry's thoughts: "He imagined the whole regiment saying: 'Where's Henry Fleming? He run, didn't 'e?'"

b. **Age**

Though the character's exact age is not mentioned, Crane hints at Henry's age in several ways. First, he most frequently refers to Henry as "the *youth*" or "the *youthful* private." We see in Chapter One that Henry still lives at home with his mother, who calls him "my boy" and "child." Further, before he leaves, he stops by the school where he is enrolled to say good-bye to his "schoolmates," including one particular girl in the crowd, two statements that suggest he is a teenager.

c. **Gender**

Henry's male gender is obvious, but the fact that this story is set in the Civil War when women were not enlisted in the army, male gender becomes key. The story would be quite different if it were about a girl, even one trying to pass herself off as male. This is a story of a young boy becoming a man by earning his "red badge of courage," a war wound.

d. **Nationality**

The setting of the story alongside Henry's name suggests that he is an American of European heritage. More importantly for this story, he is a Northerner fighting for the Union army.

e. **Appearance:**

Crane does not directly describe Henry as much as he does other characters, especially Jim Conklin, to whom he refers as "the tall man," suggesting by comparison that Henry is of average or short stature. In Chapter Five, when the regiment sees action, however, Crane describes Henry, thus:

> Perspiration streamed down the youth's face, which was soiled like that of a weeping urchin. He frequently, with a nervous movement, wiped his eyes with his coat sleeve. His mouth was still a little ways open.

f. **Mental state:**

Key to this story is Henry's mental state. Crane gives us insight into the youth's mind in Chapter Twenty-three, when the enemy approaches with their flag:

> The youth had centered the gaze of his soul upon that other flag. Its possession would be high pride. . . ..

> He plunged like a mad horse at it. He was resolved it should not escape if wild blows and darings of blows could seize it.

g. **Emotional state**

Battle is terrifying to any human being, but as a boy who wants to become a man, Henry is terribly conflicted. He does not know if he is up to the task. He fears he will run from battle. Crane tells us in Chapter Three:

> His emotions made him feel strange in the presence of men who talked excitedly of a prospective battle as of a drama they were about to witness, with nothing but eagerness and curiosity apparent in their faces. It was often that he suspected them to be liars.

NOTE: It is important to remember that people are unique. Therefore, writers pick and choose which of the approaches they will use to describe the particular person who is their topic. For example, if a person has no disabilities, the writer simply skips that approach.

Approaches to Description

Like many authors, Crane uses two methods of description.

a. **Direct description**

In this kind of description, which is the most common, authors directly state what they want their readers to see. Of course, they choose colorful vocabulary to do so, but there is no hinting at things. Look at this passage from Chapter Two of *The Red Badge of Courage* in which Crane uses direct description to tell about the enemy:

> Various veterans had told him tales. Some talked of gray, bewhiskered hordes who were advancing with relentless curses and chewing tobacco with unspeakable valor; tremendous bodies of fierce soldiery who were sweeping along like the Huns. Others spoke of tattered and eternally hungry men who fired despondent powders. "They'll charge through hell's fire an' brimstone t' git a holt on a haversack, an' sech stomachs ain't a'lastin' long," he was told. From the stories, the youth imagined the red, live bones sticking out through slits in the faded uniforms.

THINK IT THROUGH: With your classmates, identify the phrases in the above passage where Crane uses direct description.

b. **Indirect description**

To understand this kind of description, look back at a previous example where we saw various indirect ways that Stephen Crane suggested the age of Henry Fleming—that his mother called him, "my boy," for example. Another indirect method of description is the use of dialogue. In other words, an author can tell something about a character by indicating what the character says and the way in which he or she says it. For example, near the end of Chapter One, Crane includes a conversation between Henry, the tall man (Jim), and the loud man, and the talk turns to the topic of bravery. Crane writes:

> "Did you ever think you might run yourself, Jim?" he asked. On concluding the sentence he laughed as if he had meant to aim a joke.

THINK IT THROUGH: From these two lines of dialogue, what can you deduce about Henry's mental or emotional state?

EXERCISE 3.1: Describing a Person

Directions: Below is a short story set in Russia. Please read the story and then answer the questions that follow.

The Path through the Cemetery
By Leonard Q. Ross

Ivan was a timid little man—so timid that the villagers called him "Pigeon" or mocked him with the title, "Ivan the Terrible." Every night Ivan stopped in at the saloon which was on the edge of the village cemetery. Ivan never crossed the cemetery to get to his lonely shack on the other side. That path would save many minutes, but he had never taken it even in the full light of noon.

Late one winter's night, when bitter wind and snow beat against the saloon, the customers took up the familiar mockery. "Ivan's mother was scared by a canary when she carried him." "Ivan the Terrible—Ivan the Terribly Timid One."

Ivan's sickly protest only fed their taunts, and they jeered cruelly when the young Cossack lieutenant flung his horrid challenge at their quarry.

"You are a pigeon, Ivan. You'll walk all around the cemetery in this cold—but you dare not cross it."

Ivan murmured, "The cemetery is nothing to cross, Lieutenant. It is nothing but earth, like all the other earth."

The lieutenant cried, "A challenge, then! Cross the cemetery tonight, Ivan, and I'll give you five rubles—five gold rubles!"

Perhaps it was the vodka. Perhaps it was the temptation of the five gold rubles. No one ever knew why Ivan, moistening his lips, said suddenly: "Yes, Lieutenant, I'll cross the cemetery!"

The Saloon echoed with their disbelief. The lieutenant winked to the men and unbuckled his saber. "Here, Ivan. When you get to the center of the cemetery, in front of the biggest tomb, stick the saber into the ground. In the morning we shall go there. And if the saber is in the ground—five gold rubles to you!"

Ivan took the saber. The men drank a toast: "To Ivan the Terrible!" They roared with laughter.

The wind howled around Ivan as he closed the door of the saloon behind him. The cold was knife-sharp. He buttoned his long coat and crossed the dirt road. He could hear the lieutenant's voice, louder than the rest, yelling after him. "Five rubles, pigeon! *If you live!*"

Ivan pushed the cemetery gate open. He walked fast. "Earth, just earth…like any other earth." But the darkness was a massive dread. "Five gold rubles. . . ." The wind was cruel and the saber was like ice in his hands. Ivan shivered under the long, thick coat and broke into a limping run.

He recognized the large tomb. He must have sobbed–that was the sound that was drowned in the wind. And he kneeled, cold and terrified, and drove the saber through the crust into the hard ground. With all his strength, he pushed it down to the hilt. It was done. The cemetery . . . the challenge . . . five gold rubles.

Ivan started to rise from his knees. But he could not move. Something held him. Something gripped him in an unyielding and implacable hold. Ivan tugged and lurched and pulled—gasping in his panic, shaken by a monstrous fear. But something held Ivan. He cried out in terror, then made senseless gurgling noises.

They found Ivan, next morning, on the ground in front of the tomb that was in the center of the cemetery. He was frozen to death. The look on his face was not that of a frozen man, but that of a man killed by some nameless horror. And the lieutenant's saber was in the ground where Ivan had pounded it—through the dragging folds of his long coat.[15]

Direct Description

1. **Name:**

a. What is the main character's name?

b. What nicknames do the other men call him?

2. **Gender:** Obviously the gender of all the characters is male. Is this particularly important? Why or why not?

3. **Appearance:**

   a. We are given no description of Ivan except for one thing. What is he wearing?

   b. Why is it important to tell what he is wearing as he leaves the saloon?

4. **Mental or emotional state:**

   a. What are we told directly about Ivan's personality? .

   b. In what way is that personality trait important for this story?

Indirect Description

5. **Age:** Though we are not told Ivan's age directly, we can make a good guess based on certain statements in the story. What seems to be his age, and what leads you to that conclusion?

6. **Nationality:** What nationality is Ivan? How do you know?

7. **Antagonists:** What character trait is exhibited by the other men in the saloon through what they say to Ivan?

8. **Time period:** In what approximate time period does the story seem to be set? Explain your answer.

Now You Try It

Chapter 3, Essay 1
Description of a Person

Specifications

1. The purpose of this assignment is to write a description of a person employing the seven basic approaches to narrative: Name, Age, Gender, Nationality, Appearance, Mental State, and Emotional State.

2. You may choose one of the topics below or, with your teacher's approval, another similar topic:
   - the new kid at school
   - a hero from literature (Hector, Achilles, Beowulf, etc.) before he was famous
   - a member of your family
   - your best friend
   - person (choose age and gender) interacting with a pet

3. Next, complete the pre-writing activity in order to think through your character.

4. As you write, employ methods of direct and indirect description.
   - Direct Description
     - ✓ Strong word choice
     - ✓ Descriptive details
   - Indirect Description
     - ✓ What the character does
     - ✓ What the character says
     - ✓ What other characters say about him/her

5. Follow your teacher's instructions regarding the preparation of your manuscript.

Description of a Person: Pre-Writing Activity

I have chosen to describe _____.

Approach	Details
Name	
Age	
Gender	
Nationality	
Appearance	
Mental State	
Emotional State	

Approaches to Description of Objects

Often in both creative and expository writing, one needs to describe an object. For example, in science class, a student might be asked to describe a leaf; in history, a weapon; in art, a painting. There are seven main approaches to description of objects, each of which is explained in the chart below.

Approach	Details
Color	*Color* could include tint (e.g., red, blue) or degree of brightness (e.g., bright red, pale yellow, soft blue, neon green).
Size	*Size* includes measurement (inches, feet, yards, meters, etc.) or general terms for size (big, small, gigantic, miniscule, etc.).
Shape	*Shape* refers to geometric form (round, square, triangular, etc.) or to absence of shape (amorphous, formless, etc.). It may include geometrical plane (horizontal, perpendicular, etc.).
Texture	Texture differs with the object: fabric (coarse, velvety, etc.); surfaces (rough, smooth, etc.); food (lumpy, gooey, etc.); hair (fine, medium, thick, etc.).
Age	An object's age can be expressed as year of manufacture (e.g., 1957 Chevrolet); term of existence (brand new dishes, antique chair, 100-year-old knife, etc.); or period of creation (Ming Dynasty vase, Victorian candlesticks, etc.). It is also suggested by the object's condition (worn, faded, dog-eared, etc.)
Material	*Material* refers to the substance from which the object is made: wood (oak, pine, etc.), synthetics (plastic, polyester, etc.), metal (gold, brass, etc.), earthen sources (ceramic, glass, etc.).
Attribute	The term *attribute* can refer to effect (poisonous, etc.), reliability, authenticity, flexibility, mobility, transparency, etc.

Crane's *Red Badge of Courage* includes descriptions of all types:

a. **Color:**

   Chapter One: "A river, *amber-tinted* in the shadow of its banks...."

   Chapter Twelve: "Behind them *blue* smoke curled and clouded above the treetops, and through the thickets he could sometimes see a distant *pink* glare."

b. **Size:**

   Chapter Eight: "The battle was like the grinding of an *immense* and terrible machine to him."

   Chapter Fifteen: "[S]uddenly the youth remembered the *little* packet enwrapped in a faded yellow envelope...."

c. **Shape:**

   Chapter One: "A small window shot an *oblique square* of whiter light upon the cluttered floor."

   Chapter Four: "The *billowing* smoke was filled with *horizontal* flashes."

d. **Texture:**

   Chapter Seven: "Once he found himself almost into a swamp. He was obliged to walk upon bog tufts and watch his feet to keep from the *oily* mire."

e. **Age:**

   Chapter Three: "Once the line encountered the body of a dead soldier.... The youth could see that the soles of his shoes had been *worn to the thinness of writing paper*."

   Chapter Three: "The hats of a regiment should properly represent the history of headgear for a period of years. And, moreover, there were no letters of faded gold speaking from the colors. They were *new* and beautiful...."

f. **Material:**

   Chapter One: "A corporal began to swear before the assemblage. He had just put a costly *board* floor in his house," he said.

   Chapter One: "... some *tin* dishes lay upon a small pile of firewood."

Chapter One: "The smoke from the fire at times neglected the *clay* chimney and wreathed into the room, and this flimsy chimney of *clay* and *sticks* made endless threats to set ablaze the whole establishment."

g. **Attribute:**

Chapter Two: "Presently a horseman with *jangling* equipment drew rein before the colonel of the regiment."

Chapter Three: "The sun spread *disclosing* rays, and, one by one, regiments burst into view like armed men just born of the earth."

h. **Condition:**

Chapter Thirteen: "[B]its of rounded trousers, protruding from the blankets, showed *rents* and *tears* from hurried pitchings through the dense brambles."

Chapter Twenty-three: "It was a blind and despairing rush by the collection of men in dusty and *tattered* blue . . . ."

EXERCISE 3.2: Describing Objects

Directions: Below is an excerpt from Homer's *Odyssey* in which Odysseus (called here Ulysses, his Roman name) visits the home of Alcinous. Begin by reading the selection. Then analyze the Description by answering the questions that follow.

The House of Alcinous
By Homer

(1) Ulysses [Odysseus] went on to the house of Alcinous, and he pondered much as he paused a while before reaching the threshold of bronze, for the splendor of the palace was like that of the sun or moon. (2) The walls on either side were of bronze from end to end, and the cornice was of blue enamel. (3) The doors were gold, and hung on

Ulysses at the Court of Alcinous
By Francesco Haye

pillars of silver that rose from a floor of bronze, while the lintel was silver and the hook of the door was of gold. (4) On either side there stood gold and silver mastiffs which Vulcan, with his consummate skill, had fashioned expressly to keep watch over the palace of King Alcinous; so they were immortal and could never grow old. (5) Seats were ranged all along the wall, here and there from one end to the other, with coverings of fine woven work which the women of the house had made. (6) Here the chief persons of the Phaecians used to sit and eat and drink, for there was abundance at all seasons; and there were golden figures of young men with lighted torches in their hands, raised on pedestals, to give light by night to those who were at table. . . .

(7) Outside the gate of the outer court there is a large garden of about four acres with a wall all round it. (8) It is full of beautiful trees—pears, pomegranates, and the most delicious apples. . . . (9) In the furthest part of the ground there are beautifully arranged beds of flowers that are in bloom all the year round. . . . (10) Such, then, were the splendors with which the gods had endowed the house of King Alcinous.[16]

<u>Directions</u>: Beside the cue, copy the relevant word or phrase from the sentence. The first one serves as an example.

1. Sentence 1

    Material: *bronze*

2. Sentence 2

    a. **Color:**

    b. **Material:**

3. Sentences 3-4

    a. **Colors:**

    b. **Age:**

4. Sentence 5

    Texture:

5. Sentence 6

   a. **Color:**

   b. **Attributes:**

6. Sentence 7

   Size:

7. Sentence 9

   Attribute:

Now You Try It

Chapter 3, Essay 2
Description of an Object

Specifications

1. The purpose of this assignment is to demonstrate your ability to write an accurate description of an object, using the following approaches: Color, Size, Shape, Texture, Age, Material, and Attribute.

2. To do this, imagine that you are selling one of your possessions on eBay and need to write a detailed description. Since the potential buyer cannot examine the object by picking it up and looking at it, you will need to be precise in your description. Remember: Customers need to know if there are any flaws in the merchandise, so be sure to give a truthful description. Example: "There is some fading in the book jacket."

3. Next, complete the pre-writing activity in order to note all the details. If a category does not apply to the object being described, you may leave the box blank.

4. As you write, use a business-like tone, but do not hesitate to provide a bit of flair, if you like.

5. Follow your teacher's instructions regarding preparation of the manuscript.

Description of an Object: Pre-Writing Activity

What object will you describe for sale on eBay? _____.

Approach	Details
Color	
Size	
Shape	
Texture	
Age (Including condition)	
Material	
Attributes	

WRITING A GOOD PARAGRAPH

Chapter 4

Notes on Academic Writing

The purpose of this textbook is to prepare students for academic writing. But what is meant by the term *academic*? Academic writing can be defined as writing which is done for class assignments, research papers, and examinations in schools, colleges, and universities. In addition, since writing and reading are two sides of the same coin, the student who can master the writing of a paragraph becomes a student who can read even difficult academic material with mastery.

This chapter will explain the pattern of a paragraph written in the English-speaking world, which includes the United Kingdom, Ireland, the United States, Canada, Australia, New Zealand, and former territories of the British Empire, such as India, Singapore, and Hong Kong.

Topic Sentence and Controlling Idea

The most important thing to know about academic writing in English is that a paragraph is a group of sentences that discuss one clearly defined topic. This topic is usually directly stated in the first sentence of the paragraph, which is called the *topic sentence*.

A topic sentence consists of two parts: (a) the general topic you are writing about, and (b) the controlling idea, that is, the specific point you want to make about the topic.

For example, suppose that you had been studying animal life in the Arctic region and were preparing to write a summary of what you had learned about polar bears. Polar bears, of course, would be your general topic. However, as you studied, you probably learned many things about the polar bear: its eating habits, its hunting skills, the way it raises its young, its adaptation to its environment, and so on. Each one of these topics could be considered a controlling idea, and would require the writing of at least one paragraph. Let's say that for your controlling idea, you choose the latter topic: the polar bear's adaptation to its environment. In short, we could isolate the elements this way:

> General Topic: *polar bears*
>
> Controlling Idea: *adaptation to the cold environment*

The next step is to create a topic sentence by adding a subject and a verb, thus:

> The polar bear is very well-equipped to live in a cold environment.

When composing a topic sentence, one must make sure to write an idea that can be developed in the paragraph. That is to say, a topic sentence is not the same thing as a simple statement of fact. Look at the examples which follow:

STATEMENT OF FACT:

> An eBay shop is selling WigWam socks for $1.00.

TOPIC SENTENCE:

> A shopper can find great bargains in athletic clothing on eBay.

STATEMENT OF FACT:

> Pizza Hut is hiring delivery drivers.

TOPIC SENTENCE:

> There are several reasons why I like working as a delivery driver for Pizza Hut.

STATEMENT OF FACT:

> Our class went to the local art museum last week.

TOPIC SENTENCE:

> The local art museum offers a variety of educational opportunities.

With a simple statement of fact, there is no more to say. The statement needs no development. However, with a well-constructed topic sentence, there is more to say: a list of the great buys on athletic clothing on eBay, the reasons I like working as a delivery driver for Pizza Hut, and the variety of educational opportunities at the local art museum. As you continue to progress in your writing abilities, remember this tip: A topic sentence is not a simple statement of fact.

EXERCISE 4.1: Practicing Topic Sentence and Controlling Idea

<u>Directions</u>: In this exercise, there are five topic sentences. For each one, identify the general topic and the controlling idea.

1. The term *earth* refers to three distinct zones.

    General topic: _____

    Controlling idea: _____

2. The liver plays a complicated role in the body's processes.

    General topic: _____

    Controlling idea: _____

3. Though often at war with each other, the Spartans and Athenians united against the Persians.

    General topic: _____

    Controlling idea: _____

4. Greek theatre was connected to religion in several ways.

    General topic: _____

    Controlling idea: _____

5. Music was central to Greek life in several key ways.

    General topic: _____

    Controlling idea: _____

EXERCISE 4.2: Practicing Topic Sentences and Controlling Ideas

<u>Directions</u>: Below are some general topics. Choose a controlling idea for each and then compose a topic sentence. Remember: do not write a simple statement of fact when you compose the topic sentence.

1. General topic: individual sports
   Controlling idea: _____
   Topic sentence: _____
   _____

2. General topic: school uniforms
   Controlling idea: _____
   Topic sentence: _____
   _____

3. General topic: pets
   Controlling idea: _____
   Topic sentence: _____
   _____

4. General topic: shopping
   Controlling idea: _____
   Topic sentence: _____
   _____

5. General topic: Saturday activity
   Controlling idea: _____
   Topic sentence: _____
   _____

Paragraph Unity

What exactly does it mean to have a controlling idea in your paragraph? It means that this idea will control what can go into and what must be kept out of the paragraph. This is called the principle of unity. Remember that the root of the word *unity* is *uni-*, or *one*. That is, the controlling idea becomes the one idea, the only idea, which can be explored in the paragraph.

If a student decides to write about the polar bear's adaption to its environment, for example, he or she cannot digress within the paragraph and enter information about the way it raises its young or how it catches its food. Though those topics may be related in a general way to the environment, they really are different topics and should not enter this paragraph.

To understand the principle of unity, examine the following paragraph about polar bears. Notice that the controlling idea "adaptation to its environment" is clearly expressed in the topic sentence, and that all the sentences which follow stick to this idea and prove that it is true.

(1) The polar bear is very well-equipped to live in a cold environment. (2) For one thing, the thick fur of the polar bear provides special protection for life in the Arctic area, where temperatures can plummet to -45° F in the winter. (3) In fact, the undercoat of the polar bear is so thick that it can even cause the animal to overheat in the summer, when temperatures rise to 32° F. (4) The second way in which polar bears are equipped for the Arctic environment is the layer of vascularized fat called blubber, which lies just beneath the skin. (5) Blubber is loosely attached to the bear's muscles and, except for appendages, covers the entire body, again adding protection against the cold. (6) Last, the mother polar bear provides her cubs with milk which is high in fat content (31%). (7) This fat helps the cubs maintain their body temperature while they are very young.

This paragraph can be considered a well-unified paragraph because every sentence in it helps to explain how a polar bear is equipped to live in a cold environment.

One of the most serious problems experienced by beginning writers is the tendency to stray from the controlling idea. The student writer will write his or her topic sentence, add a detail or two, then forget all about the controlling idea and add material which is generally—but not specifically—related to the topic at hand. To see an example of this kind of mistake, look at the paragraph below.

> (1) Polar bears are well equipped to live in a cold environment. (2) They have an extra layer of fat and are completely covered with fur. (3) There are actually genetic variations among polar bears. (4) Some have skulls which are 37 cm. wide while others have skulls 41 cm. wide. (5) Polar bears are usually solitary animals. (6) However, sometimes they can be found in groups.

THINK IT THROUGH:

1. Which sentence(s) actually support the topic sentence, "Polar bears are well equipped to live in a cold environment"?

    A. Sentence 2

    B. Sentences 3–4

    C. Sentences 5-6

2. Though all sentences are on the general topic of "polar bears," what seem to be the controlling ideas of the other sentences?

EXERCISE 4.3: Analyzing Paragraph Unity

<u>Directions</u>: Look at the paragraph below. Several sentences have been added to the original, some of which can be considered *on the subject* and others *off the subject*. Read the paragraph and then answer the questions that follow.

The Polar Bear's Adaptation to a Cold Environment

> (1) The polar bear is very well equipped to live in a cold environment. (2) For one thing, the thick fur of the polar bear provides special protection for life in the Arctic area, where temperatures can plummet to -45° F in the winter. (3) In

fact, the undercoat of the polar bear is so thick that it can even cause the animal to overheat in the summer, when temperatures can rise to 32° F. (4) Polar climate can be subdivided into tundra climate and ice cap climate. (5) The second way in which polar bears are equipped for the Arctic environment is the layer of vascularized fat called blubber, which lies just beneath the skin. (6) Blubber is loosely attached to the bear's muscles and, except for appendages, covers the entire body, again adding protection against the cold. (7) Polar bears are one of the few animals that never drink water. (8) They receive the water their bodies need from the animals they eat. (9) Next, the mother polar bear provides her cubs with a milk which is high in fat content (31%). (10) This fat helps the cubs maintain their body temperature while they are very young. (11) Last, although the polar bear is white, its skin is actually black. (12) Since black attracts heat, this skin tone helps the polar bear to soak up heat from the sun.

1. Tell the numbers of the new sentences:

2. Which of the new sentences are *on the subject*?

3. Which of the new sentences are *off the subject*?

4. Before handing this paragraph in for a grade, what would an effective student writer be well advised to do?

   A. Remove all the new sentences.

   B. Add more details about the two types of climate.

   C. Remove Sentences 4, 7, and 8.

EXERCISE 4.4: Analyzing Paragraph Unity

Directions: In each of the paragraphs below, closely examine Sentence 1, which is the topic sentence. Underline the word or words which constitute the controlling idea. Then determine whether each sentence in the paragraph is *on the subject* or *off the subject*. In the space provided, write the numbers of sentences which are off the subject.

Paragraph 1

(1) Kansas, which is in the central United States, has four distinct seasons. (2) Summer, which lasts from June through August, has temperatures ranging upwards of 100° F. (3) The fall begins in September and lasts through November. (4) During this time, the color of the leaves changes from green to yellow and red, and the temperature drops gradually until by November the temperature is in the 50s and 40s. (5) Then with December comes the Kansas winter. (6) Temperatures are usually fairly moderate until January and February when they drop below zero. (7) Christmas is a winter holiday. (8) Spring officially arrives in March, but the lovely spring weather holds off until April or May. (9) School terms generally end late in May or early in June. (10) The temperatures in the spring range from the 60s to the 90s. (11) Kansas is a major wheat-producing state.

Sentence(s) off the subject: _____

Paragraph 2

(1) Birds vary widely with respect to size. (2) Because weight is important in flight, most birds are small. (3) The hummingbird, for example, weighs only 0.1 ounce. (4) The common sparrow weighs 1 ounce, and the robin weighs 3 ounces. (5) Robins are songbirds found in North America and Eurasia. (6) The largest flying birds are swans, pelicans, and geese, which weigh from 14 to 40 pounds. (7) If one considers wingspan, the albatross is the largest with a wingspan of 12 feet. (8) The hummingbird is again the smallest with a wingspan of only 4 inches.

Sentence(s) off the subject: _____

Paragraph Organization

Now that the concepts of topic sentence and unity have been explained, it is time to examine paragraph organization.

Deductive Pattern (General to Specific)

The first thing to recall is the principle of *unity*. That is, as explained above, the sentences which come after the topic sentence must not wander away from the controlling idea which it expresses.

To test whether a paragraph follows the principle of unity, it is possible to rearrange the sentences into a diagram. In the polar bear paragraph, all the sentences should help to explain the polar bear's adaptation to its environment. In addition, they should be arranged in a certain pattern which is characteristic of English writing. To be precise, the arrangement moves from general to specific. The first sentence, the topic sentence, is the most general, and the second sentence, which explains the topic sentence, is more specific. The third sentence can either explain the second sentence a bit more, or it can go on to add another idea about the topic sentence.

"Zigzag" Pattern

The diagram that follows imposes a zigzag line connecting the more general information to the more specific details.

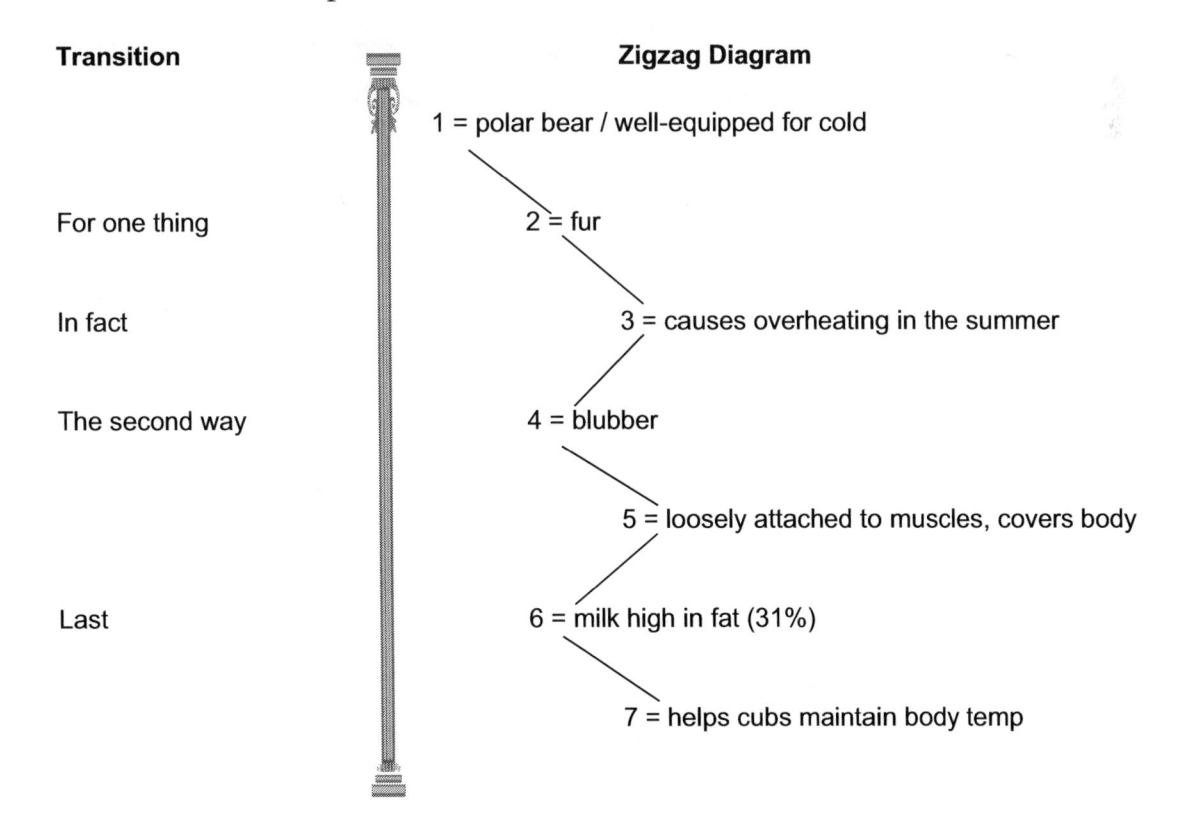

Transition	Zigzag Diagram
	1 = polar bear / well-equipped for cold
For one thing	2 = fur
In fact	3 = causes overheating in the summer
The second way	4 = blubber
	5 = loosely attached to muscles, covers body
Last	6 = milk high in fat (31%)
	7 = helps cubs maintain body temp

In the zigzag diagram, Sentence 1, which is the topic sentence, is farther to the left. It displays the general topic (polar bears) and the controlling idea (well-equipped for the cold) separated by a slash. Sentence 2 is the first point; since it is more specific, it appears farther to the right. Sentence 3 is a detail about Sentence 2; thus it appears even farther to the right. Now, when we come to Sentence 4, we see that this is the second point; thus it is at the same level as Sentence 2, the first point. The diagram continues zigging and zagging between points and details until we reach Sentence 7. Of course, it is possible to have longer paragraphs with more than seven sentences, but the zigzag pattern is almost always used for expository paragraphs. We will see longer paragraphs at a later point in the chapter.

Transitions

Just as drivers follow road signs to keep from getting lost, so readers need road signs to understand where they are in the paragraph. These "signs," which are inserted by the writer, are called transitions. The main points are often marked by words like *first, second, next,* etc. When writers wish to move the reader from the general point to the specific point, they use transitions like *for instance* or *for example.*

In the diagram above, you can see the underlying zigzag pattern of an English paragraph with transitions appearing to the left of the column and text appearing to the right.

Now, how exactly do writers signal to readers which level of generality they are on? Notice sentences 2, 4, and 6. These three sentences are on the second level of generality (that is, they are specific points supporting the topic sentence). Sentences 3, 5, and 7 are on the third level of generality (that is, they are more specific details). Reviewing the polar bear paragraph once again, we see that, to signal a move between these levels, the author inserted structure words in sentences 2, 4, and 6. Structure words that move a reader through a paragraph are called *transitions.* Please notice the transitions in the zigzag diagram (they appear to the left of the column at the appropriate sentence number).

These words operate somewhat like a leash on a dog. The phrase *for one thing* takes readers to the second level of generality. Then they are allowed to explore the topic a bit. When it is time to move to the next point, the author pulls readers back to the next point by tugging a little on the leash, that is, by inserting a structure word such as *next*. This moves readers back to the second level of generality again, making it possible to explore the second topic until the next tug on the leash, which is the structure word *last*.

EXERCISE 4.5: Zigzag Organization

Directions: Read the following paragraphs and then, on a piece of notebook paper, make zigzag diagrams for them in order to see the underlying pattern moving from general to specific to more specific. Then, to the left of the diagram, indicate the transitions that appear at the second level of generality to signal the zigzag structure.

Paragraph 1

(1) There are several modern sports which had counterparts in the ancient world. (2) The most well-known of these ancient sports is perhaps track and field. (3) Events such as discus throwing, distance running, and javelin were enjoyed in the ancient Greek Olympics in the eighth century BC. (4) Soccer is another sport which has ancient origins. (5) The Greeks and Romans played a game based primarily on the kicking of a ball, and there was a form of soccer being played in China in 200 BC as well. (6) Bowling may be the sport which has the earliest known form, however. (7) It appears to have been enjoyed in ancient Egypt nearly 7,000 years ago.

Paragraph 2

(1) Though all tornadoes have heavy winds, they vary widely in their general characteristics. (2) For one thing, tornadoes come in various sizes. (3) They may be as small as 55 yards wide but have been known to range up to a mile in width. (4) The average width of a tornado is probably 300-400 yards. (5) Second, the path of the tornado is quite variable. (6) Some tornado paths are only a few miles long, some 50 miles long, and occasionally even 300 miles long. (7) The speed of the tornadic wind is also widely variable. (8) Of course, it is difficult to measure the speed of tornadic wind because instruments of measurement are often

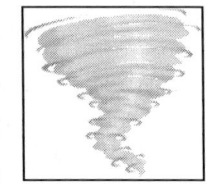

destroyed in the storm, but judging from the effects of the storm, scientists estimate that the wind of a tornado ranges from 100 to 300 mph. (9) Some may even reach speeds of 500 mph.

EXERCISE 4.6: Group Work

Directions: The teacher will divide you into groups of three or four students each. Engage in conversation with your group members to discover one thing you all enjoy—for example, reading, playing musical instruments, etc. Then compose a topic sentence which has both a general topic (e.g., "members of our group") and a controlling idea (what you enjoy). Then move through the paragraph in a zigzag fashion, identifying a group member and telling the specific thing he or she enjoys. Be sure to add transitions as you move from person to person. If time permits, read your paragraph aloud to the class.

Writing Titles

There are several things to remember when selecting a title for a paragraph. First, a title is not the same thing as a topic sentence. You will recall that a topic sentence is a grammatical unit which contains a subject and verb and identifies the topic and the controlling idea. A title, on the other hand, is not usually a sentence. Much more often it is simply a phrase. Most importantly, the title should reflect the *controlling idea*, not the general topic. For example, the topic sentence might state: "The polar bear is well equipped to live in a cold environment," but the title for such a paragraph would be "The Polar Bear's Adaptation to the Cold Environment." If a student were to title the model paragraph as "Polar Bears," it would be far too broad to identify the contents of the paragraph.

EXERCISE 4.7: Identifying Titles

Directions: Below you will find a mixture of titles and topic sentences. Put an X beside those which are titles.

_____ 1. How to Write a Business Letter

_____ 2. Mark Twain set several stories in his home state of Missouri.

_____ 3. The Highland Clans of Scotland

_____ 4. Camping equipment does not have to be expensive.

EXERCISE 4.8: Writing Titles

<u>Directions</u>: Below are five titles that would be suitable for a paragraph. Compose a topic sentence for each one.

1. Suggestions for Yearbook Photography

2. My Favorite Holiday

3. My Favorite Web Site

4. Three Characteristics of Billy Joel's Songs

5. Kids in the Bible

Capitalization in Titles

1. When writing a title, capitalize the following:

    a. the first word

    b. the last word

    c. all nouns, pronouns, verbs, adverbs, and adjectives

    d. subordinating conjunctions such as *because* and *if*

2. Do not capitalize the following parts of speech when they are not the first or last word of the title:

   a. articles such as *a, an*, and *the*

   b. prepositions such as *of* and *between*

   c. coordinating conjunctions

   d. the word *to* when it works as part of an infinitive (e.g., *to read*)

3. The word *email* is capitalized but should be entered without a hyphen between the two syllables.

   a. Organizing Your Email Files

   b. Email Address Books

4. For brand names and company names that start with a small letter, capitalize the second letter, such as *eBay, iPhone,* and *iPad*. These examples show titles that include such trademarks:

   a. iPhones in the Classroom

   b. eBay Shopping Tips

   c. Why I Love My iPad

EXERCISE 4.9: Practicing Capitalization in Titles

Directions: In the space provided, re-write these titles, capitalizing correctly.

1. life below the equator

2. the animals of the sahara

3. with love from alaska

4. how to write a paragraph

5. activities of our church youth group

6. international email addresses

7. what if it snows in august?

8. the oddball antics of my brother

9. grammar rules for the article *the*

10. ebay shopping made simple

Now You Try It

Chapter 4, Essay 1
Zigzag Paragraph

Specifications

1. The purpose of this assignment is to demonstrate your ability to write a "zigzag" paragraph, that is, one written in the deductive method moving from general to specific.

2. Your seven-sentence paragraph is to include the following:
   - a topic sentence containing a general topic and a controlling idea
   - three points
   - one detail sentence for each point

3. Review the model paragraph about polar bears before you begin.

4. Choose one of the topics below or, with your teacher's approval, another of interest to you.
   a. General topic: My family + *Controlling idea:* Activities
   b. General topic: My pet + *Controlling idea:* Three things I love about him/her
   c. General topic: Classical school + *Controlling idea:* Three characteristics
   d. General topic: _____ **+ Controlling idea:** _____

5. Plan your essay by competing the pre-writing activity.

6. Follow your teacher's instructions regarding the preparation of your manuscript.

Zigzag Paragraph: Pre-Writing Activity

I have chosen to write about _____.

1. In this space, write your topic sentence.

2. In this space, identify your first point and its detail.

   Point: _____

      Detail: _____

3. In this space, identify your second point and its detail.

   Point: _____

      Detail: _____

4. In this space, identify your third point and its detail.

   Point: _____

      Detail: _____

Paragraph Coherence

As explained above, one feature of good paragraph organization is the use of transitions. Transitions and other kinds of structure words are used to create paragraph *coherence*. That is, they help everything hang together well in the paragraph.

Coherence can be provided in several ways, but here we will only be concerned about connecting sentences with explicit markers of coordination and subordination. Basically, connecting words, or *conjunctions*, can be classified into three groups on the basis of their function in the sentence.

    a. **Group 1** words are the simple coordinating conjunctions:
and, but, or, nor, for, so, and *yet.*

        Example: The emu is a bird, *but* it cannot fly.

    b. **Group 2** words are conjunctive adverbs such as *however, on the other hand, in addition, therefore,* and *consequently.* (NOTE: Some of these transitions are two- or three-word phrases, but to keep things simple we will just call them *Group 2 words.*) There are two punctuation patterns for Group 2 words.

        Examples: The emu is a bird; *however,* it cannot fly.

        The emu is a bird. However, it cannot fly.

    c. **Group 3** words are subordinating conjunctions This group includes words like *although, because,* and *just as,* as well as time words like *before* and *after.* They normally introduce dependent (i.e., subordinate) clauses.

        Example: *Although* the emu is a bird, it cannot fly.

Note: The punctuation of a Group 3 sentence depends on the position of the subordinate clause. If the sentence begins with the subordinate clause, a comma will be used to separate it from the main clause. But if the subordinate clause is used at the end of the sentence, usually no punctuation is used.

Examples:

Because their fat makes good skin oil, emus have economic value.

Emus have economic value *because their fat makes good skin oil.*

The chart below provides a classification of transitions and cohesion words.

Function	#1 Coordinating Conjunctions	#2 Conjunctive Adverbs	#3 Subordinating Conjunctions
Addition	and or nor	in addition also moreover furthermore	(none)
Cause-Effect	so for	therefore as a result consequently	because since
Comparison	and or nor	similarly likewise	just as…, so… as as if
Contrast	but yet	however on the other hand nevertheless	although while
Chronology	and then	after that later eventually	after before

EXERCISE 4.10: Practicing Paragraph Coherence

<u>Directions</u>: Below are pairs of sentences which can be connected with structure words from Groups 1, 2, and 3. Beneath the pair of sentences, you will see three different

types of conjunctions marked *a* (a Group 1 word), *b* (a Group 2 word), and *c* (a Group 3 word). On another piece of paper, re-write the pairs of sentences using the conjunction specified. Punctuate correctly. The first one serves as an example.

1. Chris likes adventure stories. He has not read *White Fang*.

    a. (*but*) *Chris likes adventure stories, but he has not read White Fang.*

    b. (*however*) *Chris likes adventure stories. However, he has not read White Fang.*

    c. (*although*) *Although Chris likes adventure stories, he has not read White Fang.*

2. Mt. McKinley is the highest peak in North America. Mt. Fuji is the highest peak in Japan.

    a. (and)

    b. (similarly)

    c. (just as)

3. Wichita is located on the flat Kansas prairie. It is a good place to build and test airplanes.

    a. (so)

    b. (therefore)

    c. (because)

4. Julius Caesar was assassinated in 44 BC. A civil war broke out.

    a. (and then)

    b. (after that)

    c. (after)

EXERCISE 4.11: Practicing Paragraph Coherence

Directions: Read the following paragraphs and then, on another piece of paper, compose sentences as directed. A chart has been provided to assist your selection.

The Oracle at Delphi

[1] For over a thousand years, the Temple of Apollo at Delphi in ancient Greece was the site of the famous Oracle of Delphi. The Oracle (or fortune-teller) was a woman recruited from Delphi who would reside in the temple and offer prophecies about the future to people with important decisions to make. The woman who served as the Oracle was always called Pythia. She was named after the earth-dragon Python, who had been defeated by Apollo and buried deep under the Temple of Apollo. Plutarch, the famous Greek writer of the first century AD, said that the Pythia would breathe the vapors of a spring that ran under the temple. These vapors, which were said to be the breath of the Python, caused the Pythia to go into a frenzy of dancing and twirling during which she would speak incomprehensible things. The gibberish which Pythia uttered had to be "interpreted" by a priest of Apollo because it made no sense to an ordinary person.

[2] Now, Plutarch stated that in his time the vapors were decreasing, which has led modern scientists to wonder what exactly was beneath the temple that would cause a person to go into an altered state and hallucinate. In the 1980s, a team led by the geologist Jelle Zeilinga de Boer discovered that there were two fault lines that run under the Temple of Apollo. From these crevices rise a gas, probably ethylene, which could have caused the trances of the Pythia. In addition, they found ethane, methane, and ethylene in the spring water near the Oracle, which, of course, supports what Plutarch said 1,800 years before.

The Temple of Apollo as it appears today

[3] We know today that certain dosages of ethylene can cause people to lose control over their movements, thrash about wildly, and moan in strange voices. Exposure to ethane and methane can cause oxygen deprivation, which would cause the Pythia to gasp. These effects have all been recorded by people who saw the Pythia in her trance. From what we know about long-term exposure to these vapors, it is

safe to say that the unfortunate women who were chosen to be the Pythia were subjected to substances which could cause brain damage and even death. The "real" prophecies were coming from the priests. Whether the priests believed the Pythia's trance was caused by dragon's breath or not, they would have had to create an interpretation for the devotee of the Oracle. Can we conclude that the Oracle of Delphi was a very successful hoax of the ancient world?

1. **Cause/Reason.** Use information from Paragraph 1 to write correctly punctuated sentences about why the priests had to tell the prophecies to the temple visitors.

   a. therefore

   b. because

2. **Chronology:** Use information in Paragraph 1 to talk about the chronological details of the defeat and burial of the Python. Use correct punctuation.

   a. after that

   b. after

3. **Comparison:** Use information from Paragraph 3 to write correctly punctuated sentences about the similarities of behavior between the Pythia and users of methamphetamines.

   a. similarly

b. just as

4. **Contrast:** Use information from this short essay to write correctly punctuated sentences showing contrast. Consider the myth about the Python's breath and the discoveries of de Boer's team.

   a. however

   b. although

Now You Try It

Chapter 4, Essay 2
"Zigzag" Paragraph with Coherence

Specifications

1. The purpose of this assignment is to demonstrate your understanding of the following:
   - the deductive nature of an English essay, moving from general to specific to more specific
   - the conventions regarding titles
   - the topic sentence with both a general topic (GT) and a controlling idea (CI)
   - the placement of the CI near the end of the sentence where the voice is strongest
   - the principle of unity (the CI determines what can go in or must stay out of the paragraph; everything must develop the CI)
   - the principle of coherence (transition words and phrases to guide the reader through the paper)

2. Choose one of these topics or, if your teacher approves, another of interest to you:
   - equipment to protect athletes
   - places to go on a weekend that do not cost anything
   - responsibilities of taking care of a pet
   - your choice

3. Prepare a "zigzag" diagram, using phrases only.

4. When you write the essay, include a topic sentence, three points, at least one detail for each point, and transition for the main points (*first, second, third,* etc.).

5. Follow your teacher's instructions regarding the preparation of the manuscript.

"Zigzag" Paragraph with Coherence: Pre-Writing Activity

The title of my paragraph will be: _____.

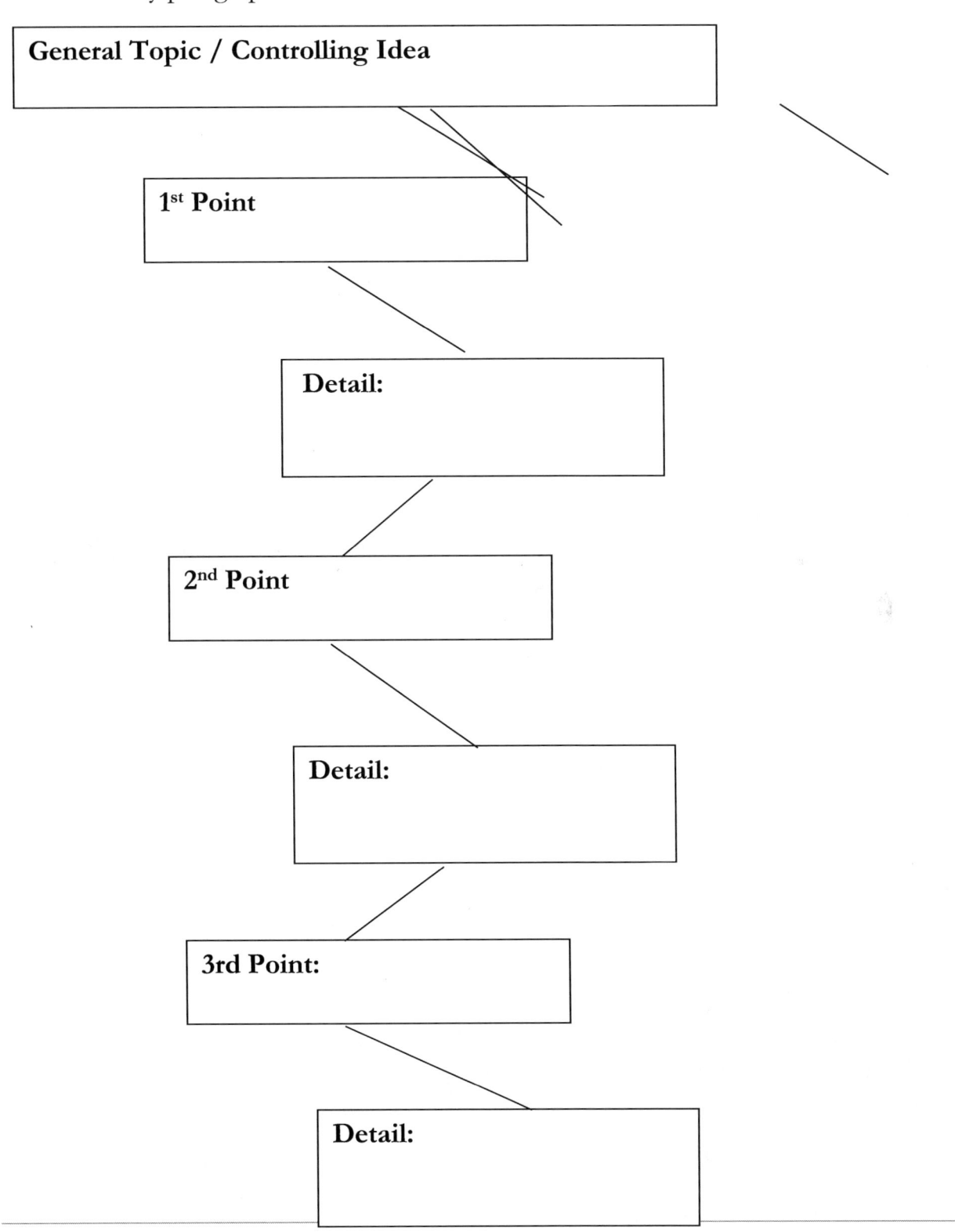

| General Topic / Controlling Idea |

| 1st Point |

| Detail: |

| 2nd Point |

| Detail: |

| 3rd Point: |

| Detail: |

Writing about Literature

In an academic setting, students are often asked to write about a piece of literature. As with other kinds of writing, this type is also arranged with a zigzag structure, starting with the topic sentence (what you are trying to prove) and proceeding with the points and details that prove it to be true.

One of the main differences with this kind of writing, however, is that the main idea is proved (or supported) with material from the book itself. This can take two forms: either quotations or paraphrasing. In either case, it is important, especially at the end of the paragraph, to comment on the quotation before rushing on. In order to drive home your point, one needs to explain to the reader the significance of the quote. The pattern can be expressed with this formula:

Idea + Quotation + Comment

Model Essay about Literature

Where Is God?

(1) In Psalm 77, David wrote about a common human weakness: questioning the existence of God when undergoing a long period of distress. (2) We often cry out to God but receive no immediate reply. (3) We may even cry out for a long period of time, perhaps even years as was the case with the Jews of Europe during the Holocaust of the twentieth century. (4) King David himself admitted to this kind of doubt, saying, "I cried out to God for help; I cried out to God to hear me. When I was in distress, I sought the Lord; at night I stretched out untiring hands." (5) His statement that he had "untiring hands," suggests that, indeed, he did pray for a long time because his hands would need to be untiring to sustain such prayer. (6) But David did not stop there. (7) Rather, he starts to think it through and adds this interesting sentence: "But my soul refused to be comforted." (8) Notice that he does not

say God refused to comfort him. (9) Rather, he acknowledges that it was his own soul that "refused" God's comfort. (10) How does a person overcome these doubts and find rest and the assurance of God's presence? (11) In verse 10, David tells us how he managed to do so: "Then I thought, 'To this I will appeal: the years of the right hand of the Most High.' I will remember the deeds of the Lord; yes, I will remember your miracles of long ago." (12) Specifically, he recalls how the Jews spent hundreds of years in captivity in Egypt. (13) No doubt during that time some of them felt abandoned by God, living their whole lives as slaves. (14) But David, speaking directly to God, acknowledges, "Your path led through the sea, your way through the mighty waters, though your footprints were not seen. You led your people like a flock by the hand of Moses and Aaron." (15) By the time we reach the end of Psalm 77, we have come to understand that God's silence does not mean God's absence and, like the Jews in Egypt, we can direct our souls to receive his comfort while we await the unfolding of his plan.

EXERCISE 4.12: Writing about Literature

Directions: The model essay above entitled "Where Is God?" uses quotations and paraphrasing to support a topic sentence. After reading the paragraph, analyze the technique by answering the questions below.

1. What is the controlling idea for this paragraph, which is expressed in Sentence 1?

2. In the chart below, list the numbers of all the sentences that contain a quotation of one or more complete sentences in the left column. Then list the numbers of all the follow-up sentences in the right column.

Sentences which have quotations	Sentences which have comments on the quotations

3. From the sentences in the right-hand column, what can you conclude about this kind of writing?

Now You Try It

Chapter 4, Essay 3
Writing about Literature

Specifications

1. The purpose of this assignment is to demonstrate that you understand how to write a paragraph about a work of literature based on the following formula:

   Idea + Quotation + Comment.

2. Read the story "Pyramus and Thisbe," which was originally written by Ovid (43 BC – AD 17).

3. The opening sentence of your essay will be: "The story 'Pyramus and Thisbe' as told by Thomas Bulfinch shows the folly of acting without knowing all the facts."

4. Begin by completing the chart in the pre-writing activity. Decide on two examples and select quotations to support each one.

5. Compose the remainder of the paragraph in zigzag style with transitions, using quotation marks when necessary.

6. Follow your teacher's instructions regarding the preparation of the manuscript.

Pyramus and Thisbe
As Told by Thomas Bulfinch

Pyramus was the handsomest youth, and Thisbe the fairest maiden, in all Babylonia, where Semiramis reigned. Their parents occupied adjoining houses; and the neighborhood brought the young people together, and acquaintance ripened into love. They would gladly have married, but their parents forbade. One thing, however, they could not forbid—that love should glow with equal ardor in the bosoms of both. They conversed by signs and glances, and the fire burned more intensely for being covered up. In the wall that parted the two houses there was a crack, caused by some fault in the structure. No one had remarked it before, but the lovers discovered it. What will not love discover! It afforded a passage to the voice; and tender messages used to pass backward and forward through the gap. As they stood, Pyramus on this side, Thisbe on that, their breaths would mingle. "Cruel wall," they said, "why do you keep two lovers apart? But we will not be ungrateful. We owe you, we confess, the privilege of transmitting loving words to willing ears." Such words they uttered on different sides of the wall; and when night came and they must say farewell, they pressed their lips upon the wall, she on her side, he on his, as they could come no nearer.

Next morning, when Aurora had put out the stars, and the sun had melted the frost from the grass, they met at the accustomed spot. Then, after lamenting their hard fate, they agreed that next night, when all was still, they would slip away from the watchful eyes, leave their dwellings and walk out into the fields; and to insure a meeting, repair to a well-known edifice standing without the city's bounds, called the Tomb of Ninus, and that the one who came first should await the other at the foot of a certain tree. It was a white mulberry tree and stood near a cool spring. All was agreed on, and they waited impatiently for the sun to go down beneath the waters and night to rise up from them. Then cautiously Thisbe stole forth, unobserved by the family, her head covered with a veil, made her way to the monument, and sat down under the tree. As she sat alone in the dim light of the evening, she descried a lioness, her jaws reeking with recent slaughter, approaching the fountain to slake her thirst. Thisbe fled at the sight and sought refuge in the hollow of a rock. As she fled she dropped her veil. The lioness after drinking at the spring turned to retreat to the woods, and seeing the veil on the ground, tossed and rent it with her bloody mouth.

Pyramus, having been delayed, now approached the place of meeting. He saw in the sand the footsteps of the lion, and the color fled from his cheeks at the sight. Presently he found the veil all rent and bloody. "O hapless girl," said he, "I have been the cause of thy death! Thou, more worthy of life than I, hast fallen the first victim. I will follow. I am the guilty cause, in tempting thee forth to a place of such peril, and not being myself on the spot to guard thee. Come forth, ye lions, from the rocks, and tear this guilty body with your teeth." He took up the veil, carried it with him to the appointed tree, and covered it with kisses and with tears. "My blood also shall stain your texture," said he, and drawing his sword plunged it into his heart. The blood spurted from the wound and tinged the white mulberries of the tree all red; and sinking into the earth reached the roots, so that the red color mounted through the trunk to the fruit.

By this time Thisbe, still trembling with fear, yet wishing not to disappoint her lover, stepped cautiously forth, looking anxiously for the youth, eager to tell him the danger she had escaped. When she came to the spot and saw the changed color of the mulberries she doubted whether it was the same place. While she hesitated, she saw the form of one struggling in the agonies of death. She started back; a shudder ran through her frame as a ripple on the face of the still water when a sudden breeze sweeps over it. But as soon as she recognized her lover, she screamed and beat her breast, embracing the lifeless body, pouring tears into its wounds, and imprinting kisses on the cold lips. "O Pyramus," she cried, "what has done this? Answer me, Pyramus; it is your own Thisbe that speaks. Hear me, dearest, and lift that drooping head!" At the name of Thisbe, Pyramus opened his eyes, then closed them again. She saw her veil stained with blood and the scabbard empty of its sword. "Thy own hand has slain thee, and for my sake," she said. "I too can be brave for once, and my love is as strong as thine. I will follow thee in death, for I have been the cause; and death which alone could part us shall not prevent my joining thee. And ye, unhappy parents of us both, deny us not our united request. As love and death have joined us, let one tomb contain us. And thou, tree, retain the marks of slaughter. Let thy berries still serve for memorials of our blood." So saying she plunged the sword into her breast.

Her parents ratified her wish, the gods also ratified it. The two bodies were buried in one sepulchre, and the tree ever after brought forth purple berries, as it does to this day.[17]

Writing about Literature: Pre-Writing Activity

General Topic / Controlling Idea:
"Pyramus and Thisbe" / folly of acting without knowing all the facts.

1st Example:

Supporting quote:

2nd Example:

Supporting quote:

OUTLINING

Chapter 5

Introduction

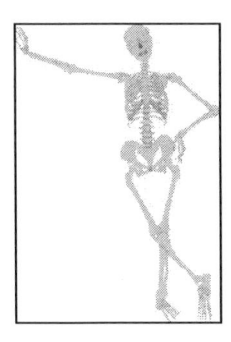

The outline is to the composition what the skeleton is to the body: it provides the structure of the work being created. When writing the outline, the writer has a chance to decide in what order the subtopics should be presented and the number of details that will be added. Then, when writing the essay, the writer simply follows his or her plan. This chapter will explain the form of the outline, the grammar of the outline, and the logic of the outline.

Form of the Outline

1. An outline contains a title and several subdivisions.

2. The subdivisions reflect levels of generality. They are arranged from general to specific.

3. The main points are listed at Roman numerals (*I, II, III,* etc.). These points will later become topic sentences.

4. The details under the main points are expressed with capital letters (*A, B, C,* etc.).

5. More specific details are expressed with Arabic numerals (*1, 2, 3,* etc.).

6. Even more specific details are expressed with small letters (a, b, c, etc.), thus:

    I. _____

        A. _____

            1. _____

                a. _____

7. I is better to have a phrase outline than a sentence outline. That is why an outline is often referred to as a skeleton. It is just a frame to which "meat" will be added.

8. After each Roman numeral, capital letter, Arabic number, and small letter, place a period. However, do not use a period after the phrases.

9. All of the periods must be aligned, one directly beneath the other. This can be accomplished by using an alphanumeric template available on your word processing software. In *Word*, outlines are called multi-level lists and can be generated automatically by using the templates available on the ribbon in the Paragraph group.

10. Capitalize only the first word in the phrase except in the case of proper nouns:

   B. Athletic shoes ⟵ Common noun: Capitalize only the first
   1. Nike
   2. New Balance ⟵ Proper noun: Capitalize both words.

```
                The Clothes in Jake's Closet
        I. Pants
            A. Uniform pants
            B. Denim pants
        II. Shirts
            A. Oxford shirts
            B. Tee shirts
        III. Shoes
            A. Dress shoes
                1. All-weather leather
                2. All-weather suede
            B. Athletic shoes
                1. Nike
                2. New Balance
```

Grammar of the Outline

Phrases vs. Sentences

Generally speaking, an outline using phrases or dependent clauses is preferable to a sentence outline, but it is always best to make the outline conform to the teacher's specifications.

Phrase Outline	Sentence Outline
I. Baseball equipment	I. Our school has baseball equipment.
A. Bases	A. We have four bases.
B. Baseballs	B. We have twelve regulation baseballs.
C. Bats	C. We own ten aluminum bats.

The advantage of the phrase outline is that it allows for more space on the page, making it easier to read and more pleasing to the eye.

Parallelism

In grammar, the term parallelism means that units joined by a conjunction must be the same grammatical type:

Parallel nouns: The most common pets are *cats, dogs,* and *fish.*

Parallel adjectives: Classical education values what is *good, true,* and *beautiful.*

In outlines, phrases must be grammatically parallel if they are at the same level of generality. That is to say, all entries at Roman numerals need to be the same grammatical type (all nouns, all dependent clauses, all adjectives, etc.) All the entries at capital letters must be the same grammatical type as each other, but do not have to be the same as that of the Roman numerals, and likewise for entries at the Arabic numbers.

INCORRECT	CORRECT
I. Types of dramatic poetry	I. Types of dramatic poetry
A. Monologues	A. As monologues
1. By Robert Browning	1. Robert Browning
2. Alfred, Lord Tennyson	2. Alfred, Lord Tennyson
B. Theatrical	B. For the theatre
1. *Oedipus Rex* (Sophocles)	1. *Oedipus Rex* (Sophocles)
2. *Othello* (Shakespeare)	2. *Othello* (Shakespeare)

THINK IT THROUGH: With your classmates, discuss the grammatical problems with the incorrect version (the outline on the left).

Logic of the Outline

1. One logical aspect of the outline is the principle of sub-division. To *divide* something means to break it into at least two points (*di-* comes from Greek and means *two*). Therefore, on an outline if you have an *A*, you must have a *B*. If you have a *1*, you must have a *2*, and so on. Compare the examples below:

INCORRECT	CORRECT
I. Perennial flowers	I. Perennial flowers
A. Roses	A. Roses
II. Annual flowers	B. Irises
A. Marigolds	II. Annual flowers
B. Geraniums	A. Marigolds
	B. Geraniums

2. In cases where there is only one example to be provided, handle it as shown at I.B. below (Rupert Brooke):

> I. British poets of World War I
>   A. Wilfred Owen
>   1. "Dulce et Decorum Est"
>   2. "Anthem for Doomed Youth"
>   B. Rupert Brooke ("The Soldier")

3. It is important to avoid duplication. You must not repeat a point—either in the same words or in a synonymous word or phrase.

INCORRECT	CORRECT
Poetry of the Civil War	Poetry of the Civil War
I. Poems	I. By Walt Whitman
A. By Walt Whitman	II. By Ambrose Bierce
B. By Ambrose Bierce	

THINK IT THROUGH: With your classmates, determine what is wrong with the left side of the above outline, "Poetry of the Civil War."

4. Similarly, make sure that points marked in the same way (e.g., *A* and *B*) are at the same level of generality.

INCORRECT	CORRECT

American Poets
 	
I. Nineteenth century
 	
  A. Walt Whitman
 	
    1. "I Hear America Singing"
 	
    2. Emily Dickinson
	American Poets
	
	I. Nineteenth century
	
	  A. Walt Whitman
	
	    1. "I Hear America Singing"
	
	    2. "O Captain! My Captain!"

THINK IT THROUGH: Regarding the outline "American Poets," determine what is wrong with the outline on the left.

5. Ideas should be presented from general to specific. It is not logical to have a specific element govern a more general one.

INCORRECT	CORRECT

Civil War Poems
 	
I. "O Captain! My Captain"
 	
  A. Poems about Abraham Lincoln
	Civil War Poems
	
	I. Poems about Abraham Lincoln
	
	  A. "O Captain! My Captain!"
	
	  B. "John Burns of Gettysburg"

THINK IT THROUGH: Regarding the outline "Civil War Poems," determine what is wrong with the outline on the left.

6. Last, the sections of the outline should be roughly equal in length. It is not logical to have, for example, ten subdivisions of *A* and only subdivision of *B*.

INCORRECT	CORRECT

I. Lyric poets
  A. Wordsworth
  B. Shelley
  C. Byron
  D. Keats
  E. Coleridge
  F. Tennyson
  G. Rossetti
II. Ballad poets
  A. Burns
  B. Scott
	I. Lyric poets
	  A. Wordsworth
	  B. Shelley
	  C. Byron
	II. Ballad poets
	  A. Burns
	  B. Scott

EXERCISE 5.1: Form of the Outline

<u>Directions</u>: Place each item on the list at the left into its proper place on the outline at the right. Two entries have been added for assistance.

Baskets	Title:
Concessions	I. *Court*
Center circle	A.
Soft drinks	B.
Perimeter	1.
Key	2.
Court	3.
Popcorn	4.
Food	5.
Features of a Basketball Arena	II.
3-point line	A.
Snacks	B.
Hot dogs	1.
Low post area	2.
Nachos	C.
Pizza	1. *Hot dogs*
Inner areas	2.

EXERCISE 5.2: Logic and Grammar of the Outline

<u>Directions</u>: The outline below contains mistakes in logic and form. On notebook paper, write a correct outline for this material. HINT: Nothing needs to be removed, just corrected.

Literature Made into Movies

I. *Hondo*

   A. Westerns

   B. *Shane*

II. Civil War

   A. *Red Badge of Courage*

   B. *Gods and Generals*

     1. Novel about four battles

        a. Movie about one battle

III. World War I

   A. *All Quiet on the Western Front.*

   B. *The African Queen.*

     1. Starring Humphrey Bogart.

   C. *The Four Horsemen of the Apocalypse.*

   D. *Four Sons*

     1. Based on a short story

     2. A silent movie

     3. Produced in 1928

     4. Written by Philip Klein

PROVERB

Chapter 6

Introduction

The most famous author and collector of proverbs was Solomon, the wisest king who ever lived. In his book, he writes to his son, warning him against folly and urging him to seek wisdom. After the first nine chapters, which demonstrate the superiority of wisdom, Solomon and other authors give proverbs for every aspect of life: money, jobs, marriage, government, child-rearing, and much more. The Book of Proverbs contains short, memorable, and often vivid advice—useful for teaching young and old.

King Solomon in Old Age
By Gustav Doré

To prove a point in an argument, the Greeks usually took their wise sayings from the works of their poets, as here in the *Republic*, where Plato argues the rude nature of the gods with a quote from Homer's *Iliad*:

> O heavens! Verily in the house of Hades there is soul and ghostly form but no mind at all![18]

That the Greeks loved their poets was also known by the apostle Paul, who had had a classical education. Therefore, when he spoke about God to the men of Athens on Mars Hill, he was able to substantiate his message by employing proverbs from the Greek poets Epimenides and Aratus, as when he said:

> He is not far from each one of us; *"for in Him we live and move and exist,"* as even some of your own poets have said, *"For we also are His children"* (emphasis added) (Acts 17:28a).[a]

As in most matters, the Romans imitated the Greek use of proverbs and quoted them frequently, so many Roman sayings originated with Latin poets, such as Virgil's famous maxim "Love conquers all" *("Amor vincit omnia")*. Roman proverbs were

---

[a] The first italicized quote is from Epimenides; the second, from Aratus.

frequently also taken from the works of their philosophers such as Seneca, who once penned, "Where fear is, happiness is not."

Definition and Purpose of the Proverb

A *proverb* (also known as a *maxim*) is a short statement that gives advice. It is used to urge the hearer to good or bad behavior. Unlike the fable, the proverb simply states a moral without a story. In this chapter, you will learn how to expand a proverb, that is, to demonstrate that a proverb is worth following.

Proverbs, or maxims, are popular in all cultures and time periods. For example, *The Maxims of Ptahhotep* originated in Egypt when the vizier Ptahhotep was serving the government around 2375-2350 BC. Similarly, many famous sayings originated among the Chinese, such as "Give a man a fish, and you feed him for a day. Teach a man to fish, and you feed him for a lifetime." And in more modern times the American Benjamin Franklin generated dozens of wise and witty sayings, such as, "Early to bed and early to rise, makes a man healthy, wealthy, and wise."

Benjamin Franklin 1705-1790

Regardless of the origin of a proverb, its purpose is to help people, especially the young, to find their way in a world they may not know is a troubled place. As Solomon said, "Get wisdom; get insight" (Proverbs 4:5).

EXERCISE 6.1: Proverbs in the Ancient World

Directions: The website *Wikiquote* lists proverbs by topic and language. For each language of the ancient world, select one you like and copy it in the space provided. The first one serves as an example.

URL: < https://en.wikiquote.org/wiki/Category:Proverbs_by_language>

1. Chinese: *A book holds a house of gold.*

2. Greek

3. Hebraic (Hebrew)

4. Latin

Approaches to Expanding a Proverb

Because proverbs develop wisdom, teachers in the ancient world provided instruction on the key ways to examine a proverb. The resulting composition is termed an Expanded Proverb. In his handbook for the progymnasmata, Aphthonius listed seven ways to approach a proverb (see chart below):

Approach	Details
Citation	Cite, or state, the proverb about which you are writing. If necessary, provide context. That is, explain.
Encomium	Praise the wisdom of the person who created or reported the proverb.
Paraphrase	Restate the proverb in your own words.
Cause	Explain why this proverb was created.
Comparison	Compare the subject under discussion to something similar by means of a simile or metaphor.

Contrast	Compare the subject under discussion to its opposite.
Example	Give an example from fact or fiction to prove the truth of the proverb.
Testimony of the Ancients	Quote an authority from the past to corroborate the wisdom of the saying.
Exhortation	Encourage readers to conduct themselves according to the teaching of the proverb.

Special Note: Techniques of Paraphrasing

Paraphrasing is the art of explaining what another person has said or written, using different (usually simpler) words without changing the meaning of the original. In the Expanded Proverb, paraphrasing is used to make the meaning more clear to others. There are basically seven techniques for paraphrasing, which are listed below, though it is important to note that one change often requires another.

1. Re-phrase a simile or metaphor.

   Original: The pen is mightier than the sword.
   Mark-up: The pen is mightier than the sword.
   Paraphrase: Persuading is mightier than fighting.

2. Use synonymous words or phrases.

   Original: All that glitters is not gold.
   Mark-up: All that glitters is not gold.
   Paraphrase: Not all pretty things that attract us are valuable.

3. Use a different form of the same word.

   Original: Beggars can't be choosers.
   Mark-up: <u>Beggars</u> can't be <u>choosers</u>.
   Paraphrase: If you <u>beg</u>, you can't <u>choose</u>.

4. Change verbs from active to passive.

   Original: Don't count your chickens before they hatch.
   Mark-up: Don't <u>count</u> your chickens before they <u>hatch</u>.
   Paraphrase: Chickens shouldn't <u>be counted</u> before they <u>are hatched</u>.

5. Change verbs from passive to active.

   Original: Bloom where you are planted.
   Mark-up: Bloom where you <u>are planted</u>.
   Paraphrase: Bloom where God <u>plants</u> you.

6. Change complex sentences to compound sentences.

   Original: If you can't beat 'em, join 'em.
   Mark-up: <u>If</u> you can't beat 'em, join 'em.
   Paraphrase: You can't beat 'em, <u>so</u> you should join 'em.

7. Change compound sentences to complex sentences.

   Original: The early bird gets the worm, but the second mouse gets the cheese.
   Mark-up: The early bird gets the worm, <u>but</u> the second mouse gets the cheese.
   Paraphrase: <u>Although</u> the early bird gets the worm, the second mouse gets the cheese.

These seven techniques have been applied in isolation from each other, but in reality, a good paraphrase typically employs several techniques. For an example, look at the following variations of an English proverb.

   Proverb: You can lead a horse to water, but you can't make it drink.

- **Removal of metaphor:** You can counsel people, but you can't make them accept what you say.

- **Use of synonymous words and phrases:** You can give people advice, but you can't force them to accept it.

- **Change in verb from active to passive:** People can be advised, but they cannot be forced to accept the advice.

- **Change in structure from compound to complex:** Although you can give people advice, you cannot force them to accept it.

EXERCISE 6:2: Practicing Paraphrase

Directions: In the space provided, practice the suggested paraphrasing technique.

1. You can't change a leopard's spots.

    Remove the metaphor:

2. No man can serve two masters.

    Re-phrase with synonymous words or phrases:

3. Curiosity killed the cat.

    Change from active to passive:

4. Rome wasn't built in a day.

    Change passive to active:

5. Zeal without knowledge is a runaway horse.

   Re-phrase by changing the form of the word:

6. Away goes the devil if he finds the door shut against him.

   Change from complex to compound:

7. Everyone talks about the weather, but nobody does anything about it.

   Change from compound to complex:

Special Note: Comparison Techniques

The comparison approach to Expanded Proverb again has the purpose of making the meaning more clear. To draw meaningful comparisons, the ancients suggested using literary techniques such as simile, metaphor, and analogy. These tools show similarities between two things that might not, at first glance, seem alike. Writers can use similes and metaphors as one-sentence comparisons. Though both are used for description, simile says that A is like B, while metaphor simply says that A is B. The Bible abounds in literary techniques of this type, which are used for various purposes:

1. To help people understand the nature of God:

   "How often would I have gathered your children together as a hen gathers her brood under her wings, and you were not willing!" (Matthew 23:37b)

2. To teach us about righteous and unrighteous behavior:

   Do not look at wine when it is red,
     when it sparkles in the cup

and goes down smoothly.
In the end it bites like a serpent
and stings like an adder (Proverbs 23:31-32).

3. To help us envision something we have not yet seen:

The hairs of his head were white like wool, like snow. His eyes were like a flame of fire" (Revelation 1:14).

Another option for a comparison is an analogy, which both makes a comparison and explains it. Some of the parables in the Bible are in the form of an analogy, as in Matthew 13:31-32 where verse 31 employs a simile and 32 explains its meaning:

[31]He put another parable before them, saying, "The kingdom of heaven is like a grain of mustard seed that a man took and sowed in his field. [32]It is the smallest of all seeds, but when it has grown it is larger than all the garden plants and becomes a tree, so that the birds of the air come and make nests in its branches."

Many similes, metaphors, and analogies that have come down to us from the ancient world employ themes of nature, as in these passages which used serpents, fire, and mustard seeds. Such comparisons were easily understood in a largely agrarian society where people lived close to nature and were able to observe animals and plants quite easily. However, in our time, the population is more urban than rural, and common culture is shared not through the barnyard experience, but through the commercial world of television and the Internet.

As a result, today's writers and speakers who wish to make a point with a comparison can draw easily upon commercial products For example, Lay's potato chips used to promote their product with the line, "Betcha can't eat just one," so when counseling young people to avoid addiction to methamphetamines, one might say, "They're like Lay's potato chips: you can't stop at just one."

The exercises below will help you invent comparisons using nature or commercial products in the progymnasmata exercise of Proverb.

EXERCISE 6.3: Making Comparisons with Nature

Directions: Below are comparisons that use nature to help someone understand a moral principle. Each quotation is followed by a question, which is designed to draw attention to the spiritual truth behind the natural phenomenon. Please read each quotation and respond to the question that follows it.

1. **Quotation:** The wolf shall dwell with the lamb, . . .
   and a little child shall lead them (Isaiah 11: 6).

   Question: Under what conditions would a wolf dwell peacefully with a lamb? Who is the little child that will bring this condition about?

2. **Quotation:** In the parable of the weeds, an enemy sowed weeds into a man's field. Jesus explained that the enemy was the devil and that ultimately the weeds (evil ones) would be thrown into the fire. The disciples asked if they should root out the weeds (the evil ones) in the world, and Jesus said, "No, lest in gathering the weeds you root up the wheat along with them" (Matthew 13:29).

   Question: What are followers of Christ advised *not* to do when evil seems to be winning?

3. **Quotation:** "I will remove from you your heart of stone and give you a heart of flesh" (Ezekiel 36:26).

   Question: What is the difference between stones and flesh? Knowing that, can you understand what God is saying here?

EXERCISE 6.4: Making Comparisons with Commercial Products

Directions: Below is a list of products which people buy to fill a need. In some cases, a particular product is named (as in the Lay's potato chip example above), and in others a generic product is named. Following each is a question which should help you consider applications of these needs and products to other aspects of life. If your teacher permits, brainstorm your ideas with a partner or in a small group.

1. To strengthen our fingernails, we might use Keranique.

   What can we do to strengthen our families?

2. To reward dogs for obeying commands, we give them treats.

   To encourage improved study skills among students, what could a school or teacher do?

3. To perk up our hair-dos on a "bad hair day," we use dry shampoo, though it really is not a permanent solution.

   If we have a problem to solve, how effective is a temporary solution?

4. If we learn that the weed killer Round-up causes cancer, we stop using Round-up.

   If drug addicts want to restore their lives, what can they do?

5. To keep algae out of the swimming pool, we use chlorine.

   If arguments are wrecking family life, what spiritual application might be helpful?

Special Note: Finding Testimony of the Ancients

Testimony of the ancients can be particularly difficult to find. For this section of the expanded proverb, it is not enough to ask parents or friends for their opinion on the proverb. You must find a published quote by a famous person to support your proverb. Since wisdom is often determined by how long something lasts, the supporting testimony is usually from a person who is no longer living, hence the term: testimony of the *ancients*.

There are several places where you can find an authoritative quotation:

- a Bible concordance
- a book of quotations
- Internet websites

EXERCISE 6.5: Finding Testimony of the Ancients on the Internet

Directions: This exercise will give you practice finding proverbs and maxims from various sources on the Internet.

Bible

Go to the *Topical Bible* web site at <www.openbible.info/topics>. In the search bar, type the topic that appears in each prompt. Click "Search." Then skim the verses that appear and choose one that you like. Write it in the space below, being sure to give the verse reference (such as John 3:16). The first set will serve as an example.

1. a. **Topic:** Idleness

    b. **Verse:** *Go to the ant, O sluggard; consider her ways, and be wise.*

    c. **Reference:** *Proverbs 6:6*

2. a. **Topic:** Kindness

   b. **Verse:**

   c. **Reference:**

3. a. **Topic:** Forgiveness

   b. **Verse:**

   c. **Reference:**

Book of Quotations

<u>Directions:</u> Go to the web site for *Bartlett's Familiar Quotations* at <www.bartleby.com/348/>. Then do the two searches below.

1. Scroll down to the Category Index. You will see "Featured Entries" in alphabetical order. These represent some of the most frequent topic searches. Click on the topic *Beauty*. On the next screen, choose a quotation you like. Copy it in the space provided and include the name of the person to whom the quote is attributed.

   a. Quote:

   b. Person:

2. Return to the "Category Index." Click on the word *Ability*. On the next screen, you will see an alphabetical list of topics. Scroll down to *Diligence* and click on it. On the next page, select a quotation you like. Copy it in the space provided and include the name of the person to whom the quote is attributed.

   a. Quote:

   b. Person

Model Essay on a Proverb

Preserving Tranquility

Citation

I appreciate the proverb that says, "Let sleeping dogs lie."

Encomium (Praise of the Speaker)

The person who originated this saying showed wisdom by observing how the simple incidents of home life can teach us about getting along in the world.

Paraphrase

The saying "Let sleeping dogs lie" means that when our circumstances are comfortable and trouble-free, we should not introduce discomfort and troubles. we should not introduce discomfort and troubles.

Cause

The person who originated this saying was probably a dog owner who noticed that when his dog was sleeping, he had a tendency to pet it or tickle its ears. Though he did not mean to invite the dog to interact with him, he discovered that the dog, now awake, wanted to play or sit on his lap and lick his face. In short, he saw that waking the dog brought him unintended troubles and removed the pleasant moment that had led him to pet the dog in the first place.

Comparison

Waking a sleeping dog is a little like stirring up a hornet's nest. At first, the environment is peaceful. But after stirring the nest or waking the dog, one finds the environment is no longer peaceful and has even become dangerous.

Contrast

The opposite of waking a sleeping dog is letting the dog alone. One can admire the dog's loveable nature by simply observing the dog.

Example

One afternoon a grandmother was taking care of her grandchildren. The children were at the art table coloring and making greeting cards, and the atmosphere was quiet and pleasant. The grandmother approached them and said, "Why don't we put on a play?" The children, thinking this a grand idea, sought her help in choosing a play, creating costumes, gathering props, rearranging the furniture, and rehearsing the play. Of course, all this activity led to conflicts among the siblings about who would play the hero and who the villain and required countless decisions, such as whether to have a curtain on the stage, whether to apply stage make-up, how to get cooperation from grandmother's cat, who was cast in the role of a lion. The afternoon passed, but when the parents came for the children, the grandmother was completely exhausted. How she wished she had just let the children work cooperatively at the art table!

Testimony of the Ancients (Corroboration)

The Bible also addresses the issue of disturbing a dog with whom one is at peace: "Whoever meddles in a quarrel not his own is like one who takes a passing dog by the ears" (Proverb 26:17). As before, we see that one's peace can be changed to conflict through one's own interference.

Exhortation

Life has enough problems without creating problems for ourselves. We should try always to preserve tranquility and not bring unintended problems on ourselves.

EXERCISE 6.6: Analyzing an Expanded Proverb

<u>Directions</u>: After reading the model essay, analyze Expanded Proverb by answering the questions below, one for each approach.

1. **Encomium:** For what does the writer praise the originator of the proverb?

2. **Paraphrase:** What part of the paraphrase concisely expresses the idea of the proverb?

3. **Example:** How does the example prove the point of the proverb?

4. **Comparison:** What similar proverb is used in this section?

5. **Contrast:** What is the opposite of waking the sleeping dog?

6. **Cause:** How is the creation of the proverb explained?

7. **Testimony of the Ancients:** What ancient source is quoted to corroborate the proverb?

8. **Exhortation:** What are we advised not to do?

Now You Try It

**Chapter 6 Essay
Proverb**

Specifications

1. The purpose of this assignment is to demonstrate your ability to write an expanded proverb, employing the nine approaches: Citation (and Narrative, if needed), Encomium, Paraphrase, Cause, Comparison, Contrast, Example, Testimony of the Ancients, and Exhortation.

2. Begin by choosing a proverb. In a library or on the Internet, search for a proverb or maxim in one of these resources:
   - *The Topical Bible* (web site) <www.openbible.info/topics>
   - *Bartlett's Familiar Quotations* (web site) <www.bartleby.com/348/>

3. Begin by completing the pre-writing activity on the next page, or, if your teacher prefers, prepare a formal phrase outline. This will help you think through the full meaning of your proverb before you write.

4. Follow your teacher's instructions regarding the preparation of the manuscript.

Proverb: Pre-Writing Activity

The proverb I have chosen is on the subject of _____.

Approach	Details
Citation	
Narrative (if needed)	
Encomium	
Paraphrase	
Cause	
Comparison	
Contrast	
Example	
Testimony of the Ancients (Corroboration)	
Exhortation	

CHREIA

Chapter 7

Introduction

What was there about that famous line—"Toto, I don't think we're in Kansas anymore"—which was uttered by Dorothy (Judy Garland) in the 1939 movie *The Wizard of Oz*? What gave it staying power and allowed it to slip so definitely into popular culture, known by all and used with the power of a proverb?

In addition to words, there are real-life actions that have hung around, too. One of the most touching was Lou Gehrig's famous line from his farewell speech of July 4, 1939, "Today, I consider myself the luckiest man on the face of the earth." This sentiment was made especially poignant by the fact that one of the greatest baseball players of all time was announcing his resignation from baseball due to a totally debilitating muscular disease called amyotrophic lateral sclerosis (ALS), known ever since as Lou Gehrig's disease. Certainly the basic oxymoron that underlay the statement helped to make it so memorable. In what way could a man with such a disease and in such a situation consider himself the luckiest man alive?

As human beings, we possess the ability to express feelings in words, and when someone packs a deep emotion experienced in common by many people everywhere into a few brief words, people will remember it and pass it on to others in the way of encouragement—or possibly a warning.

In some cases, words fail. The poet T. S. Eliot used the term *ineffable* to refer to feelings that run so deep they can barely be put into words. We know that there are such situations because Paul states in Romans 8:26 that the Holy Spirit can intercede for us when we do not know what to say: "Likewise the Spirit helps us in our weakness. For we do not know what to pray for as we ought, but the Spirit himself intercedes for us with groanings too deep for words."

It is our shared experience as human beings that allows these nuggets of wisdom or the noble actions of another person to resonate in hearts and minds for years to come. They tug at the heartstrings, so to speak, or bring a tear to the eye.

Definition and Purpose of a Chreia

A Chreia [KRĀ-ə] is either a detailed explanation of a wise saying made by a specific person, or an anecdote, a brief narrative about something that once happened. It differs from a proverb, whose author is often unknown and often emerges from a specific context. The example above by Lou Gehrig of the New York Yankees forever links the history of baseball to the humble gratitude of a stricken athlete. It is worthy of remembrance—which leads us to the next point: the purpose of a Chreia.

To understand the purpose of a Chreia, it is helpful to consider the Greek adjective from which it is derived: *chreiodes* [KRĀ-ə-dēz], or *useful*. A detailed explanation of what a fellow human being has observed about life is useful to us in that it can help us to understand our world and find the courage to navigate the often troubled waters of life. In the Judeo-Christian world, individual believers often encourage and counsel one another by quoting Scripture or reminding a discouraged friend of the stories of David and Goliath or Joseph's rising influence in Egypt. As Americans, we often remember and take heart from George Washington's men at Valley Forge or Abraham Lincoln's reading by the firelight as a boy. Since these are the stories of actual people who overcame great obstacles, they can be very influential.

Types of Chreia

There are two basic types of chreia. The first is the Verbal Chreia (or verbal anecdote). This is the explication of a famous quotation made by a named person who faced an opportunity, a fear, or a hardship. One great example from the ancient world is Julius Caesar's famous line, *"Veni, vidi, vici"* ("I came, I saw, I conquered"), a line he wrote to the Roman Senate in 47 BC after defeating the troops of Pharnaces II of Pontus at the Battle of Zela. Caesar had been outnumbered two-to-one, so the succinct nature of the quote shows the character of Caesar and makes it a memorable saying.

The second type of chreia is the Action Chreia. This can be defined as the communication of what a real person has done in a challenging situation. Because it is a short narrative, it is sometimes called an *anecdote*, which is a brief story that proves a point. The Greek and Roman historians frequently employed anecdotes both to prove a point and to make their histories enjoyable reading. One such example is that written by Plutarch in his *Life of Alexander*, where Plutarch records that the Battle of Issus in 333 BC was a decisive victory for Alexander against the Persians under the command of Darius III. Although Darius was not killed in the battle, the victory nonetheless went to Alexander, whose men seized for him the tent of Darius, "full of splendid furniture and quantities of gold and silver," yet it was Alexander's treatment of the women in Darius' family which Plutarch took pains to record, believing it an excellent example of the character of Alexander:

> But as he was going to supper, word was brought him that Darius' mother and wife and two unmarried daughters, being taken among the rest of the prisoners, upon the sight of his chariot and bow, were all in mourning and sorrow, imagining him to be dead.
>
> After a little pause, more lively affected with their affliction than with his own success, he sent Leonnatus to them, to let them know Darius was not dead, and that they need not fear any harm from Alexander, who made war upon him only for dominion; they should themselves be provided with everything they had been used to receive from Darius.
>
> This kind message could not but be very welcome to the captive ladies, especially being made good by actions no less humane and generous.
>
> For he gave them leave to bury whom they pleased of the Persians, and to make use for this purpose of what garments and furniture they thought fit out of the booty. He diminished nothing of their equipage, or of the attentions and respect formerly paid them, and allowed larger pensions for their maintenance than they had before.
>
> But the noblest and most royal part of their usage was, that he treated these illustrious prisoners according to their virtue and character, not suffering them to hear, or receive, or so much as to apprehend anything that was

unbecoming. So that they seemed rather lodged in some temple, or some holy virgin chambers, where they enjoyed their privacy sacred and uninterrupted, than in the camp of an enemy.[19]

As discussed in Chapter 2, good writers are always said to show, rather than simply to tell, and Plutarch's use of this Action Chreia indeed goes much farther in making the author's point about Alexander than any simple statement of Alexander's fair-mindedness could do.

Approaches to Expanding a Chreia

Approach	Details
Citation / Narrative	Cite the saying or briefly narrate the anecdote.
Encomium	Praise the wisdom of the person who originated the saying or who performed the action.
Paraphrase	For a verbal chreia, re-state the proverb in your own words. For an action chreia, explain what is to be learned from the anecdote.
Cause	Explain why the saying or action was wise. What were its benefits?
Comparison	Indicate a position or action similar to the one you are explaining, or use a simile or metaphor to explain the idea.
Contrast	Indicate a position or action opposite the one you are explaining.
Example	Give an example from fact or fiction to prove the truth of the saying.

Testimony of the Ancients (Corroboration)	Quote an authority from the past to confirm the wisdom of the saying. A truth that has stood the test of time is powerful support.
Exhortation	Encourage your readers to follow the teaching of the saying or anecdote.

When students write a composition explaining the meaning of a saying or anecdote, they are said to be expanding a Chreia. The nine basic parts of the expansion are explained in the accompanying chart.

Model of a Verbal Chreia

Shakespeare's "Viperous Worm"

Citation + Narrative + Encomium

In William Shakespeare's play *King Henry VI, Part One*, the king tries to persuade the Dukes of Gloucester and Winchester to bring an end to their quarrels, saying: "Civil dissension is a viperous worm / That gnaws the bowels of the commonwealth" (Act III, scene 1, lines 77-78). Shakespeare is to be praised for his understanding of the delicate nature of human organizations.

Paraphrase

Specifically, what Shakespeare is trying to say is that when individuals and factions within a group stir up hatred and discord, the organization they seek to improve is actually destroyed.

Cause

Shakespeare had a strong motive to express this point of view in his play because at the time this play was written, Queen Elizabeth I, a Protestant, was on the throne of England. She came to be queen in a time period when

Catholics and Protestants were at each other's throats. The reigns of her father, sister, and brother before her had all been politically turbulent. Thus, when Elizabeth came to the throne, she vowed to reduce the trouble between the two groups. She even went so far as to suppress the performance of plays which seemed to stir up trouble. Thus, Shakespeare, a playwright, was always careful in his plays to support Elizabeth's way of looking at things. The members of his audience would certainly have understood what Henry VI was saying to the quarreling dukes.

Comparison

Englishman Sir Samuel Garth (1661-1719) once conveyed a similar notion but used the metaphor of a stream instead of that of a worm:

> Dissensions like small streams, at first begun,
> Scarce seen they rise, but gather as they run.[20]

As a small stream rises, it can become bigger and, by implication, more destructive, just as the small worm can cause great damage by burrowing deep.

Contrast

The opposite of dissension is harmony. When people deal with others in a harmonious way, the results are generally pleasing to both parties. This does not mean that people must never express disagreement when they think improvement is needed. But it does mean that people should approach one another with respect and try to find common ground. In a reasonable society, people will cultivate an attitude of "give-and-take." No one has all the power, nor is anyone completely powerless. There is a desire among people on both sides to keep peace in order to promote those values which they *do* hold in common.

Example

History is full of examples where dissension brought about destruction. The fall of Jerusalem in AD 70 can be attributed as much to internal factions as to the Roman conquest. The Jewish historian, Josephus, makes it quite clear that

John of Giscala and other zealots were directly responsible for the fall of Jerusalem. Their feuds had created such great disorder that it was relatively easy for the Roman general Titus to march in and take control. For some, it may almost have seemed a blessing.

Testimony of the Ancients (Corroboration)

Abraham Lincoln shared Shakespeare's opinion about civil dissension. He once observed that "a house divided against itself cannot stand." This observation came directly from the teachings of Jesus, recorded in Matthew 12:25. Thus, for Christians, Lincoln's words go beyond mere opinion and achieve the status of truth.

Exhortation

As we go through life, we all encounter times when we disagree with family members, friends, or authorities. It is hoped that all of us can remember Shakespeare's warning about the "viperous worm" and seek cordial ways to bring about change without destroying what we seek to improve.

EXERCISE 7.1: Analyzing a Verbal Chreia

Directions: After reading "Shakespeare's 'Viperous Worm,'" analyze a Verbal Chreia by answering these questions, one for each approach.

1. **Citation / Narrative:** We see the quotation about civil dissension is being applied to the kingdom of what English king?

2. **Encomium:** The writer praises Shakespeare for understanding what?

3. **Paraphrase:** The thirteen-word quotation is reduced to what three words?

4. **Cause:** Why did Shakespeare include such sentiments in his English history play?

5. **Comparison:** What different metaphor was used by Sir Samuel Garth to convey the idea of dissension?

6. **Contrast:** We are told that the opposite of civil dissension is what?

7. **Example** What historical event is used to illustrate civil dissension?

8. **Testimony of the Ancients:** What two persons are cited?

9. **Exhortation:** We are encouraged to seek what?

The Art of Paraphrasing: Review

As in the previous chapter, Proverb, a writer will include paraphrasing as one of the key approaches in Chreia. Below is an exercise to help you practice paraphrasing.

Exercise 7.2: Paraphrasing Practice

Directions: Below are some famous quotations. In the space provided, write a paraphrase of the quotation. The first one serves as an example.

1. "The hand that rocks the cradle rules the world" (William Ross Wallace).

   Mothers have an important influence on the world.

2. "There are no gains without pains" (Benjamin Franklin).

3. "Man shall not live by bread alone" (Jesus Christ, Matthew 4:4a).

4. "A person's a person, no matter how small" (Dr. Seuss, *Horton Hears a Who!*).

5. "Preach the gospel at all times, and when necessary use words" (St. Francis of Assisi).

6. "A blow with a word strikes deeper than a blow with a sword" (Robert Burton).

Model of an Action Chreia

The Extremes of Diogenes of Sinope

Narrative

Diogenes of Sinope (d. 323 BC) was one of the founders of the Cynic philosophy, which was famed for its ascetic ideals. Diogenes, for example, would roll himself in hot sand during the summer and cling to snow-covered statues during the winter in order to prepare himself to endure any adversity that might come his way in the future.

Diogenes of Sinope (d. 323 BC)

Encomium

The Cynic philosophy has long been abandoned, but Diogenes did show wisdom in his understanding that it is important to prepare for all eventualities.

Paraphrase

By his extreme preparations in hot and in cold seasons, Diogenes was demonstrating that a life of ease never prepared a person to handle hardship.

Cause

Preparing for the worst circumstances is beneficial because it satisfies the survival instinct in all of us. Muscles grow weak and flabby when we loll about on the sofa in an air-conditioned room, which only makes muscles undependable allies in times when natural disaster, war, or criminal assault threatens our safety and our lives. It is much better to spend some time exercising or practicing self-defense so that we are not the helpless playthings of the winds.

Comparison

The Spartans had a similar philosophy to that of Diogenes. Theirs was a warrior culture, and boys were taken from their families at the age of seven to be sent away for military training. The boys were subject to harsh living. The trainees were exposed to the elements and to fierce animals so that they could learn to handle themselves in all circumstances. The older boys were told to beat the younger boys in order for them to develop toughness. So famous were the Spartans for lives of toughness and asceticism that the adjective *spartan* is used in English to refer to a life of deprivation.

Contrast

The opposite philosophy was delineated by Aesop in his fable "The Ant and the Grasshopper." The grasshopper made music all summer and did no work to set food aside, while the ant was busy storing food for the winter. In the autumn, the grasshopper asked the ant for food, but the ant, not impressed with the grasshopper's lack of preparation, refused.

Example

Brent Gleeson, the author of *TakingPoint [sic]*, has written that one of the sayings among Navy SEALS is to get comfortable being uncomfortable. He explains that one part of Navy SEAL training is what they call "surf torture." That is to say, a group of trainees will link arms and remain together in frigid zones of the Pacific Ocean until they reach the point of hypothermia. Then they cover themselves with sand and remain so for the rest of the day. The idea is to push the extremes out of the mind and focus on the task at hand. This kind of activity prepared him for business life, Gleeson says, making it easier for him to handle the kinds of discomfort that arise when interacting with people in stressful situations.[21] Indeed, almost anything would seem do-able after serving as a Navy SEAL.

Testimony of the Ancients (Corroboration)

In his epistle to the Ephesians, the apostle Paul wrote of the necessity of preparation for spiritual battle. He counseled believers to be fully prepared by taking up "the whole armor of God":

> Therefore take up the whole armor of God, that you may be able to withstand in the evil day, and having done all, to stand firm. Stand therefore, having fastened on the belt of truth, and having put on the breastplate of righteousness, and, as shoes for your feet, having put on the readiness given by the gospel of peace. In all circumstances take up the shield of faith, with which you can extinguish all the flaming darts of the evil one; and take the helmet of salvation, and the sword of the Spirit, which is the word of God (Ephesians 6:13-17).

Exhortation

Ultimately, all of us need to be better about getting off the couch and engaging in activities that keep us strong and fit both physically and spiritually so that we are ready to handle whatever challenges come our way in the future.

EXERCISE 7.3 Analyzing an Action Chreia

<u>Directions</u>: Answer these questions about the model Action Chreia, "The Extremes of Diogenes of Sinope."

1. **Citation/Narrative:** Why did Diogenes of Sinope roll in hot sand in summer and embrace snow-covered statues in the winter?

2. **Encomium:** The writer praises Diogenes for understanding the importance of what?

3. **Paraphrase:** What does the author say never prepared anyone for hardship?

4. **Cause:** Summarize in your own words why such preparation is advisable?

5. **Comparison:** What is said to be similar to Diogenes' methods?

6. **Contrast:** Who or what is said to be the opposite of Diogenes' methods?

7. **Example:** What twenty-first century example of Diogenes' methods is cited?

8. **Testimony of the Ancients:**

    a. What Biblical person is cited?

    b. What particular metaphor is cited?

9. **Exhortation:** What are we encouraged to do?

EXERCISE 7.4: Analyzing a Published Chreia

<u>Directions</u>: Below is a real-life example of a Chreia, which appeared on *Got Questions,* a web site sponsored by Got Questions Ministries. (Sentences have been numbered for instructional purposes.) Since it was not written for a classroom exercise but is a "real-life" example of the approaches to a verbal anecdote, the approaches appear in the order that suited the writer, not in the standard textbook format, which is typical of "real world" writing. Please read the essay and then in the questions that follow try to determine which sentences constitute each approach. Two of the approaches were not used by the writer of this essay, which, once again, shows that writers adapt the approaches to their needs.

> **Question: What did Jesus mean when he said, "The eye is the lamp of the body"?**
>
> **Answer: (1)** Jesus said, "The eye is the lamp of the body. (2) If your eyes are good, your whole body will be full of light" (Matthew 6:22). (3) Here our Lord describes the eye as a lamp which lights the entire body. (4) Our eyes are the entrance to our hearts and minds and, as such, they provide a doorway to our very souls. (5) When He referred to "good" eyes, He meant eyes that not only see well, but also perceive well. (6) It is not only what we see, but how we perceive what we see that makes the difference between godliness and ungodliness, between light and darkness. (7) Bad eyes lead to bad perception, but if our eyes are good, our whole person will be illuminated. (8) If we are in a lighted room, we see everything clearly. (9) We can move around obstacles and locate whatever we're looking for. (10) But walking in darkness results in stumbling, falling, and groping for some secure thing to hang on to. (11) Our eyes can be used to see that which is good or evil, that which is beneficial or harmful, and the things we see and perceive affect our whole being. (12) If we perceive goodness, that will radiate outward from within our hearts and minds.

(13) But if we allow our eyes to linger on evil, we are so affected by what we see that darkness actually begins to emanate from within and can corrupt us and those around us.

(14) The Bible tells us that Satan disguises himself as an angel of light. (15) That's his great deception—to make people think they've found the light when in fact it's the darkness of false light (2 Corinthians 11:14). (16) His intention is to blind us to truth and corrupt our minds, and he uses our eyes to gain entrance to our hearts. (17) He parades before us all manner of evil, from the deluge of pornography on the internet to the endless barrage of the world's goods that appeal to our materialistic impulses. (18) He deludes us into believing that these things will make us happy, fulfilled people, when all the while they are robbing us of the very joy we long for. (19) He wants us to allow more and more darkness into our minds through the books we read, the movies we watch, and the images we allow our eyes to linger upon. (20) In that way, the light of the glory of God shining in the face of Jesus Christ is obscured to us. (21) Although the light is everywhere, like the sun at noonday—blazing, blinding light—if our eyes are continually focusing on sin, the light we perceive is no light at all. (22) If we want to be filled with the true light, we have to turn from sin and repent and ask God to forgive and cleanse us and open our spiritual eyes. (23) Then we must commit to being careful where we allow our eyes to go. (24) We guard our hearts and souls by guarding our eyes.[22]

In the blank, write the letter that corresponds to the approach used in the specified sentences.

A. Citation / Narrative

B. Encomium

C. Paraphrase

D. Cause

E. Comparison

F. Contrast

G. Example

H. Testimony of the Ancients

I. Exhortation

_A_____ 1. Sentences 1-2

_C_____ 2. Sentences 3-10

_D_____ 3. Sentences 11-13

_G_____ 4. Sentences 14-21

_I_____ 5. Sentences 22-24

_B, E, F, H_ 6. Unused approaches

Now You Try It

Chapter 7 Essay
Chreia

Specifications

1. The purpose of this assignment is to demonstrate your ability to write an Expanded Chreia.

2. Begin by choosing a quotation from a work of literature with which you are familiar. Examples from some well-known works include the following:

   - "There's no place like home." (Dorothy in *The Wizard of Oz* by Frank Baum.)

   - "You see but you do not observe. The distinction is clear." (Sherlock Holmes in *A Scandal in Bohemia* by Arthur Conan Doyle)

3. Begin by completing the pre-writing activity or by preparing a formal phrase outline, if your teacher prefers.

4. Follow your teacher's instructions regarding the preparation of the manuscript.

Chreia: Pre-Writing Activity

I will write about _____.

Approach	Details
Citation	
Narrative (if needed)	
Encomium	
Paraphrase	
Cause	
Comparison	
Contrast	
Example	
Testimony of the Ancients	
Exhortation	

REFUTATION

Chapter 8

Introduction

The city of Rome was founded by twin brothers, Romulus and Remus. Born of the priestess Rhea Silvia and the god Mars, the boys were hated by their uncle the king. He left them in a basket in the Tiber River, hoping they would drown. However, the basket washed up on shore, and the boys were nursed by a she-wolf. Eventually, the boys were found by a shepherd, who raised them as his own children. Romulus and Remus grew up to kill their wicked uncle and build the city of Rome.

Do you believe that this story is true? Is it convincing? In previous chapters, you have learned to retell narratives and fables. In this chapter, you will move on to the higher step of analyzing a narrative to see whether it is true or not.

THINK IT THROUGH: Have you ever been told a far-fetched story that someone was passing off as the truth? Be ready to relate that story to your classmates, identifying what seemed "fishy" to you. If you know, indicate whether the story turned out to be true or not—and how you were able to find out.

Definition and Purpose

Refutation is a form of rhetoric that attempts to prove that a story is false. Since much of Greek and Roman oratory took place in the courtroom, this exercise was very important. A Roman lawyer like Cicero might use refutation to prove that his client could not have committed a crime and that his opponent's version of the story was false. Historians such as Livy and Herodotus might use it to show why an ancient myth was false and then prove that his readers should consider other explanations for a historical event.

In addition, historians often write refutations to stop the spread of false information about historical events. As long ago as 440 BC, the Greek historian Herodotus was working to set the record straight on the Trojan War, pointing out that Homer had historical inaccuracies in his great epic poem, *The Iliad*.

But is refutation used today? Certainly.

- In elections, one candidate for public office might use refutation to disprove another's position on a controversial issue such as climate change.
- In a late-night disputation in a college dormitory, one student might use refutation to point out flaws in another's account of the world's origins.
- In law enforcement, a police detective relies on elements of refutation to eliminate suspects.
- In school, a teacher might ask students to confirm or refute the ideas in a work they are studying.

THINK IT THROUGH: With your classmates, make a list of situations where you have used or could use facts to refute what someone else has said—in your family, school, church, community, state, or country.

The mirror image of Refutation is Confirmation, rhetoric that attempts to prove that a story is true. This chapter will focus on Refutation; the next, on Confirmation, but it is important to see that these two exercises employ the same approaches.

Choosing a Narrative for Refutation

Narratives that make themselves ripe for refutation are those which are neither *certainly* true nor *certainly* false. Instead, they are narratives in which one or more elements are uncertain, perhaps even sketchy or "fishy." For example, if the entire seventh grade sees on a daily basis that Johnny enthusiastically eats a banana at lunch, it would be silly to argue later that Johnny never eats bananas. There is nothing in doubt about Johnny and the bananas. However, she-wolves do not raise human children every day, so the story of Romulus and Remus needs to be subjected to proof.

Choosing to Refute All or Part of a Narrative

Sometimes it is necessary to refute an entire narrative; other times, only a part of the narrative requires scrutiny. In the case of Romulus and Remus, one could try to prove that Romulus and Remus never actually existed, refuting the entire narrative. On the other hand, one could refute only the fantastic elements, arguing that the twins may have been real enough but were not raised by a she-wolf. This has, in fact, been done by writers who point out that the Latin word *lupa* could mean either *she-wolf* or *woman of ill repute*. According to this argument, the twins were rescued not by a wild animal, but by a local woman, albeit one with a bad reputation like that of Mary Magdalene before her encounter with Jesus.

Asking Questions to Winnow out the Truth

One can begin the process of refutation by asking Yes/No questions about a suspicious narrative.

- *Did the event happen at all?*
- *Does the narrative contradict what we know to be true?*
- *Are there more logical explanations for farfetched elements in the narrative?*

To apply these to the story of Romulus and Remus, one could ask:

- Did Romulus and Remus even exist?
- Has the word *lupa* been understood correctly?
- Is there a more logical explanation for the rescue of the twins?

Approaches to Refutation

Classical teachers of rhetoric Aphthonius and Hermogenes gave six categories for refuting or confirming arguments:

- Is the narrative *possible* or *impossible*?
- Is the narrative *probable* or *improbable*?

- Is the narrative *clear* or *unclear*?
- Is the narrative *consistent* or *inconsistent*?
- Is the narrative *appropriate* or *inappropriate*?
- Is the narrative *expedient* or *inexpedient*?

Since Refutation attempts to show that something is *not* true, it focuses on the negative form of each pair: *im*possible, *im*probable, *un*clear, *in*consistent, *in*appropriate, and *in*expedient. The first four of these approaches challenge the factual truth of a story, as shown in the chart below:

Approach	Details
Impossible	The event violates the laws of nature.
Improbable	The events are too unusual to be accepted.
Unclear	There are not enough details to be convincing.
Inconsistent	There are contradictory elements.

In today's Internet world, stories pass rapidly around the country—and even the world—by email transmission, but how are we to believe everything we read? One way to check out whether a story is true, false, or a mixture of both, is to consult a web site called *Snopes.com*, which addresses the veracity, or truth, of "urban legends." Here are some narratives that have circulated the country and the responses *Snopes* supplied.

- In May 2002, a story circulated that an 83-year-old grandma had beaten up six airport security guards, employing a motorized wheelchair, an oxygen canister, a knitting needle, a cigarette lighter, and a skinny-fisted jab at a jaw! Grounds for rejecting? The story was just too *improbable* to be true. *Snopes* tracked down the source of the story and learned that it

152

originated as a humorous piece by writer Bob Wallace, who termed the piece a "traveler's daydream" in an era when people are frustrated by airport security.[23]

- Second, in October 2010, a rumor began circulating that mandarin oranges imported from China were causing health problems. An American identified only as "a lady" was said to have broken out in a rash after eating mandarin oranges and was told by her doctor that the Chinese "are using a new pesticide that is causing a reaction for a lot of people." Grounds for rejection? The facts of this narrative are *unclear* (vague). Neither the pesticide nor the physical reactions were named.[24]

- Third, a February 2006 email warned that drinking cold water after a meal could cause cancer. This email did offer details, saying that the cold water solidified oily food from a dinner, which, in turn, slowed digestion, forming a kind of "sludge." The sludge then would react with stomach acid, causing faster absorption into the intestine where it would turn into fats and cause cancer. Grounds for rejecting? This is simply *impossible*. According to *Snopes*, no medical literature exists to support the scenario outlined in the email. In fact, *Snopes* reports that "chilled liquids do not solidify ingested fats when the two meet in the stomach: the internal heat of the human body quickly nullifies any temperature differences among the various items that have been swallowed.. . ."[25]

- Fourth, many of us have heard the explanation that the nursery rhyme "Ring around the Rosie" originated in the Middle Ages when the Black Plague was decimating the population of Europe in the fourteenth century. As the story goes, the opening line, "ring around the rosie," referred to the red rash that would break out on the skin. The next phrase, "a pocket full of posies," was a reference to herbs and flowers which would be carried in the pocket to ward off the disease. The conclusion ("Ashes! Ashes! We all fall down!") was a reference to sneezing ("a-choo!") and to falling down in death. Grounds for rejection? *Inconsistency*. The researcher at *Snopes* points out that there are widely various explanations for each line. The "pocket full of posies," for example, has been explained five different ways: they warded off the disease, they masked the smell of death, they were buried with the dead, they were placed on the grave, and they represented pockets of pus under the skin. With so many explanations, *Snopes* says, the truth of the story is doubtful.[26]

The last two approaches focus less on the facts of a case and more on the speaker or writer's attitude toward the effects of the narrative:

Approach	Details
Inappropriate	The narrative fosters bad behavior, encourages the unthinkable, and/or violates the tenets of civilization.
Inexpedient	The narrative is not advantageous or edifying.

An example of an *inappropriate* narrative would be a wild-eyed story claiming that one's neighbor is a cannibal. This is such a shocking crime that it would be difficult to believe that it happened in the house next door. Of course, as Christians we recognize that people are sinful and capable of many evil deeds. Therefore, this category should be used with care. However, when a person is known to have good character, the proof of inappropriateness can be a powerful refutation of false charges. Moreover, in our system of law, a mere accusation is not proof of guilt.

Expediency may also sound a little foreign to our modern ears. A synonym for *expediency* is *advantageous*. In other words, we should ask if a story is edifying or helpful for us to hear. If we do not gain any valuable information or learn lessons from a narrative, then it is not worth studying. The term *yellow journalism* is often applied to lurid stories that serve to arouse the baser instincts in the reader. For example, reputable newspapers often omit the gory details of a homicide. People today mostly see narratives as having value for entertainment. However, the world does not center on us—we are called to love God and serve our neighbor. If the narrative encourages vice, then that would be good grounds to condemn it. As Christians, we are to hold all things up to the light of God's word. If something falls short, then we can legitimately say that it is not expedient (i.e., not advantageous).

Organizing a Refutation

When writing a Refutation, begin by writing a brief narrative of the suspicious story. Next, state your own position on the issue. Then write one paragraph for each of the approaches (either the first four or all six, depending on your audience). Conclude with a summary of your points.

Model Refutation

Did Joseph of Arimathea Come to England?

Narrative

There have long been legends about the Biblical figure Joseph of Arimathea coming to Britain (or Albion) in the first century AD. According to the narrative, Joseph went to Glastonbury and buried the Holy Grail, the cup from which Jesus drank at the Last Supper, at the foot of Glastonbury Tor (Hill), which was deemed an entrance to the Underworld. As the narrative goes, a spring burst forth from the place where the cup was buried, and water from this spring (called the Chalice Well) would give everlasting youth to those who drank of it. In addition, Joseph thrust his staff into the ground in the area where Glastonbury Abbey now stands, and overnight the staff turned into a thorn bush.

Writer's Position

Though these are pleasant legends, they must be considered as part of the folklore of ancient Britain, not actual history.

Improbable

First, it is highly *improbable* that a man of Joseph's age would undertake a trip of this type. Though we cannot be certain of his exact age, *The Jewish Encyclopedia* indicates that one of the qualifications for a member of the Sanhedrin (which

Joseph most certainly was) is that he be "of advanced age." This is supported by the further requirement that all Sanhedrin judges were to have significant experience before serving on the Sanhedrin. What is more, there have also been persistent statements that Joseph was the uncle of Mary, the mother of Jesus, which would have made him the approximate age of Jesus' earthly grandfather. Whether the latter is true or not, we know enough about the Sanhedrin to state that Joseph of Arimathea was not a young man at the time of Jesus' crucifixion. Therefore, it is unlikely that he would have taken a trip as far afield as Britain at that time.

Unclear

Second, there are numerous *unclear* elements in the narrative. When exactly did Joseph make this trip? Are there any records of it in, say, Scripture or other sources? Furthermore, why did Joseph remove the cup from Jerusalem in the first place? And why specifically did he select Britain as his destination rather than some place nearer to Jerusalem? These unanswered questions suggest that the story is merely legendary.

Impossible

Third, some elements of the narrative are simply *impossible*. Staffs do not magically turn into bushes. It is true that miracles can happen, but Biblical miracles always involve the betterment of God's people; they are not just showy tricks of magic with no specific purpose. Similarly, it is not possible for water from Glastonbury to give eternal youth to those who drink it. If that were so, there would be citizens of Glastonbury today who had been alive in the early first century—and there most certainly are not!

Inconsistent

Fourth, elements of this story are *inconsistent* with passages of Scripture. Mark records that Joseph of Arimathea was "a respected member of the Council, who was also himself looking for the kingdom of God" (Mark 15:43). The association of Joseph of Arimathea with magic is inconsistent with this

Joseph of Arimathea among the Rocks of Albion

description of Joseph as a respected Jew. No Jewish person with such respect in first-century Jerusalem would use magic to turn material objects into objects of veneration. Such would have been anathema to such a man.

Inappropriate

Next, it is *not appropriate* in the Judeo-Christian tradition to ascribe magical qualities to objects or to give them special powers. To do so would be a violation of the Second Commandment, which says, "You shall not make for yourself a carved image, or any likeness of anything that is in heaven above, or that is in the earth beneath, or that is in the water under the earth. You shall not bow down to them or serve them, for I the LORD your God am a jealous God, visiting the iniquity of the fathers on the children to the third and the fourth generation of those who hate me, but showing steadfast love to thousands of those who love me and keep my commandments" (Exodus 20:4-6). In the face of such an injunction, a respected member of the Sanhedrin would be scandalized to think that centuries later people would ascribe magic powers to him.

Inexpedient

Last, the legends about Joseph of Arimathea in Britain should be taught as simply that: legends. Allowing children to believe that obvious legends are true leads them only to spiritual error and, thus, should be avoided.

Conclusion

The story of Joseph Arimathea's journey to and activities in ancient Britain is unclear, improbable, impossible, and inconsistent with Scripture. Moreover, if taught as factual history, the legend would be inappropriate for Christian life and inexpedient in the education of Christian children. Thus, the story should not be treated as anything more than a fairy tale.

EXERCISE 8.1: Analyzing a Refutation

Directions: Answer the following questions about the essay.

1. **Impossible**

    a. Did the writer say the story was impossible in its entirety or in some parts? If parts, please provide details.

    b. What does the writer say regarding the possibility of a miracle?

2. **Improbable**

    a. Which aspect of the Character is investigated in this paragraph—gender, age, or nationality?

    b. Did the writer speculate or do research to help investigate this issue? If research was used, indicate the source(s).

3. **Unclear**

    a. To state the unclear parts of the narrative, what kind of statement does the writer use—indicative, interrogative, or imperative?

    b. Why do you suppose that form was chosen?

4. **Inconsistent**

    a. The writer uses testimony of the ancients (in this case the Bible) to show an inconsistency. Which "ancient" is quoted?

    b. How does the "testimony" strengthen the refutation?

5. Inappropriate

  a. The writer also uses the Bible to discuss the inappropriateness of teaching the legend as though it were true. What verse is cited?

  b. What exactly does the writer deem inappropriate?

6. Inexpedient

In what way is the story about Joseph of Arimathea deemed inexpedient?

EXERCISE 8.2: Looking for "Holes" in a Narrative

<u>Directions</u>: The first step in writing a refutation is to study the narrative closely, looking for what we often call "holes" in the story. For this purpose, we will use Livy's version of the remarkable story of "Mucius the Left-Handed." Please begin by reading the introduction and the excerpt from Livy's book. Next, generate some yes/no questions to test the truth of the narrative, and then complete the Refutation chart.

INTRODUCTION: *When the Clusian king Lars Porsena attacked Rome in 508 BC, he established a blockade of the city, creating a scarcity of corn. An assassination attempt by a young Roman named Mucius failed, but what he did next is still being talked about today.*

Mucius the Left-Handed
By Livy

[1] The blockade . . . continued, and with it a growing scarcity of corn at famine prices. Porsena still cherished hopes of capturing the City by keeping up the investment. There was a young noble, C. Mucius, who regarded it as a disgrace that whilst Rome in the days of servitude under her kings had never been blockaded in any war or by any foe, she should now, in the day of her freedom, be besieged by those very Etruscans whose armies she had often routed. Thinking

that this disgrace ought to be avenged by some great deed of daring, he determined in the first instance to penetrate into the enemy's camp on his own responsibility. On second thoughts, however, he became apprehensive that if he went without orders from the consuls, or unknown to any one, and happened to be arrested by the Roman outposts, he might be brought back as a deserter, a charge which the condition of the City at the time would make only too probable.

[2] So he went to the senate. "I wish," he said, "Fathers, to swim the Tiber, and, if I can, enter the enemy's camp, not as a pillager nor to inflict retaliation for their pillagings. I am purposing, with heaven's help, a greater deed." The senate gave their approval.

[3] Concealing a sword in his robe, he started. When he reached the camp, he took his stand in the densest part of the crowd near the royal tribunal. It happened to be the soldiers' pay-day, and a secretary, sitting by the king and dressed almost exactly like him, was busily engaged, as the soldiers kept coming to him incessantly. Afraid to ask which of the two was the king, lest his ignorance should betray him, Mucius struck as fortune directed the blow and killed the secretary instead of the king. He tried to force his way back with his blood-stained dagger through the dismayed crowd, but the shouting caused a rush to be made to the spot; he was seized and dragged back by the king's bodyguard to the royal tribunal.

[4] Here, alone and helpless, and in the utmost peril, he was still able to inspire more fear than he felt. "I am a citizen of Rome," he said, "men call me C. Mucius. As an enemy I wished to kill an enemy, and I have as much courage to meet death as I had to inflict it. It is the Roman nature to act bravely and to suffer bravely. I am not alone in having made this resolve against you; behind me there is a long list of those who aspire to the same distinction. If then it is your pleasure, make up your mind for a struggle in which you will every hour have to fight for your life and find an armed foe on the threshold of your royal tent. This is the war which we the youth of Rome, declare against you. You have no serried ranks, no pitched battle to fear; the matter will be settled between you alone and each one of us singly."

[5] The king, furious with anger, and at the same time terrified at the unknown danger, threatened that if he did not promptly explain the nature of the plot which he was darkly hinting at, he should be roasted alive. "Look," Mucius cried, "and learn how lightly those regard their bodies who have some great glory in view." Then he plunged his right hand into a fire burning on the altar. Whilst he kept it roasting there as if he were devoid of all sensation, the king, astounded at his preternatural conduct, sprang from his seat and ordered the youth to be removed from the altar. "Go," he said, "you have been a worse enemy to yourself than to me. I would invoke blessings on your courage if it were displayed on behalf of my country; as it is, I send you away exempt from all rights of war, unhurt, and safe."

[6] Then Mucius, reciprocating, as it were, this generous treatment, said, "Since you honor courage, know that what you could not gain by threats you have obtained by kindness. Three hundred of us, the foremost amongst the Roman youth, have sworn to attack you in this way. The lot fell to me first, the rest, in the order of their lot, will come each in his turn, till fortune shall give us a favorable chance against you."

[7] Mucius was accordingly dismissed; afterwards he received the sobriquet of Scaevola [left-handed], from the loss of his right hand. Envoys from Porsena followed him to Rome. The king's narrow escape from the first of many attempts, which was owing solely to the mistake of his assailant, and the prospect of having to meet as many attacks as there were conspirators, so unnerved him that he made proposals of peace to Rome. . . . [Once the peace was] concluded, Porsena moved his troops from the Janiculum and evacuated the Roman territory.[27]

Directions: After reading the narrative, we begin by questioning it. For each numbered section, propose at least one question that challenges the narrative. The first one serves as an example.

1. Paragraph 2:

Did the Senate know Mucius would attempt an assassination?

2. Paragraph 3:

3. Paragraphs 4:

4. Paragraph 5:

5. Paragraph 6:

Refutation Chart: After considering these questions, jot down points you could use to refute all or part of Mucius' story.

Approach	Details
Impossible	
Improbable	
Unclear	
Inconsistent	

EXERCISE 8.3: Analyzing a Classical Refutation (More Challenging)

<u>Directions</u>: Socrates taught philosophy to all who would listen to him, but many Athenians did not like this and, in 399 BC, took him to court, charging him with atheism and corrupting the youth of Athens. Plato, who had been Socrates' student, wrote a record of the trial, an excerpt of which appears below. Please read the selection and answer the questions that follow.

Excerpt from *Apology*
By Plato

SOCRATES: I have said enough in my defense against the first class of my accusers; I turn to the second class, who are headed by Meletus, that good and patriotic man, as he calls himself. And now I will try to defend myself against them: these new accusers must also have their affidavit read. What do they say?

Something of this sort: That Socrates is a doer of evil, and corrupter of the youth, and he does not believe in the gods of the state and has other new divinities of his own. That is the sort of charge; and now let us examine the particular counts. He says that I am a doer of evil, who corrupts the youth; but I say, O men of Athens, that Meletus is a doer of evil, and the evil is that he makes a joke of a serious matter, and is too ready at bringing other men to trial from a pretended zeal and interest about matters in which he really never had the smallest interest. And the truth of this I will endeavor to prove....

Response to the First Charge

SOCRATES: Come hither, Meletus, and let me ask a question of you. You think a great deal about the improvement of youth?

MELETUS: Yes, I do.

SOCRATES: Tell the judges, then, who is their improver; for you must know, as you have taken the pains to discover their corrupter and are citing and accusing me before them. Speak, then, and tell the judges who their improver is. Observe, Meletus, that you are silent, and have nothing to say. But is not this rather disgraceful, and a very considerable proof of what I was saying, that you have no interest in the matter? Speak up, friend, and tell us who their improver is.

MELETUS: The laws.

SOCRATES: But that, my good sir, is not my meaning. I want to know who the person is, who, in the first place, knows the laws.

MELETUS: The judges, Socrates, who are present in court.

SOCRATES: What do you mean to say, Meletus, that they are able to instruct and improve youth?

MELETUS: Certainly they are.

SOCRATES: What, all of them, or some only and not others?

MELETUS: All of them.

SOCRATES: By the goddess [Hera], that is good news! There are plenty of improvers, then. And what do you say of the audience? Do they improve them?

MELETUS: Yes, they do.

SOCRATES: And the senators?

MELETUS: Yes, the senators improve them.

SOCRATES: But perhaps the members of the citizen assembly corrupt them? Or do they too improve them?

MELETUS: They improve them.

SOCRATES: Then every Athenian improves and elevates them; all with the exception of myself; and I alone am their corrupter? Is that what you affirm?

MELETUS: That is what I stoutly affirm.

SOCRATES: I am very unfortunate if that is true. But suppose I ask you a question: Would you say that this also holds true in the case of horses? Does one man do them harm and all the world good? Is not the exact opposite of this true? One man is able to do them good, or at least not many. The trainer of horses, that is to say, does them good, and others who have to do with them rather injure them? Is not that true, Meletus, of horses, or any other animals?

MELETUS: Yes, certainly.

SOCRATES: Whether you and Anytus say yes or no, that is no matter. Happy indeed would be the condition of youth if they had one corrupter only, and all the rest of the world were their improvers....

Response to the Second Charge

SOCRATES: Then, by the gods, Meletus, of whom we are speaking, tell me and the court, in somewhat plainer terms, what you mean! for I do not as yet understand whether you affirm that I teach others to acknowledge some gods, and therefore do believe in gods and am not an entire atheist. This you do not lay to my charge; but only that they are not the same gods which the city recognizes. The charge is that they are different gods. Or, do you mean to say that I am an atheist simply, and a teacher of atheism?

MELETUS: I mean the latter—that you are a complete atheist.

SOCRATES: That is an extraordinary statement, Meletus. Why do you say that? Do you mean that I do not believe in the godhead of the sun or moon, which is the common creed of all men?

MELETUS: I assure you, judges, that he does not believe in them; for he says that the sun is stone, and the moon earth. . . .

SOCRATES: I should like you, O men of Athens, to join me in examining what I conceive to be his inconsistency; and do you, Meletus, answer. . . . Did ever man, Meletus, believe in the existence of human things, and not of human beings? . . . . I wish, men of Athens, that he would answer, and not be always trying to get up an interruption. Did ever any man believe in horsemanship, and not in horses? or in flute-playing, and not in flute-players? No, my friend; I will answer to you and to the court, as you refuse to answer for yourself. There is no man who ever did. . . .

What Should be Done to Socrates?

SOCRATES: And so [Meletus] proposes death as the penalty. And what shall I propose on my part, O men of Athens? Clearly that which is my due. . . . What would be a reward suitable to a poor man who is your benefactor, who desires leisure that he may instruct you? There can be no more fitting reward than maintenance in the Prytaneum,[a] O men of Athens![28]

1. What are the two charges against Socrates?

2. In response to the first charge, Meletus says that (a) Socrates is the only person who corrupts the youth and that (b) all the other citizens of Athens improve the youth. Does Socrates challenge Meletus' argument on the grounds that this charge is unlikely, impossible, or inconsistent? Explain your answer.

3. Socrates says all men, including himself, believe that the sun and moon are gods. However, Meletus says that Socrates is an atheist. Why does Socrates believe that Meletus is making an inconsistent argument in the second charge?

4. Which of the approaches is Socrates using when he insists that the citizens of Athens should reward him rather than punish him?

---

[a] A public hall for religious and state purposes

Now You Try It

Chapter 8 Essay
Refutation

Specifications

1. The purpose of this assignment is to demonstrate your ability to write a refutation, arguing that a historical narrative is Unclear, Unlikely, Impossible, and/or Inconsistent.

2. Refute the narrative using *at least three* of the approaches in Group 1 and *at least one* of the approaches in Group 2.

   Group 1
   - Unclear
   - Unlikely
   - impossible
   - inconsistent

   Group 2
   inappropriate
   inexpedient

3. Begin by reading the introduction and the excerpt entitled "Parfact." As you read, look for weaknesses in the text and determine how "Parfact" can be refuted in part or in whole.

4. Next, on the pre-writing activity, jot down three debatable Yes/No questions. Then choose the one which you consider to be the best grounds for refutation and, in the boxes on the chart, indicate why you consider the narrative to be doubtful.

5. Follow your teacher's instructions regarding preparation of the manuscript.

Reading

INTRODUCTION: The free encyclopedia Wikipedia *is an online encyclopedia in which the articles are written and edited primarily by volunteers all over the world. As a result,* Wikipedia *often falls victim to hoaxes. That is to say, sometimes an anonymous person enters a fake article which conforms to* Wikipedia's *format and style, sometimes even including pictures, and enters it online where it may successfully remain for months or years. The article below, entitled "Parfact," is an example. It survived for over two years on the web site before it was determined to be false and taken down. Though slightly edited for educational purposes here, the article retains some of the original author's errors in punctuation and spelling. (British spellings have been retained and are not considered spelling errors.) As you read, look for statements that appear doubtful.*

Parfact

"Parfact" is an example of a cryptolect[b] originating from the Worcestershire area of the UK. Similar to the use of "Cant" (a secret language supposedly used by rogues and vagabonds in Elizabethan England), "Parfact" is thought to have been devised by a group of local teenagers in the mid-1990s as a secret language to conceal true meaning from their peers. Elements of the cryptolect have, however, crept into mainstream use in Worcester and can often be overheard within general conversation in the historic city.

Rules and variations

Characterised by the word *parfact* itself (thought to be a corruption of the word "perfect"), Parfact encompasses a wide range of covert principles, from the most basic use of opposites (ie. "yes" becomes "no", albeit pronounced in a rather obnoxious, exaggerated tone (eg. "NNNOOOOOOOOOO"), through to the addition of extra syllables to add hidden meaning to words ("loser" becomes *losazer*, pronounced "LOO-ZA-ZEER"). Controversially, the use of Parfact tends often to aim insults at an oblivious victim, much to the amusement of those who comprehend the elements of the cryptolect.

---

[b] In a separate article, *cryptolect* is defined as "the jargon or language of a group, often employed to exclude or mislead people outside the group."

The Parfact salute

A non-verbal element of Parfact also exists in the form of a military-style salute. Usually accompanying the word *parfact* with the intention of adding emphasis, the exact technique of the salute often varies from user to user. Original proponents of Parfact apparently insist upon a single, right-handed salute, but witnesses have reported many different techniques:

- frenzied **multiple, single-handed salute** accompanied by a face of strained determination
- limp, single-handed flourish ending with the reverse of the hand **striking the forehead** with considerable force
- disguised salute whereby the user mimicks **scratching his/her head vigorously** behind the right ear
- elaborate asynchronous double-handed salute accompanied by a **peculiar dance**, often as the user runs at speed
- synchronized **double-handed salute**, with the user maintaining the final position for several seconds

Integration of backslang

Parfact is often used in conjunction with speaking backwards, whereby words are pronounced as if the letters reversed. For example, "permission" becomes *noissimrep*, and is thus pronounced NO-IH-SIM-REP. Users of Parfact have even been known to combine some of the cryptolect's trademark words with the methodology of rechtub klat, resulting in such words as *tcafrap* and *gnilrets*. Whole sentences can also be reversed in this manner, although it takes rather quick thinking to employ this technique in spoken conversation. *Egnellahc a taht si? Orez!*

Selected translations

Parfact phrase	English translation	Pronunciation
Is that a sars?	I consider your contextual significance to be negligible, but don't wish to overtly communicate my opinion.	(As spelled)
Can say!	I consider your comment(s) and/or implication(s) to be inappropriate, unfounded or in some other way offensive.	(As spelled)
yrc nac, rezatawt! (can cry, twatazer!)	Although I have little respect for you, I'd like you to adopt a more positive outlook.	English pronunciation: /ɪrknæk rɛzətɔːt/
God count: low!	I hold the (usually human) subject of conversation in extremely high regard.	(As spelled)
I'm the goit!!!	I consider you to be of a lower social status to myself and/or my companions and do not wish to converse with you any further.	(As spelled)
Twat count... LOW!!!	There appear to be an above average number of disagreeable persons in my vicinity.	(As spelled)

Linguist magazine

In 2004 as "Parfact" begun to attract attention from language experts in Worcestershire, "Linguist" magazine responded accordingly by featuring an article on the cryptolect. Written by a James P. Rushton, the article featured an interview with a local Worcester man named Dan Wilesmith, who claimed to have created the language with an unnamed co-conspiritor [*sic*]. "Parfact" has been the subject of many a heated debate among Midlands-based intellectuals but, as of October 2006, the article in "Linguist" magazine remains the only printed reference to the phenomenon.

This is part of a series of local slang terms which, while widely understood in Worcester, can puzzle those not from the area. Use of this word has occasionally spread from the Worcester area, and there have been recorded incidences of it being used as far afield as Bristol, Fulham, and Newquay. The meaning of "Parfact" has been the subject of many a heated debate by local historians and linguists in Worcester, and has even been the subject of an article pondering its origins in the respected "Linguist" magazine. It is now accepted that the word is a corruption of "perfect," and is used when you might want express sarcastic appreciation for something or someone.

Examples of use could include – "You win PARFACT" ie sarcastically expressing that the person in question hasn't won at all. This would be correctly used if shouted at someone [who] had just come last in a race, or hadn't won anything with some element of competition.

Sources and further supporting examples to follow. [NOTE: None appeared.]

Refutation: Pre-Writing Activity

1. Compose three debatable Yes/No questions generated by your reading. In other words, find three statements that seem questionable to you and write a Yes/No question to address it, such as, "Does Dan Wilesmith exist?"

   a.

   b.

   c.

2. Brainstorm your thoughts by completing the chart:

	Grounds for Refutation (Choose at least three.)
Approach	**Details**
Impossible	
Improbable	
Unclear	
Inconsistent	
	Your Assessment (Choose at least one.)
Inappropriate	
Inexpedient	

CONFIRMATION

Chapter 9

Introduction

When Abraham Lincoln was a young man, he worked as a store clerk in New Salem, Illinois. As he closed the store one day, he discovered that he had overcharged a customer six and a quarter cents. Too honest to pass over such an error, the young Lincoln walked six miles to return a few pennies.[29]

Since there were only two eyewitnesses for the original story (Lincoln and the customer), what evidence could you find to prove that this story is true? In this chapter, you will learn how to confirm a suspicious narrative to demonstrate that it is believable. Because Confirmation is the reverse of Refutation, the approaches for proof are the opposite of the six approaches in the previous chapter. In some ways, Confirmation is the more difficult exercise, because one has to explain to others what they may categorically reject.

Definition and Purpose

This chapter primarily covers the judicial and historical uses of Confirmation. When the Roman senator Cicero gave his great speech against the conspirator Catiline, he used Confirmation to prove that Catiline was actively plotting to destroy the Roman Republic. The historian Livy used Confirmation on a smaller scale to explain the legend of Romulus and Remus. He did not believe that Romulus and Remus were raised by a she-wolf, but suggested that the legend arose from the family that took the children in. The farmer's wife was nicknamed "she-wolf," Livy said, and this is perhaps how the legend began. Today, historians still use parts of the exercise of Confirmation to compare conflicting accounts of an event and to choose the most probable story.

Choosing a Narrative for Confirmation

As in the exercise of Refutation, you must first choose a narrative to confirm. It must not be a story that is certainly true or certainly false. Instead, you should choose a story that has one or more elements that are probably (but not certainly) true. For example, if a bank robber wore a mask and then was caught after he took off his mask, it would take some work to prove that he was the guilty criminal, since no one saw his face in the bank. Still, there are other clues which could be pursued.

Once a narrative is chosen, you must decide whether it is necessary to confirm the entire narrative or only a part of the narrative. If the whole narrative is questioned, then you must confirm all aspects of the narrative. If only a few details are in doubt, then you should limit your essay to those details. This can be seen in the classic game of Clue. At first, you must prove the suspect, weapon, and room. Later in the game, you may know that the criminal is Miss Scarlet and the weapon is the candlestick, so you only need to confirm the room.

Approaches to Confirmation

After narrowing the question, you will consider approaches that prove the truth of the narrative. Aphthonius and Hermogenes give six categories for confirming arguments, which are the opposites of those used in refuting arguments. Please note that all the questions are in a Yes/No format.

- Is the narrative possible?
- Is the narrative probable?
- Is the narrative clear?
- Is the narrative consistent?
- Is the narrative appropriate?
- Is the narrative expedient?

As in the Refutation, you may not decide to use every approach in your final essay, but you should consider all the approaches to discover the best arguments to support your case.

The first four of these approaches are still in common usage today. The chart below explains the approaches one would take when confirming the facts of a narrative.

Approach	Details
Possible	The event does not violate the laws of nature.
Probable	The events are common enough to be believed.
Clear	There are enough details to be convincing.
Consistent	There are no contradictory elements.

Here are some real-life examples that may help demonstrate these four approaches:

First, let's revisit the case of the Roman legend about Romulus and Remus. Most people would dismiss it altogether as "just a myth." Similarly, even though the *Jungle Book* by Rudyard Kipling is fiction, where the rules of historical truth do not apply, some might object that it is just impossible for Mowgli to have been raised by wild animals. Yet even the most skeptical must admit that there are on record numerous examples of children who have been raised apart from other human beings. Such persons have been given the name *feral children*, and the term *wild child* has even slipped into our everyday usage over the years. The most remarkable case is that of an eighteenth-century French girl named Marie-Angélique Memmie Le Blanc, who survived alone in the forest for ten years. She was even educable and later learned to read and write. Because examples of such children have been documented, the story of Romulus and Remus must be considered as *possible*.[30]

Second, after 9/11, President George W. Bush stated that the terrorist organization al-Qaeda was responsible for the attacks on the World Trade Center and the Pentagon. While he did not have absolute proof that day, his statement was a highly *probable* explanation of events because al-Qaeda had committed similar atrocities before and had frequently threatened the United States. Although this proof was not confirmed until al-Qaeda claimed responsibility for the attacks, the President's claim had a good probability of being true and thus was expressed as truth.

Third, archaeology as a scientific pursuit has proved the truth of many details provided in historical narratives about the alleged locations. Although the *Iliad* provides several **clear** details about the geographic location of Troy, many scholars doubted the existence of Troy because the gods and heroes in the epic were larger than life. But in the late 1800s, Frank Calvert and Heinrich Schliemann followed the clear geographic clues in the *Iliad* and began uncovering the ancient city of Troy, proving its historical existence to modern skeptics. Today, archaeologists have uncovered a layer of the city that seems to have been burned by the departing Greeks.

Heinrich Schliemann (1822-1890)

Last, let us look at the confirmation of a passage in the *History* of the Greek historian Herodotus. In 450 BC, after a journey up the Nile, Herodotus described an unusual boat called a *baris*, which he observed while it was undergoing construction. He explained that the builders cut acacia trees into planks two cubits (36 inches) long and arranged them like bricks, attaching them by ties to long stakes until the hull was complete. Then they lay cross-planks on the top from side to side. He said they did not give the boats any ribs, but caulked the seams with papyrus on the inside. Each *baris*, he said, had a single rudder, which was driven straight through the keel, and the sails were made of papyrus.[31] However, until recently no one had ever found proof of such a ship, and some historians even claimed that Herodotus had never actually visited Egypt and had just made up some of the things in his book. Then in the year 2019 archaeologists working at Thonis-Heracleion, a now-sunken port city in Egypt northeast of Alexandria, discovered a ship whose structure was entirely *consistent* with what Herodotus described. In fact, one writer, Alexander Belov, has even stated that it was so similar to Herodotus' ship that it could even have been built in the shipyard the historian visited. It took 2,469 years, but Herodotus is at last proven right.[32]

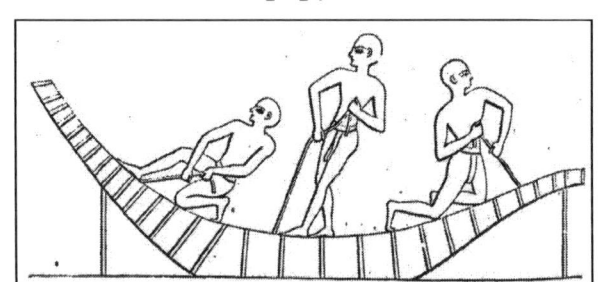

As with Refutation, the last two ways to confirm a narrative focus on the speaker or writer's attitude toward the narrative. They can be charted as follows:

Approach	Details
Appropriate	The narrative encourages what is in accordance with civilized behavior and the better side of human nature.
Expedient	The narrative is edifying.

If a story is *appropriate,* it portrays actions that are fitting for human nature. Livy retells the story of Horatius, who defended the bridge to Rome against an entire army. This is consistent with human nature because it shows courage and love of country. History is full of stories about brave men who nobly defended their countries against seemingly impossible odds, and thus, Horatius' action is an appropriately praiseworthy example of human behavior.

What makes a narrative *expedient?* The story is told that when George Washington was a young boy, he received a hatchet. Like any other young boy, he had to try his hatchet on every piece of wood in sight, including his father's prized cherry tree. Mr. Washington was unhappy when he discovered that his cherry tree was dead, and he demanded to know who had done the crime. Young George replied, "Father, I cannot tell a lie. I chopped it with my little ax." This narrative is expedient because it teaches the importance of truthfulness.

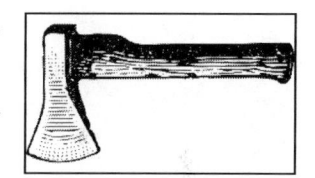

Analyzing a Professional Confirmation Essay

Skeptics often question Bible narratives which seem impossibilities to them. One example is the narrative of Jonah in the Old Testament. To see a persuasive confirmation of the Book of Jonah, begin by reading the Bible excerpt and then move on to the Confirmation, which was written by a professional writer at the *Got Questions* web site (reprinted here with permission).

Jonah 1:1 – 2:10
Jonah Flees the Presence of the Lord

1 Now the word of the Lord came to Jonah the son of Amittai, saying, 2 "Arise, go to Nineveh, that great city, and call out against it, for their evil has come up before me." 3 But Jonah rose to flee to Tarshish from the presence of the Lord. He went down to Joppa and found a ship going to Tarshish. So he paid the fare and went down into it, to go with them to Tarshish, away from the presence of the Lord.

4 But the Lord hurled a great wind upon the sea, and there was a mighty tempest on the sea, so that the ship threatened to break up. 5 Then the mariners were afraid, and each cried out to his god. And they hurled the cargo that was in the ship into the sea to lighten it for them. But Jonah had gone down into the inner part of the ship and had lain down and was fast asleep. 6 So the captain came and said to him, "What do you mean, you sleeper? Arise, call out to your god! Perhaps the god will give a thought to us, that we may not perish."

Jonah Is Thrown into the Sea

7 And they said to one another, "Come, let us cast lots, that we may know on whose account this evil has come upon us." So they cast lots, and the lot fell on Jonah. 8 Then they said to him, "Tell us on whose account this evil has come upon us. What is your occupation? And where do you come from? What is your country? And of what people are you?" 9 And he said to them, "I am a Hebrew, and I fear the Lord, the God of heaven, who made the sea and the dry land." 10 Then the men were exceedingly afraid and said to him, "What is this that you have done!" For the men knew that he was fleeing from the presence of the Lord, because he had told them.

11 Then they said to him, "What shall we do to you, that the sea may quiet down for us?" For the sea grew more and more tempestuous. 12 He said to them, "Pick me up and hurl me into the sea; then the sea will quiet down for you, for I know it is because of me that this great tempest has come upon you." 13 Nevertheless, the men rowed hard to get back to dry land, but they could not, for the sea grew more and more tempestuous against

them. ¹⁴ Therefore they called out to the LORD, "O LORD, let us not perish for this man's life, and lay not on us innocent blood, for you, O LORD, have done as it pleased you." ¹⁵ So they picked up Jonah and hurled him into the sea, and the sea ceased from its raging. ¹⁶ Then the men feared the LORD exceedingly, and they offered a sacrifice to the LORD and made vows.

A Great Fish Swallows Jonah

¹⁷ And the LORD appointed a great fish to swallow up Jonah. And Jonah was in the belly of the fish three days and three nights.

Jonah's Prayer

2 Then Jonah prayed to the LORD his God from the belly of the fish, ² saying,

"I called out to the LORD, out of my distress,
    and he answered me;
out of the belly of Sheol[a] I cried,
    and you heard my voice.
³ For you cast me into the deep,
    into the heart of the seas,
    and the flood surrounded me;
all your waves and your billows
    passed over me.
⁴ Then I said, 'I am driven away
    from your sight;
yet I shall again look
    upon your holy temple.'
⁵ The waters closed in over me to take my life;
    the deep surrounded me;
weeds were wrapped about my head
⁶   at the roots of the mountains.
I went down to the land
    whose bars closed upon me forever;

---

[a] The dwelling place of the dead, in Hebrew writing

> yet you brought up my life from the pit,
>   O Lord my God.
> ⁷ When my life was fainting away,
>   I remembered the Lord,
> and my prayer came to you,
>   into your holy temple.
> ⁸ Those who pay regard to vain idols
>   forsake their hope of steadfast love.
> ⁹ But I with the voice of thanksgiving
>   will sacrifice to you;
> what I have vowed I will pay.
>   Salvation belongs to the Lord!"
> ¹⁰ And the Lord spoke to the fish, and it vomited Jonah out upon the dry land.

After reading the narrative, we begin by asking debatable Yes/No questions of the narrative. By *debatable,* we mean questions that elicit different answers depending on a person's point of view. Here are some debatable Yes/No questions for this passage:

Yes/No Questions

- Are storms on the Mediterranean Sea this bad?
- Did God really send a big fish to swallow Jonah?
- Was the big fish a whale, as commonly portrayed?
- Did Jonah die?
- Was Jonah alive in the belly of the fish?
- Can a person survive in the belly of a fish for three days and three nights?
- Has anyone else in history recorded this narrative?
- Is there any physical evidence to support this narrative?

Professional Confirmation of the Jonah Narrative

Since many people have questions about the narrative of Jonah, the web site *Got Questions* has composed a confirmation of the Book of Jonah, which appears below. The various approaches to Confirmation have been inserted as headings to assist your analysis of the Confirmation. The parenthetical documentation is part of the original essay. (NOTE: Because this is a professional essay, it does not follow the basic educational format: Possible, Probable, Clear, Consistent, Appropriate, and Expedient. However, though it follows the author's own outline, one can still see the presence of all approaches.)

<h3 style="text-align:center">Question: "Was Jonah truly swallowed by a whale?"</h3>

Narrative

The book of Jonah recounts the story of a disobedient prophet who, upon being swallowed by a whale (or a "great fish") and vomited upon the shore, reluctantly led the reprobate city of Nineveh to repentance. The Bible's plain teaching is that, yes, Jonah was truly swallowed by a whale (or a great fish).

The biblical account of Jonah is often criticized by skeptics because of its miraculous content. These miracles include the following events:

- A storm is summoned and dissipated by God (1:4–16).

- A massive fish swallows the prophet after he is thrown into the sea by his ship's crew (1:17).

- Jonah survives in the belly of the fish for three days and three nights—or he dies and is resurrected, depending on how you interpret the text (1:17).

- The fish vomits Jonah upon the shore at God's command (2:10). . . .

Probable (Considering Nineveh's Beliefs)

God's use of a whale or great fish as Jonah's mode of transportation was sure to capture Nineveh's attention, given the prominence of Dagon worship in that particular area of the ancient world. Dagon was a fish-god who enjoyed popularity among the pantheons of Mesopotamia and the eastern Mediterranean coast. He is mentioned several times in the Bible in relation to the Philistines (Judges 16:23–24; 1 Samuel 5:1–7; 1 Chronicles 10:8–12). Images of Dagon have been

Drawing of Dagon, based on the "oannes" relief at Khorsabad

found in palaces and temples in Nineveh and throughout the region. In some cases he was represented as a man wearing a fish. In others he was part man, part fish—a merman, of sorts.

Orientalist Henry Clay Trumbull observes: "What better heralding, as a divinely sent messenger to Nineveh, could Jonah have had, than to be thrown up out of the mouth of a great fish, in the presence of witnesses, say on the coast of Phoenicia, where the fish-god was a favorite object of worship? Such an incident would have inevitably aroused the mercurial nature of Oriental observers, so that a multitude would be ready to follow the seemingly new avatar of the fish-god, proclaiming the story of his uprising from the sea, as he went on his mission to the city where the fish-god had its very centre of worship" ("Jonah in Nineveh," Journal of Biblical Literature, Vol. 2, No.1, 1892, p. 56).

Some scholars have speculated that Jonah's appearance, bleached white from the action of the fish's digestive acids, would have been of great help to his cause. It could be that the Ninevites would have been greeted by a man whose skin, hair, and clothes were bleached ghostly white—a man accompanied by a crowd of frenetic followers, many who had witnessed him being vomited upon the shore by a great fish. Given the piscine nature of Jonah's arrival, Nineveh's repentance follows from a logical progression.

Consistent (with Berosus' Narrative)

Apart from the Bible, there is no conclusive historical proof that Jonah was ever swallowed by a fish and lived to tell about it; however, there is some provocative corroboratory evidence. In the third century BC, a Babylonian priest/historian named Berosus wrote of a mythical creature named Oannes who, according to Berosus, emerged from the sea to give divine wisdom to men. Scholars generally identify this mysterious fish-man as an avatar of the Babylonian water-god Ea (also known as Enki). The curious thing about Berosus' account is the name he used: Oannes.

Berosus wrote in Greek during the Hellenistic Period. Oannes is just a single letter removed from the Greek name Ioannes, which happens to be used in the

Greek New Testament for Jonah. As for the *I* being dropped from Ioannes, Professor Trumbull writes, "In the Assyrian inscriptions the J of foreign words becomes I, or disappears altogether; hence Joannes, as the Greek representative of Jona, would appear in Assyrian either as Ioannes or as Oannes" (ibid., p. 58).

Nineveh was an Assyrian city. What this essentially means is that Berosus wrote of a fish-man named Jonah who emerged from the sea to give divine wisdom to man—a remarkable corroboration of the Hebrew account.

Possible (Transmission of Narrative)

Berosus claimed to have relied upon official Babylonian sources for his information. Nineveh was conquered by the Babylonians under King Nabopolassar in 612 BC, more than 300 years before Berosus. It is quite conceivable that record of Jonah's success in Nineveh was preserved in the writings available to Berosus. If so, it appears that Jonah was deified and mythologized over a period of three centuries, first by the Assyrians, who no doubt associated him with their fish-god, Dagon, and then by the Babylonians, who appear to have hybridized him with their own water-god, Ea.

Consistent (with Other Old Testament Passages)

Jonah was not an imaginary figure invented to play the part of a disobedient prophet, swallowed by a fish. He was part of Israel's prophetic history. Jonah appears in the chronicles of Israel as the prophet who predicted Jeroboam II's military successes against Syria (2 Kings 14:25).[b] He is said to be the son of Amittai (cf. Jonah 1:1) from the town of Gath-hepher in lower Galilee. Flavius Josephus reiterates these details in his *Antiquities of the Jews* (chapter 10, paragraph 2).

---

[b] He restored the border of Israel from Lebo-hamath as far as the Sea of the Arabah, according to the word of the LORD, the God of Israel, which he spoke by his servant Jonah the son of Amittai, the prophet, who was from Gath-hepher.

Consistent (with Archaeological Discoveries)

The city of Nineveh was rediscovered after more than 2,500 years of obscurity. It is now believed to have been the largest city in the world at the time of its demise (see Tertius Chandler's *Four Thousand Years of Urban Growth: An Historical Census*). According to Sir Austen Henry Layard, who chronicled the rediscovery of Nineveh, the circumference of Greater Nineveh was "exactly three days' journey," as recorded in Jonah 3:3 (*A Popular Account of Discoveries at Nineveh*, New York: J. C. Derby, 1854, p. 314). Prior to its rediscovery, skeptics scoffed at the possibility that so large a city could have existed in the ancient world. In fact, some skeptics denied the existence of Nineveh altogether. Its rediscovery in the mid-1800s proved to be a remarkable vindication for the Bible, which mentions Nineveh by name eighteen times and dedicates two entire books (Jonah and Nahum) to its fate.

Clear (Linguistic Evidence)

It is interesting to note where the lost city of Nineveh was rediscovered. It was found buried beneath a pair of tells in the vicinity of Mosul in modern-day Iraq. These mounds are known by their local names, Kuyunjik and Nabi Yunus [see Fig. 1]. *Nabi Yunus* happens to be Arabic for "the prophet Jonah."

Consistent (with Marine Biology)

As for the whale or great fish that swallowed Jonah, the Bible doesn't specify what sort of marine animal it was. The Hebrew phrase used in the Old Testament, *gadowl dag*, literally means

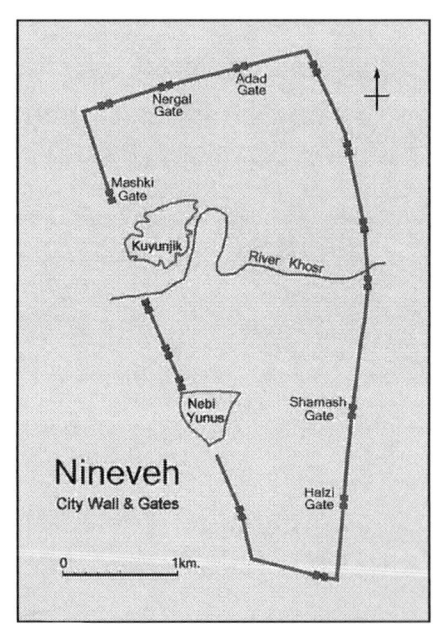

Fig. 1. Plan of the walls and gates of Nineveh based on archaeological evidence

"great fish." The Greek used in the New Testament is *këtos*, which simply means "sea creature." There are at least two species of Mediterranean marine life that are able to swallow a man whole. These are the cachalot (also known as the sperm whale) and the white shark. Both creatures are known to prowl the

Mediterranean and have been known to sailors since antiquity. Aristotle described both species in his fourth-century-BC *Historia Animalium*.

Expedient (Edifying to Our Knowledge of God)

Skeptics scoff at the miracles described in the book of Jonah as if there were no mechanism by which such events could occur. That is their bias. We are inclined, however, to believe that there is One who is capable of manipulating natural phenomena in such supernatural ways. We believe that He is the Creator of the natural realm and is not, therefore, circumscribed [limited] by it. We believe God sent Jonah to Nineveh to bring about their repentance and that, in the process, Jonah was swallowed by a whale or great fish.

Probable (as a Metaphor for Christ's Crucifixion and Resurrection)

Jesus spoke of Jonah's ordeal as a real historical event. He used it as a typological metaphor for His own crucifixion and resurrection: "As Jonah was three days and three nights in the belly of a huge fish, so the Son of Man will be three days and three nights in the heart of the earth. The men of Nineveh will stand up at the judgment with this generation and condemn it; for they repented at the preaching of Jonah, and now something greater than Jonah is here" (Matthew 12:40–41).

Conclusion

The evidence is such that any Christian should have confidence to believe that Jonah was truly swallowed by a whale, and any skeptic should think twice before dismissing the story of Jonah as a fairy tale.[33]

EXERCISE 9.1: Analyzing the Professional Confirmation

Directions: Answer the questions below in order to analyze the professional Confirmation of the Jonah narrative.

1. **Possible:** How was it possible that the Jonah narrative was available to Berosus?

2. **Probable:**

   a. God could have chosen any method he wanted to deliver Jonah to Nineveh. According to Henry Clay Trumbull, why is it probable that God deliberately chose to have a fish vomit his prophet forth on the land?

   b. In what way is it probable that the Jonah narrative is a metaphor for the crucifixion and resurrection of Jesus?

3. **Clear:** In the archaeological dig at Nineveh, what clear linguistic evidence was found that linked Jonah to that city?

4. **Consistent:**

   a. The Jonah narrative is consistent with what other historical record?

   b. In Jonah 1:1, Jonah is identified as "the son of Amittai." Is this consistent with any other Old Testament passage?

   c. Some people have doubted Jonah 3:3, which says that "Nineveh was an exceedingly great city, three days' journey in breadth." Were archaeological discoveries made by Sir Austen Henry Layard in the nineteenth century consistent with the Biblical account?

d. Is the reference to a "great fish" consistent with marine biology of the Mediterranean Sea? Explain your answer.

5. **Expedient:** In what way is the Jonah narrative edifying?

6. **Appropriate:** In the professional essay, the appropriateness of the narrative is not directly stated. However, in your own opinion, after reading and analyzing the essay, how might we consider the Jonah narrative appropriate for readers in our time?

Analyzing a Narrative for Confirmation

INTRODUCTION: *The narrative below, which is about Alexander the Great and his horse, Bucephalus, was written by Plutarch (AD 46-120), a Greek author famous for a collection of biographies called* Plutarch's Lives. *As you read, keep in mind that Alexander was a boy of ten at the time his father, Philip of Macedonia, was examining a horse for a possible purchase. As you read, look for things that are a bit hard to believe a young boy could do.*

The Taming of Bucephalus
By Plutarch

Philonicus the Thessalian brought the horse Bucephalus to Philip of Macedonia, offering to sell him for thirteen talents; but when they went into the field to try him, they found him so very vicious and unmanageable that he reared up when they endeavored to mount him, and would not so much as endure the voice of any of Philip's attendants. Upon which, as they were leading him away as wholly useless and untractable, Alexander (his ten-year-old son), who stood by, said, "What an excellent horse do they lose, for want of address and boldness to manage him!"

Philip at first took no notice of what he said; but when he heard him repeat the same thing several times and saw he was much vexed to see the horse sent away, asked, him, "Do you reproach those who are older than yourself, as if you knew more and were better able to manage him than they?"

"I could manage this horse," replied he, "better than others do."

"And if you do not," said Philip, "what will you forfeit for your rashness?"

"I will pay," answered Alexander, "the whole price of the horse." At this the whole company fell a-laughing; and as soon as the wager was settled amongst them, he immediately ran to the horse, and taking hold of the bridle, turned him directly towards the sun, having, it seems, observed that he was disturbed at and afraid of the motion of his own shadow; then letting him go forward a little, still keeping the reins in his hand, and stroking him gently when he found him begin to grow eager and fiery, he let fall his upper garment softly, and with one nimble leap securely mounted him, and when he was seated, by little and little drew in the bridle, and curbed him without either striking or spurring him.

Presently, when he found him free from all rebelliousness, and only impatient for the course, he let him go at full speed, inciting him now with a commanding voice, and urging him also with his heel. Philip and his friends looked on at first in silence and anxiety for the result, till seeing him turn at the end of his career, and come back rejoicing and triumphing for what he had performed, they all burst out into acclamations of applause; and his father, shedding tears, it is said, for joy, kissed him as he came down from his horse, and in his transport, said, "O my son, look thee out a kingdom equal to and worthy of thyself, for Macedonia is too little for thee."[34]

EXERCISE 9.2: Analyzing a Narrative for Confirmation

Directions: Keeping in mind Alexander's age and the temperament of the horse, begin by writing three debatable Yes/No questions about the narrative. Next, read the Research Source, which gives information about training horses. Then using information from the source along with your own observations, fill in the chart with arguments that will confirm the narrative as true.

Yes / No questions leading to confirmation:

1.

2.

3.

Research Source

The paragraph below will serve as research on how horses interact with humans. It should help you decide if Alexander's seemingly easy training of a spirited wild horse is believable. You may do additional research if you like.

Horse Behavior and Humans

The ability of humans to work in cooperation with horses is based on the strong social bonds that horses have with each other. Horses resist being separated from the herd, because to be alone is to be exposed to predators on all sides. Horse training principles are based upon having the horse accept a person as the dominant herd member, not through force, but by virtue of ability and confidence. In pastures, it is the rule that horses tend to gravitate around the most mature and confident members. Those attributes are highly valued because they point the way to survival. A horse that is afraid more than necessary will expend energy needlessly and may not be able to escape when the threat is real.[35]

Confirmation Chart: Using your own observations and information in the Research Source, jot down points for any approaches you could use to confirm the story about Alexander and Bucephalus.

Approach	Details
Possible	
Probable	
Clear	
Consistent	
Appropriate	
Expedient	

Organization

Although there are possible arguments in each category, some arguments are stronger than others. Of the six approaches, you may want to choose the three or four that best support your point of view. These approaches will become the body of your essay. You may also choose to support the approaches with specific quotations or page references. The best organization plan is as follows:

1. Briefly retell the narrative.

2. State your position on the narrative, that is, indicate whether you consider it believable or not.

3. Write one well-developed paragraph to explain each argument.

4. Write a conclusion in which you summarize your key points.

Model Confirmation

Can a Ten-Year-Old Boy Break a Spirited Stallion in Minutes?

Narrative

When Alexander the Great was ten years old, his father received a horse that was considered too spirited to be tamed. However, the boy told his father the horse could be managed by addressing it properly and handling it confidently. He said he could do it and would pay the price of the horse if he could not. He had noticed the horse was afraid of its shadow, so he turned the horse so that he was looking into the sun. He showed gentleness by stroking the horse. He then mounted the horse in one leap and gradually drew in the bridle. He did not strike the horse, and when the animal was relaxed, he allowed it to run at full speed. When he returned, the adults were amazed, and his father made a prediction that Alexander would be masterful in the world.

Writer's Position

Although it is hard to believe a ten-year-old boy could master such a spirited horse, I believe the story can be confirmed.

Possible

According to an article in the *New World Encyclopedia*, wild horses can be tamed "not through force, but by virtue of ability and confidence." This is exactly what Alexander meant when he said it was a pity to lose such a horse because of "want of address and boldness to manage him." Alexander's ability to communicate with the horse gently and handle it confidently made it possible for him to break the horse.

Probable

Even as a child, Alexander knew he first had to overcome the horse's fear. Having noticed the horse's fear of its shadow, he turned it to face into the sun. He also spoke gently to the horse and stroked it soothingly. He did not beat the horse, but simply used the pressure of his heel to communicate his intent.

These actions show he probably had a natural understanding of animal behavior.

Clear

From the reaction of the men who witnessed this event, it is clear that Alexander had a unique talent. They laughed at him at first, but when Alexander mastered the horse, they cheered and burst into applause. His father even shed some tears and said to his small son, "O my son, look thee out a kingdom equal to and worthy of thyself, for Macedonia is too little for thee."

Consistent

From the time he saw the horse until the time Bucephalus allowed himself to be mastered, Alexander showed consistent confidence and skill. He approached confidently, sensed what the horse needed, gave the animal no reason to distrust him, and never wavered. In addition, the story is consistent with our knowledge of Alexander's later achievements, which persuades us that even as a child, Alexander had a natural ability to lead.

Appropriate

This narrative about Alexander and Bucephalus is appropriate for all readers because it teaches us that we can manage animals without abusing them. It is in line with Biblical teaching: "Whoever is righteous has regard for the life of his beast" (Proverbs 12:10a).

Expedient

The narrative is expedient (advantageous) because it helps us to learn that even the most difficult tasks can be performed with the right methods. Some people may have a natural talent with animals, but we can all learn something from Alexander's example.

Conclusion

At first, it is hard to believe a ten-year-old boy could tame such a spirited animal almost effortlessly. However, the details of what he did along with our understanding of the animal-human connection confirm the truth of the narrative. Considering his natural talents, what Alexander did is possible and probable. The details of the incident are clear and consistent, and the story is appropriate and expedient for all readers.

EXERCISE 9.3: Analyzing a Confirmation

Directions: Draw out the characteristics of the student's essay about Alexander and Bucephalus by answering the following questions.

1. **Narrative / Writer's Position:** Which of these two paragraphs is neutral in tone, and which one expresses an opinion?

2. **Possible / Probable:** What facts from the Research Source were used in each of the following approaches?

   a. Possible:

   b. Probable:

3. **Clear:** This paragraph is developed without any reference to Bucephalus. What did the writer focus on here to find clear evidence of Alexander's ability?

4. **Consistent:** The writer proves consistency in two different ways. What are they?

   a.

   b.

5. **Appropriate:** As shown in the chapters on Proverb and Chreia, one good way to support an idea is with Testimony of the Ancients. Though not required in Confirmation, it is used in the Appropriate approach in the model Confirmation. What support from the ancient world is included? Why do you suppose it was included?

6. **Expedient:** What advantage to readers is identified in this paragraph?

7. **Conclusion:** Which of the following best describes the writer's conclusion?

    A. It repeats the six approaches that were used in the essay.

    B. It repeats each approach and includes a brief reminder for each.

    C. It begins with a two-sentence observation about what one sees at first glance and what one sees after examination. Then it repeats each approach and includes a brief reminder of each.

Now You Try It

**Chapter 9 Essay
Confirmation**

Specifications

1. The purpose of this assignment is to write a Confirmation of a theory which cannot be absolutely proven but can be supported with facts and logical reasoning.

2. In your essay, confirm the narrative on *at least three* of the approaches in Group 1 and *at least one* of the approaches in Group 2:

Group 1
- possible
- probable
- clear
- consistent

Group 2
- appropriate
- expedient

3. The subject of the confirmation will be based on an incident that is recorded in the narrative of Jesus' arrest in Gethsemane. It is found only in the gospel of Mark:

"And a young man followed him, with nothing but a linen cloth about his body. And they seized him, but he left the linen cloth and ran away naked" (14:51-52).

4. Over the years, various theories have been put forward regarding the identity of this young man. Your task will be to examine three of those theories and decide

which you believe to be the most probable. You will then write an essay confirming the theory.

5. Begin by reading the three theories which appear in the pre-writing activity. Then compose three Yes/No questions that will help you focus on the debatable points in the theories. If time permits, discuss the various theories as a class or with a teacher familiar with the story. Then choose which of the theories you would like to confirm. Write your choice in the space above the chart. Then on the chart, jot down the points that best support the candidate you chose and begin writing.

6. Follow your teacher's instructions regarding preparation of the manuscript.

Confirmation: Pre-writing Activity

1. Three theories regarding the identity of the young man in Mark 14:51-52:

   a. **Lazarus of Bethany:** Professor E. H. Plumptre argued that the young man who fled from Gethsemane was Lazarus of Bethany. Here are his reasons: Lazarus was a young man, so the age is right. Though not a disciple, Lazarus is likely to have had an interest in abiding near Jesus. We know the chief priests wanted to arrest and kill him (John 12:9-10). The *sindon* (linen cloth) wrapped around him was a winding-sheet for bodies of the dead; Lazarus would be in possession of his. The *sindon* was expensive, and Lazarus seems to have been from a wealthy family. Bethany was near Gethsemane, so Lazarus could have reached the garden rather easily.[36]

   b. **First resurrected body:** Keeping in mind that God revealed his name as I AM (Exodus 3:14), Rev. Jeff Dixon wrote: "When Jesus said, 'I AM [John 18:4-6],' the power that was released was so tremendous that it knocked the soldiers backward (go back and read the story again for that moment). But it may have also caused a rumbling in the local cemetery! When the blast of power was released, a young boy, draped in a linen burial cloth in accordance with the tradition of that time, crawled out from his tomb—raised from the dead!"[37]

   c. **Mark:** Henry Spence-Jones and Joseph Exell argued that the young man was Mark himself: Since Mark is the only evangelist who mentions this incident, he was probably the lad who fled. Only he would have known what had happened. By tradition, it is reckoned that the house where Jesus celebrated the Passover was the house of Mark's mother, which had previously been used as a meeting place, as we know from Acts 12. After Jesus and the disciples withdrew to Gethsemane, the young Mark would have gone to bed. He could later have been awakened by the tumult of the soldiers led by Judas passing his house on their way to Gethsemane to arrest Jesus. The lad who fled had a linen cloth called a *sindon* cast about his naked body. The *sindon* was made of fine linen, which suggests it belonged to a person from a wealthy family. Though the word is used elsewhere in the New Testament to refer to a burial cloth, it could also refer to a kind of light cloak frequently worn in hot weather.[38]

2. **Debatable Yes/No Questions:**

   a.

   b.

   c.

3. Circle one: I have chosen to confirm theory: a   b   c.

	Grounds for Confirmation (Choose at least three.)
Possible	
Probable	
Clear	
Consistent	

	Your Assessment (Choose at least one.)
Appropriate (Encourages Right Behavior)	
Expedient (Advantageous, Edifying)	

COMMONPLACE

Chapter 10

Introduction

Have you ever heard of the "ladder of success"? This phrase expresses the idea that each step people take as they strive for success is like taking a step up a ladder. Often as people climb toward success, they receive the assistance of others, but what about the guy who receives help, reaches the top, and then considers himself better than those who gave him a helping hand—or, worse, those he stepped on to move himself upward?

This is the concept that William Shakespeare was working with in his play *Julius Caesar*. Brutus, a well-respected senator, knows that Caesar has made many enemies who are conspiring against him, and in this speech from Act 2, Shakespeare reveals Brutus' private reflections on the ingratitude of the man he once admired:

> But 'tis a common proof,
> That lowliness is young ambition's ladder,
> Whereto the climber upward turns his face;
> But when he once attains the upmost round,
> He then unto the ladder turns his back,
> Looks in the clouds, scorning the base degrees
> By which he did ascend.[39]

In this passage, Shakespeare has distilled the sin of ingratitude: the successful man's "scorning the base degrees by which he did ascend" the ladder of his success. The very thought of it was enough to turn Brutus into an enemy.

Ingratitude has the power to affect human relationships to such an extent that stories and proverbs exposing and opposing it can be found in all time periods and in all cultures. Thus, we can conclude that human beings everywhere find it necessary to focus attention on certain behaviors in an effort to mold a better society.

THINK IT THROUGH: What Bible teachings deal with the sin of ingratitude? What books, plays, or movies have characters who fail to show gratitude? What are some famous quotations about ingratitude?

Definition and Purpose

A Commonplace is a writing or a speech which praises a virtue or assails a vice. It differs from the Encomium and the Invective, respectively, in that it concerns the behavior itself, not the person who exhibits it.

The purpose of the Commonplace is to draw attention to an issue of vital importance and arouse in the reader or listener a proper emotional response—a decision to avoid vice and to cultivate virtue. Historically, the Christian homily has served this purpose. A homily is a sermon which focuses on a behavior with the intent to persuade believers to a life that is pleasing to God. However, the Commonplace can also be found in the secular culture when, say, the First Lady of the United States advocates her cause. Examples include Melania Trump's campaign against cyberbullying, Michelle Obama's campaign to improve health through diet, Laura Bush's campaign for literacy, and Nancy Reagan's "Just Say No" campaign against drug abuse.

Approaches to the Commonplace

When writing a Commonplace about a vice, one begins with a simple, direct statement about the evil of the behavior. During the reign of Queen Elizabeth I in the sixteenth century, the Anglican Church presented homilies on moral issues. The homily against drunkenness began with the statement, "Now you shall hear how foul a thing gluttony and drunkenness is before God. . . ."[40] Similarly, in our own times, Karen P. Tandy, an administrator with the U. S. Drug Enforcement Administration, spoke to an international gathering about drug abuse in 2005, saying, "We are all shared partners in the travesty that [drug abuse] wreaks upon our children and all the future generations for all our countries."[41]

Classical teachers of rhetoric Aphthonius and Hermogenes established five approaches to the Commonplace, which are explained in the chart below:[42]

Approach	Details
Comparison	Compare the vice to one that is worse (e.g., plagiarism to felony theft).
Contrast	Make a statement about the opposite of the vice (e.g., honesty and dishonesty).
Cause	Explain why someone would engage in this vice.
Example(s)	Offer examples from history which prove the evil of the vice or the advantage of the virtue; or, if dealing with a hypothetical case, offer a profile of the type of person who would engage in this behavior.
For a Vice: **Rejection of Pity**	Argue that the vice deserves punishment. Below are specific approaches one can take in this section. <table><tr><td>*a. Description*</td><td>*Describe the evil effects of the vice.*</td></tr><tr><td>*b. Illegality*</td><td>*Discuss in terms of the law.*</td></tr><tr><td>*c. Justice*</td><td>*Argue that the severest possible punishment be applied.*</td></tr><tr><td>*d. Expediency*</td><td>*Show that things will be better the sooner the vice is eliminated.*</td></tr><tr><td>*e. Honor*</td><td>*Show how those who eliminate the vice will be honored.*</td></tr><tr><td>*f. Practicality*</td><td>*Argue that the public desires retribution.*</td></tr><tr><td>*g. Immediacy*</td><td>*Argue that swift action will be a warning to others.*</td></tr></table>

Organization

Although it is possible to use each of the approaches, some writers choose those approaches which are the strongest. These approaches will become the body of your essay. The best organization plan is as follows:

1. Write a general statement about the virtue or vice you will discuss, and clearly state your position on the issue.

2. Write one well-developed paragraph to explain each approach.

3. Write a conclusion in which you summarize your key points.

Model Commonplace

INTRODUCTION: *Pliny the Elder (AD 23-79) was a Roman naturalist whose work entitled* Natural History *is considered the first encyclopedia. It concerned mathematics and the sciences. In the section on medicine, Pliny includes a commonplace against the way the Greeks practiced medicine (Book 29, Chapters 1-27). The paragraphs below are an adapted version of the nineteenth-century English translation by John Bostock and H. T. Riley.*

Evils Attendant upon the Practice of Medicine
By Pliny the Elder

General Statement + Writer's Position

Cato the Younger once warned his son Marcus about the Greeks, especially forbidding him "to have anything to do with Greek physicians." It was not so much that Cato condemned medicine itself, but rather the art of medicine as it was practiced by the Greeks. And it was horrid indeed!

Comparison

To advance his cause, Cato made a comparison to literature. "Whenever Greece shall bestow its literature upon Rome," he warned his son, "it will mar everything!" But he really drove home his point when he compared Greek physicians to racist enemies who "conspired among themselves to murder all barbarians with their medicine." He felt they practiced their profession for lucre, in order that they might win our confidence and dispatch us all the more easily, considering us nothing but bumpkins who would be easy to fool and wipe out.

Contrast

Why is it that Romans, who normally want to understand those things that affect them, value nothing as much as a doctor who speaks Greek! The less intelligible it is, the more they crave it. Roman physicians can even lose the esteem of their patients if they do not speak to them in Greek, which they themselves often do not understand. Similarly, why is it that with all the other arts, a person cannot simply declare himself an expert and be believed, but with medicine, the moment a man declares himself to be an adept in medicine, he is immediately believed? We should not allow doctors simply to self-declare their skill.

Example

There is no other profession that has perpetrated more fraud and quackery in the exercise of its work. To understand the harm it sometimes runs to, we need only consider the success of the doctor in poisonings. Medical murder has even been committed in the houses of our princes. Who can forget the Roman physician Eudemus, for example, who connived with Livia to poison her husband Drusus Caesar [AD 23]?

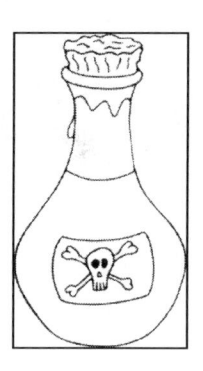

Cause

What exactly is it that drives physicians to such lengths? Although there is enough rivalry among physicians to keep their prices down, it is a well-known fact that Charmis, a physician from Massilia, made a bargain with a patient in the provinces that he would cure the man if he (the sick man) agreed to pay 2,000 sesterces. Even emperors seem to have no control over these profits. For example, what happened when the Emperor Claudius, angered at some malpractice of his surgeon Alcon, fined the man 10 million sesterces and exiled him to Gaul? Was Alcon put out of business for his quackery? No. After being recalled from exile, he made the ten million sesterces back in the course of a few years, and then went on to make more!

Rejection of Pity (Description)

Just look at what we submit to even when we are in good health. We rub the body with wax and oil which, though they might provide good preparation for a wrestling match, do not really preserve our health. We take hot baths because we are told they are necessary for digestion when, in fact, they leave us weak. In fact, the patients who submit the most are often carried from the baths to their tombs! We take potions when fasting. We vomit to clear the stomach only to immediately drench it with a series of drinks. We stop at nothing with their ridiculous "cures."

Rejection of Pity (Illegality/Immorality)

Greek medical practitioners have also been known to engage in immoral and illegal behavior. Patients have to disrobe, which contributes to the decline in public morals. Physicians also commit fraud. For example, they sell an expensive preparation named *theriace*, which is made from 600 different costly ingredients, when Nature has bestowed many remedies (nearly free for the taking) that work just as well.

Conclusion

To sum it all up, in order to make a better future, we must stop considering the ancient Greeks superior to us. We must stop physicians from taking outrageous profit for foolish treatments and unnecessary medications. We must stop them from using their knowledge of poisons to murder individuals and even to bring about the doom of our race. In brief, as things stand now, no art is as cruel as the "art" of the Greek physician.[43]

EXERCISE 10.1: Analyzing Pliny's Commonplace

Directions: After reading Pliny's remarks about the evils of the practice of medicine, familiarize yourself with the techniques of Commonplace by answering the questions below.

1. **General Statement / Writer's Position:**

    a. In the first paragraph, we see the general statement that Cato did not condemn medicine itself, but what?

    b. What was the writer's position on the subject?

2. **Comparison:** In the second paragraph, we see two *comparisons*. What are they?

    a.

    b.

3. **Contrast:** In the third paragraph, Pliny makes two *contrasts*.

    a. Sadly, a Roman doctor who speaks Latin is *not as good as who?*

    b. Sadly, what can a doctor do that a person in any other art cannot?

4. **Example:** In the fourth paragraph, what specific Roman physician is singled out as an example? What had he done?

5. **Cause:** What does Pliny say motivates doctors?

6. **Rejection of Pity (Description):** What five bad medical treatments are described? (Be brief.)

a.

b.

c.

d.

e.

7. **Rejection of Pity (Illegality/Immorality):** What two accusations does Pliny make?

   a. What must patients do?

   b. What might physicians do?

EXERCISE 10.2: Brainstorming Approaches to the Commonplace

Directions: With a classmate, begin by choosing a vice about which you could write a Commonplace. Then complete the chart to indicate the various approaches you could take toward the subject. It is not necessary to write up the essay.

Choose one:

1. Cheating

2. Telling a lie about a person

3. Being "two-faced"

4. Being ashamed of one's family

5. Cruelty to animals

Approach	Details
Comparison	

Contrast	
Cause	
Example	

Rejection of Pity (Choose two.: Description, Illegality, Justice, Expediency, Honor, Practicality, Immediacy)

1st Choice:	
2nd Choice:	

Now You Try It

**Chapter 10 Essay
Commonplace**

Specifications

1. The purpose of this assignment is to demonstrate your ability to write a Commonplace.

2. In Paul's second letter to the church at Corinth, he listed some vices which he considered pitfalls for the church, urging the believers to avoid them. Your task will be to select one of these vices from 2 Corinthians 12:20 and compose a Commonplace which will help readers understand why these vices are so destructive.

Quarreling	Anger	Slander	Conceit
Jealousy	Hostility	Gossip	Disorder

3. Complete the pre-writing activity, or, if you teacher prefers, prepare a formal phrase outline. Then compose your essay.

4. Follow your teacher's instructions regarding the preparation of the manuscript.

Commonplace: Pre-Writing Activity

I have chosen to write about _____.

Approach	Details
Comparison	
Contrast	
Cause	
Example	
Rejection of Pity (Choose two: Description, Illegality, Justice, Expediency, Honor, Practicality, Immediacy)	
1st Choice	
2nd Choice	

ENCOMIUM

Chapter 11

Introduction

Psalm 150:1-6
Let Everything Praise the LORD

> Praise the LORD! Praise God in his sanctuary;
>   praise him in his mighty heavens!
> Praise him for his mighty deeds;
>   praise him according to his excellent greatness!
>
> Praise him with trumpet sound;
>   praise him with lute and harp!
> Praise him with tambourine and dance;
>   praise him with strings and pipe!
> Praise him with sounding cymbals;
>   praise him with loud clashing cymbals!
> Let everything that has breath praise the LORD!
> Praise the LORD!

When a Christian thinks of praise, perhaps the first thing that comes to mind is David's lavish praise of the Lord, which is apparent in Psalm 150 above. The New Testament as well gives ample praise to the Lord Jesus Christ and concludes in the Book of Revelation with everyone in heaven praising God's name.

Knowing that we humans are in a fallen condition, the authors of works collected in the Bible afford little in the way of praising humankind, but occasionally Paul would offer a word of thanksgiving to the first generation of Christian believers, as in this passage at the very outset of I Corinthians 1:4-5, which says: "I give thanks to my God always for you because of the grace of God that was given you in Christ Jesus, that in every way you were enriched in him in all speech and all knowledge." However, even here Paul's praise for the church at Corinth was couched in language that referred to the work of Christ in them, which immediately provides us with a gauge as we undertake to praise our fellow travelers on planet earth: we can extend praise to a person insofar as the person conducts himself in a way that is not at loggerheads with the teachings of the Bible.

"Well," you might ask, "if that is the case, how could I possibly praise Achilles or Hector, who were both created by a pagan author who never heard the gospel?" The answer is that one should develop the habit of holding all literature up to the truth of Scripture. Inasmuch as Hector goes down fighting on behalf of his countrymen at the end of the *Iliad*, we acknowledge his willingness to do so as consistent with the teachings of Christ, who said, "Greater love has no one than this, that someone lay down his life for his friends" (John 15:13).

Similarly, in a great work of the fourteenth century entitled *Inferno*, the author, Dante Alighieri, seems also to have acknowledged this quality in Hector, placing him in the first circle of hell, Limbo, where the virtuous pagans dwell in relative peace. Seeing there the shade of Hector, Dante noted, "I feel myself exalted to have seen him"—high praise indeed.

Definition and Purpose of the Encomium

An Encomium is a piece of writing whose purpose is to offer praise. In an Encomium, the writer or speaker will dwell on the good qualities of the person or thing being praised.

The passage below comes from a Hebrew writing called *The Wisdom of Ben Sira* from the early second century BC. It speaks of the responsibility of men to acknowledge the deeds of their ancestors.

> [1] Let us now praise famous men, and our fathers in their generations.
> [2] The Lord apportioned to them great glory, his majesty from the beginning.
> [3] There were those who ruled in their kingdoms, and were men renowned for their power, giving counsel by their understanding, and proclaiming prophecies;

⁴ leaders of the people in their deliberations and in understanding of learning for the people, wise in their words of instruction;

⁵ those who composed musical tunes, and set forth verses in writing;

⁶ rich men furnished with resources, living peaceably in their habitations –

⁷ all these were honored in their generations, and were the glory of their times.

⁸ There are some of them who have left a name, so that men declare their praise.

⁹ And there are some who have no memorial, who have perished as though they had not lived; they have become as though they had not been born, and so have their children after them.

¹⁰ But these were men of mercy, whose righteous deeds have not been forgotten;

¹¹ their prosperity will remain with their descendants, and their inheritance to their children's children.

¹² Their descendants stand by the covenants; their children also, for their sake.

¹³ Their posterity will continue for ever, and their glory will not be blotted out.

¹⁴ Their bodies were buried in peace, and their name lives to all generations.

¹⁵ Peoples will declare their wisdom, and the congregation proclaims their praise.[44]

THINK IT THROUGH: Name some people whom you think "fit the bill" for persons described in:

Lines 3-4:

Line 5a or 5b:

Line 6:

Line 9:

Subjects and Occasions of the Encomium

Most of us have been present on occasions when a speaker has taken the microphone and offered an Encomium of some kind. Some examples might be a religious event, a holiday, a wedding celebration, a birthday, or a funeral.

THINK IT THROUGH: Name a couple of American holidays when a particular person or group of persons might be praised.

Approaches to Encomium

An Encomium of a person has five basic approaches, which are listed and explained in the chart below.

Approach	Details
Background	Here one provides the person's date of birth, place of birth, parents, and ancestors.
Education and Influences	Here one indicates the person's interests, course of study, and talents. Influential teachers and religious training might also be mentioned.
Character	Here one may comment on the person's faith, persistence, kindness, devotion, and/or courage—in short, any positive aspect of the figure's personality.
Achievements	Here one lists the person's life achievements.
Comparison	Here one compares the subject of the Encomium to another, perhaps more well-known figure from the past.

As with all progymnasmata exercises, depending on your particular subject and occasion, you may or may not need to include all five approaches of the Encomium. This will be discussed later in this chapter.

Organization

The most typical organization plan for an Encomium is as follows:

1. Write an Introduction which introduces the person you are writing about and places him or her in historical context (time, place, etc.). In a short work, the Introduction can be combined with the Background.

2. Write one paragraph for each of the approaches.

3. Write a clincher that wraps up the essay and generates a positive feeling in the reader. (This may be simply the last sentence of the final paragraph.)

Model Encomium

INTRODUCTION: *Below is an Encomium to St. Boniface (c. 672-754), known in history as Apostle to the Germans. It was written by an Englishman of the sixteenth century, John Foxe (d. 1587), whose famous work* Foxe's Book of Martyrs *is a classic anthology of encomia to martyred Christians. Please read Foxe's encomium of Boniface and then answer the questions that follow.*

St. Boniface: Apostle to the Germans
By John Foxe

Introduction + Background

Boniface, archbishop of Mentz and father of the German church, was an Englishman, and is, in ecclesiastical history, looked upon as one of the brightest ornaments of this nation. Originally, his name was Winfred, or Winfrith, and he was born at Kirton, in Devonshire, then part of the West Saxon kingdom.

Education

When he was only about six years of age, he began to discover a propensity to reflection, and seemed solicitous to gain information on religious subjects. Wolfrad, the abbot, finding that he possessed a bright genius, as well as a strong inclination to study, had him removed to Nutscelle, a seminary of learning in the diocese of Winchester, where he would have a much greater opportunity of attaining improvement than at Exeter.

Achievements

After due study, the abbot, seeing him qualified for the priesthood, obliged him to receive that holy order when he was about thirty years old. From that time he began to preach and labor for the salvation of his fellow creatures; he was released to attend a synod of bishops in the kingdom of West Saxons. He afterwards, in 719, went to Rome, where Gregory II, who then sat in Peter's chair, received him with great friendship, and finding him full of all the virtues that compose the character of an apostolic missionary, dismissed him with commission at large to preach the gospel to the pagans wherever he found them. Passing through Lombardy and Bavaria, he came to Thuringia, which country had before received the light of the gospel. He next visited Utrecht, and then proceeded to Saxony, where he converted some thousands to Christianity.

Archbishop Boniface (AD 672-754)

During the ministry of this meek prelate, Pepin was declared king of France. It was that prince's ambition to be crowned by the most holy prelate he could find, and Boniface was pitched on to perform that ceremony, which he did at Soissons, in 752. The next year, his great age and many infirmities lay so heavy on him, that, with the consent of the new king, the bishops, &c. of his diocese, he consecrated Lullus, his countryman, and faithful disciple, and placed him in the see of Mentz. . . .

Character

Having left these orders, he took boat [*sic*] to the Rhine, and went to Friesland, where he converted and baptized several thousands of barbarous natives, demolished the temples, and raised churches on the ruins of those superstitious structures. A day being appointed for confirming a great number of new converts, he ordered them to assemble in a new open plain, near the river Bourde. Thither he repaired the day before; and, pitching a tent, determined to remain on the spot all night, in order to be ready early in the morning. Some pagans, who were his inveterate enemies, having intelligence of this, poured down upon him and the companions of his mission in the night, and killed him and fifty-two of his companions and attendants on June 5, 755.[a] Thus fell the great father of the Germanic church, the honor of England, and the glory of the age in which he lived.[45]

EXERCISE 11.1: Analyzing the Model Encomium

Directions: To examine the techniques of Encomium, please answer the questions below, which concern Foxe's essay on Boniface.

1. Do elements of praise appear in the Introduction as well as in the subsequent paragraphs?

2. Try "reading between the lines" a bit. What age does Boniface seem to have been at the end of the section called "Achievements"?

3. Considering his age, what is remarkable about what you learn in the section entitled "Character"?

4. Why do you suppose Foxe did not end his essay after he provided the date of Boniface's death, June 5, 755?

The Adapted Encomium

Exactly which of the Encomium approaches might be employed depends on a number of factors, such as the age of the person being praised, the time period in which he or she lived, and the immediate context of the Encomium. For example, if you sat down today to write an Encomium of Julius Caesar, you would probably do

---

[a] Foxe gave the date as 755, but most sources now say 754.

research to find his dates of birth and death, some information about his family, education, achievements, and so on. However, authors with different purposes and different subjects will begin differently. For example, the immediate situation of a scene in a play or a novel would influence the way the author composed the encomium. Because it would need to fit the context of the play, it would praise the subject of the Encomium but would not use the discrete paragraphs of a standard Encomium.

Model Adapted Encomium

INTRODUCTION: *In Book XI of the* Odyssey, *Odysseus must descend into the Underworld to meet with the shade of Tiresias, priest and prophet, in order to discover how he can return to his home, Ithaca. While there, he encounters the shade of Achilles, who enquires about his father. The following is Odysseus' response.*

Odysseus' Encomium of Achilles' Son
By Homer

(1) "I have heard nothing," I answered, "of Peleus, but I can tell you all about your son Neoptolemus, for I took him in my own ship from Scyros with the Achaeans. (2) In our councils of war before Troy, he was always first to speak, and his judgment was unerring. (3) Nestor and I were the only two who could surpass him; and when it came to fighting on the plain of Troy, he would never remain with the body of his men, but would dash on far in front, foremost of them all in valor. (4) Many a man did he kill in battle—I cannot name every single one of those whom he slew while fighting on the side of the Argives, but will only say how he killed that valiant hero Eurypylus, son of Telephus, who was the handsomest man I ever saw except Memnon; many others also of the Ceteians fell around him by reason of a woman's bribes. (5) Moreover, when all the bravest of the Argives went inside the horse that Epeus had made, and it was left to me to settle when we should either open the door of our ambuscade, or close it, though all the other leaders and chief men among the Danaans were drying their eyes and quaking in every limb, I never once saw him turn pale nor wipe a tear from his cheek; he was all the time urging me to break out from the horse—grasping the handle of his sword and his bronze-

shod spear, and breathing fury against the foe. (6) Yet, when we had sacked the city of Priam, he got his handsome share of the prize money and went on board (such is the fortune of war) without a wound upon him, neither from a thrown spear nor in close combat, for the rage of Mars is a matter of great chance."[46]

EXERCISE 11.2: Analyzing an Adapted Encomium

Directions: The questions below direct your attention to specific statements of praise from the excerpt. Indicate how Odysseus praises Neoptolemus in each of the numbered sentences.

1. **Sentence #2:** How did Neoptolemus perform as an advisor in war counsels?

2. **Sentence #3:** In battle, he was foremost in what?

3. **Sentence #4:** How is Neoptolemus praised as a warrior?

4. **Sentence #5:** During the long wait inside the Trojan horse, how did he compare to the others?

5. **Sentence #6:** After the sack of the city, what was his condition he returned to the ship?

6. Because the excerpt above is an Adapted Encomium, the various approaches do not appear in separate paragraphs with tidy labels, yet three of the five approaches have been used. Which approach is stated or implied in the following sentences—Background, Education/Influences, Character, Achievements, Comparison?

   a. Sentences 2, 3b, and 5:

   b. Sentence 3a:

c. Sentences 4 and 6:

Now You Try It

Chapter 11, Essay 1
Encomium to a Person

Specifications

1. The purpose of this assignment is to demonstrate your ability to write an Encomium of a person.

2. For a topic, you can choose a person from this list:
   - a Biblical figure
   - a family member
   - a character from literature
   - a historical figure
   - a sports figure
   - a person who sacrificed for others
   - a person who overcame a difficulty in his or her life

3. If necessary, do some research in the library or on the Internet to find information for each category of the Encomium:
   - Background
   - Education/Training
   - Character
   - Achievement
   - Comparison

4. Complete the chart in the pre-writing activity, or, if your teacher prefers, prepare a formal phrase outline.

5. Follow your teacher's instructions regarding preparation of the manuscript.

Encomium to a Person: Pre-Writing Activity

I have chosen to write an Encomium of _____.

Approach	Details
Background	
Education and/or Training	
Character	
Achievements	
Comparison	

Other Encomia

Because it is natural to praise anything we love, humans are not the only subjects of Encomium. First-century rhetorician Hermogenes of Tarsus wrote, "We also praise things; for example, justice, and dumb [mute] animals, for example, a horse; and there have even been encomia of plants and mountains and rivers."[47] To help students with these encomia, Hermogenes listed suitable topics, which appear in the chart below.

Subject of Encomium	Hermogenes' Topics
Animals	<ul><li>The place where they occur</li><li>The gods to whom they are dedicated (e.g., the owl to Athena)</li><li>How they are nurtured</li><li>What kind of mind they have</li><li>What kind of body they have</li><li>What functions they have</li><li>How they are useful</li><li>How long they live</li></ul>
Plants	<ul><li>The place where they grow</li><li>The gods to whom they are dedicated (e.g., the olive to Athena)</li><li>How they are raised</li><li>What care they need</li><li>What structure they have</li><li>In what ways they are beautiful</li><li>How they are useful</li></ul>
Cities	<ul><li>How they were founded</li><li>How they have grown</li><li>How they were nurtured by the gods</li><li>The education they offer</li><li>The manners and customs characteristic of their people</li><li>What sort of institutions they have</li><li>What pursuits they follow</li><li>What they have accomplished</li></ul>

One thing to note in Hermogenes' lists is the importance of the role of the gods. As he explained, "The term *enkômion* . . . comes from the fact that poets sang hymns praising the gods in *kômai* (villages) in ancient times. . . ."[48] Certainly in Judeo-Christian civilization, the God of Abraham, Isaac, and Jacob is not overlooked in encomia. Since God is the Creator of all things and the Director of history, His hand will naturally come to the mind of a believer. Take, for example, the case of the lowly donkey. When most people think of a donkey, they deem it a stubborn animal more suitable for comedy than praise, yet the Bible includes several narratives in which God used the donkey as a part of his plan: Balaam's donkey actually "explained things" to Balaam, Samson once killed a thousand men with the jawbone of a donkey; and, of course, the donkey colt was used by Jesus for his triumphal entry into Jerusalem (not what Hollywood would probably use for a movie hero).In short, references to the Creator are always appropriate in an Encomium. An Encomium to the Lord Himself, however, is normally called a *hymn*.

Model of an Adapted Encomium to an Animal

INTRODUCTION: *As with an Encomium to a person, an Encomium to an animal, plant, or city can appear in adapted form. In the model below, we see encomiastic remarks about dogs, which are used in a discussion about the characteristics of a good guardian of a city. It comes from Book II of Plato's* Republic. *The speaker is Socrates, who is in conversation with Glaucon. Glaucon's words are in italics in the selection.*

Excerpt from *The Republic*
By Plato

. . . [I]t will be our duty to select if we can natures which are fitted for the task of guarding the city.

It will.
And the selection will be no easy matter, I said, but we must be brave and do our best.

We must.
Is not the noble youth very like a well-bred dog in respect of guarding and watching?

What do you mean?
I mean that both of them ought to be quick to see, and swift to overtake the enemy when they see him; and strong too, if, when they have caught him, they have to fight with him.

All these qualities, he replied, will certainly be required by them.
Well, and your guardian must be brave if he is to fight well?

Certainly.
And is he likely to be brave who has no spirit, whether horse or dog or any other kind of animal? Have you never observed how invincible and unconquerable is spirit and how the presence of it makes the soul of any creature to be absolutely fearless and indomitable?

I have.
Then now we have a clear notion of the bodily qualities which are required in the guardian.

True.
And also the mental ones; his soul is to be full of spirit?

Yes.
But are not these spirited natures apt to be savage with one another and with everybody else?

A difficulty by no means easy to overcome, he replied.
Whereas, I said, they ought to be dangerous to their enemies and gentle to their friends; if not, they will destroy themselves without waiting for their enemies to destroy them.

True, he said.
What is to be done then? I said; how shall we find a gentle nature which has also a great spirit, for the one is the contradiction of the other.

True.

He will not be a good guardian who is wanting in either of these two qualities; and yet the combination of them appears to be impossible; and hence we must infer that to be a good guardian is impossible.

I am afraid that what you say is true, he replied.
Here, feeling perplexed, I began to think over what had preceded. My friend, I said, no wonder that we are in a perplexity, for we have lost sight of the image which we had before us.

What do you mean? he said.
I mean to say that there do exist natures gifted with those opposite qualities.

And where do you find them?
Many animals, I replied, furnish examples of them; our friend the dog is a very good one; you know that well-bred dogs are perfectly gentle to their familiars and acquaintances, and the reverse to strangers.

Yes, I know.
Then there is nothing impossible or out of the order of nature in our finding a guardian who has a similar combination of qualities?

Certainly not.
Would not he who is fitted to be a guardian, besides the spirited nature, need to have the qualities of a philosopher?

I do not apprehend your meaning.
The trait of which I am speaking, I replied, may be also seen in the dog and is remarkable in the animal.

What trait?
Why, a dog, whenever he sees a stranger, is angry; when an acquaintance, he welcomes him although the one has never done him any harm, nor the other any good. Did this never strike you as curious?

The matter never struck me before, but I quite recognize the truth of your remark.

And surely this instinct of a dog is very charming. Your dog is a philosopher!

Why?
Why, because he distinguishes the face of a friend and of an enemy only by the criterion of knowing and not knowing. And must not an animal be a lover of learning who determines what he likes and dislikes by the test of knowledge and ignorance?

Most assuredly.
And is not the love of learning the love of wisdom, which is philosophy?

They are the same, he replied.
And may we not say confidently of man also that he who is likely to be gentle to his friends and acquaintances must by nature be a lover of wisdom and knowledge?

That we may safely affirm.
Then he who is to be a really good and noble guardian of the State will require to unite in himself philosophy and spirit and swiftness and strength.

Undoubtedly.[49]

EXERCISE 11.3: Analyzing an Adapted Encomium

Directions: After reading the excerpt about the ideal guardian of the city, analyze Adapted Encomium by answering these questions.

1. Hermogenes suggested praising the nurture of the animal. What does Socrates say about the proper nurturing of dogs?

2. Hermogenes suggested praising the mind of the animal. How does Socrates praise the mind of a dog?

3. Hermogenes suggested praising the body of the animal. What characteristics does Socrates list for the body of the dog?

4. Hermogenes suggested praising the functions of the animal. What functions are specified for the dog? What features make the dog suited for that function?

Now You Try It

Chapter 11, Essay 2
Encomium to an Animal, Plant, or City

Specifications

1. The purpose of this assignment is to demonstrate your ability to write an Encomium on a subject other than a person.

2. You can write your Encomium about one of these topics:
   - an animal (either a specific pet or a species)
   - a plant (e.g., the flower which is the symbol of your state)
   - a city (your own city, a city famous in history, a city you like to visit)

3. After selecting a topic, begin by completing the chart in the pre-writing activity (or, if your teacher prefers, by writing a formal outline). Under *Topics,* select five of Hermogenes' topics from the chart on p. 220. For example, if you are writing about elephants, you could write "Place where they occur" under *Topics.* Then, under *Details,* you would indicate the specific places: Africa, India. If your teacher prefers, prepare a formal phrase outline.

4. Follow your teacher's instructions regarding preparation of the manuscript.

Encomium to an Animal, Plant or City: Pre-Writing Activity

I have chosen to write an Encomium of _____.

Hermogenes' Topics (Choose three from p. 220.)	Details

INVECTIVE

Chapter 12

Introduction

After Nazi Germany was defeated in 1945 by the Allied Forces under the command of United States General Dwight D. Eisenhower, the Nazi leaders were put on trial at Nuremberg, Germany, in 1946. In his summation, Robert H. Jackson, the United States' chief prosecutor, reviewed the roles of each of the men in the Nazi regime, employing strong language to persuade the judge that these men should be executed for crimes against humanity. As he proceeded, he catalogued the role of each defendant, among which were the following:

Robert H. Jackson
(1892-1954)

- Wilhelm Frick, "the ruthless organizer"
- Hermann Göring, the "half militarist and half gangster"
- Joachim von Ribbentrop, "the salesman of deception"
- Alfred Rosenberg, "the intellectual high priest of the 'master race'"
- Fritz Sauckel, the "cruelest slaver since the Pharaohs of Egypt"
- Julius Streicher, "the venomous vulgarian"

As a result of the judgment at Nuremberg, these men (with the exception of Göring, who committed suicide in prison) were all executed on October 16, 1946, and the Third Reich which they had served lay broken in the ash can of history, a prime example of the truth of Proverbs 22:8, which says, "Whoever sows injustice will reap calamity, and the rod of his fury will fail."

Definition and Purpose of Invective

Good manners dictate that we not dwell on another's weaknesses, and logicians counsel us to avoid *ad hominem* attacks. However, there is a place in the public square for public censure (severe disapproval). Nazism in Germany and Stalinism in Russia were two political movements in twentieth-century Europe that were responsible for the deaths of tens of millions of people and acts of cruelty and cultural ruin that cannot be passed by in silence. It is for such cases that the ancients devised the Invective, a writing or a speech in which a person is held accountable by reasonable people for the excesses of heartless behavior.

What sets the Invective apart from Encomium and the Commonplace? Whereas the Encomium praises people for their good deeds, the Invective blames them for their evil deeds. Whereas the Commonplace deals with bad behavior (racism, injustice, cruelty), the Invective deals with the individual who exhibited the behavior (e.g., Adolf Hitler, Joseph Stalin, Saddam Hussein).

THINK IT THROUGH: Who are some historical figures who have reputations for evil? What about Biblical figures?

Approaches to Invective

An Invective of a person has five basic approaches, which are listed and explained in the chart below.

Approach	Details
Background	Note (a) that the evil person had the advantage of a good upbringing but turned against it, or (b) note that the evil person was the product of an evil environment.
Education and Influences	Either (a) identify the good influences that the subject turned against, or (b) identify the evil influences in the person's life.
Vices	List the bad character traits of the person (e.g., greed, selfishness, cruelty, bigotry, etc.).

Evil Deeds	List the person's evil deeds: either inward motivations (e.g., self-love, cowardice) or outward acts (e.g., cruelty, murder).
Comparison	Compare the subject either to (a) someone with a similar background who took a better path, or (b) another villain of history whose infamy is well known.

Organization

The organization plan of the Invective is similar to that of the Encomium, and, as with Encomium, it is not necessary to use all of the approaches. You may select those which are suited to your topic.

1. Write an Introduction which identifies the person you are writing about and places him or her in historical context (time, place, etc.). In a short work, the Introduction can be combined with the Background.

2. Write one paragraph for each of the approaches you choose to use.

3. Write a Conclusion that wraps up the essay and leaves the reader with a feeling of disdain.

Model Invective

Invective against the Emperor Nero

Introduction + Background

Nero Claudius Caesar Augustus Germanicus, commonly known as Nero, was the last Roman emperor in the line beginning with Julius Caesar. Born in AD 37, Nero was the son of Domitius Ahenobarbus and Julia Agrippina, who was the niece of the Emperor Claudius. Agrippina was a plotter and conniver and must have shown signs of her wickedness during her marriage to Domitius, as Suetonius records that upon the birth of Nero, Domitius prophesied "that nothing

Nero (AD 37–68)

but what was detestable, and pernicious to the public, could ever be produced of him and Agrippina."[50] After the death of two husbands, Agrippina married her uncle Claudius, who adopted her son Nero as his own. Nero's evil reputation begins perhaps with his mother, who murdered several and drove others to suicide in her efforts to promote her own cause and that of her son. It is widely believed that she dispatched her husband, the Emperor Claudius, by way of poisoned mushrooms so that her son could begin his reign as emperor at the age of seventeen. However, her evil ways rubbed off on Nero, who, in AD 59, murdered her.

Education and Influences

When Nero was twelve, Agrippina arranged for the philosopher Seneca to be returned from exile in order to undertake the education of her son. Suetonius records that, "When a boy, he took up almost all the liberal arts; but his mother turned him from philosophy, warning him that it was a drawback to one who was going to rule, while Seneca kept him from reading the early orators, to make his admiration for his teacher endure the longer. Turning therefore to poetry, he wrote verses with eagerness . . . . He likewise had no slight interest in painting and sculpture."[51] Nero also "gained some knowledge of music" as a boy and shortly after becoming emperor, brought Terpnus, the most accomplished master of the lyre, to the palace, engaging him to play and sing while Nero dined. Then, after listening to the master at dinner, he would practice singing late into the night. Eventually considering himself to be a master singer, Nero would force vast audiences to listen to him sing for hours on end, not allowing anyone to leave the theatre until he was finished. "And so it is said," notes Suetonius, "that some women gave birth to children there, while many who were worn out with listening and applauding, secretly leaped from the wall, since the gates at the entrance were closed, or feigned death and were carried out as if for burial."[52]

Vices

Suetonius characterizes Nero with references to his "acts of wantonness, lust, extravagance, avarice and cruelty." He was jealous to the point of murder; resentful of any criticism; boastful, merciless, self-indulgent, immoral, and frightened by omens and dreams—not a good mix for a man with unlimited power.

Evil Deeds

One of Nero's earliest acts of cruelty was the murder of his mother, Agrippina, whom he invited to a party at Baiae, a pleasure resort on the Bay of Naples. Unbeknownst to her, he had rigged the ship to be sunk, but when that plot failed, he ordered her to be beaten to death in her home. He ordered the beheadings of two relatives of the Emperor Augustus as well as his own wife. With his companions, he would riot through the city during the night, attacking men and women he encountered along the way. However, Nero's infamy lies primarily in his persecution of the early Christians. In AD 64, the city of Rome burned. Suetonius records that "under cover of displeasure at the ugliness of the old buildings and the narrow, crooked streets [of Rome], he set fire to the city," a conflagration that raged for six days and seven nights for which he blamed the Christians of Rome, a lie which gave impetus to a severe persecution against Christians.[53] According to Tacitus, "Mockery of every sort was added to their deaths. Covered with the skins of beasts, they were torn by dogs and perished, or were nailed to crosses, or were doomed to the flames and burnt, to serve as a nightly illumination, when daylight had expired.".[54] It was in this general mayhem that the apostle Peter was crucified, and the apostle Paul beheaded.

Nero fiddling as the smoke rises behind him.

Comparison

In his immorality and perversions, Nero was much like his uncle, the mad emperor Caligula. In his persecution of the Christians from AD 64 to 68, he was more like the Emperor Diocletian under whom 20,000 Christians were martyred in the early fourth century. Still, the vivid mental image of Nero fiddling while Rome burned has made Nero himself the villain against whom many subsequent tyrants have been compared.

Conclusion

In short, Nero's desensitizing education, the evil influence of his mother, his arrogance and cruelty, and his persecution of innocents have all combined to give Nero Claudius Caesar Augustus Germanicus a spot on any list of history's most cruel men.[55]

EXERCISE 12.1: Analyzing the Model Invective

Directions: After reading the Invective against the Emperor Nero, analyze the techniques of the Invective by answering the questions that follow.

1. **Background:** What member of Nero's family is also described as vicious?

2. **Education and Influences:**

   a. What two tutors are specifically named, and what did they teach?

   b. What two things did Suetonius identify that Nero did *not* study?

   c. Why do you think Suetonius found it important to mention things *not* studied?

3. **Vices:** How many vices are specified for Nero?

4. **Evil Deeds:**

   a. What does the author of the Invective consider to be Nero's most evil deed?

b. Testimony of the Ancients is not a required approach for Invective, but which ancient writers have been cited in "Evil Deeds"? Why do you suppose they were chosen?

5. **Comparison:** To which two tyrants is Nero compared?

Model Classical Invective

INTRODUCTION: *Aphthonius of Antioch was a Greek scholar and rhetorician who lived in the second half of the fourth century AD. He is best remembered for his textbook entitled* Progymnasmata, *whose purpose was to prepare students for their future study of rhetoric. Please read his model invective of Philip of Macedonia and then answer the questions that follow.*

In Dispraise of Philip of Macedonia
By Aphthonius of Antioch

Introduction

It is not fitting to leave virtue apart from praise or evil without blame, because profit is gained from both the praise of good men and the reproach of wicked men. Therefore, it is just to hear a bad report about those who are inclined to evil, but about Philip more than anyone else, to the extent that he surpassed all wicked men.

Background

His nation [Macedonia] was first in prominence among all nations, ordained to be the worst of the barbarians, one that sought to move constantly from place to place out of cowardice. For the Argives first expelled them, then wandering toward the place they now possess, they fled there for refuge but plunged into misfortune. They made their homes, yielding to the stronger and casting out the weaker. Because of their cowardice and greed, they could not make permanent homes.

Influences

Having been born of such a nation, he came from a more vulgar city. For the Macedonians are the worst of the barbarians, but Pelle is the worst city of the Macedonians. Men who are enslaved from there are not at all pleasant. Born of such a land, his ancestors were more ill-tempered than the land. His ancestor Philip was not permitted to rule over the land because of his birth. Then Amyntas [III], his father, came into the kingdom with the help of others, for the Athenians led him back when he was cast out [by the Illyrians].

Vices

Since he was seen to have such ancestors, he stayed in Thebes as a hostage. And passing time in the middle of Greece, he did not change his behavior in that society, but he brought barbarian incontinence into Greek customs. Although the Greeks and barbarians are completely different, he himself was over each, working equal licentiousness among peoples that were not alike.

Evil Deeds

First, he reduced his relatives to slavery, exhibiting disloyalty to those from whom he came. For the same reason, he attacked and utterly destroyed his neighbors. Taking the Paeonians, he imposed them upon the Illyrians. Snatching and attacking the land of the Triballi, he took as many of the nations as were so unfortunate as to lie before him. Although he captured the bodies of the barbarians, he did not snatch their minds with their bodies; those enslaved by force of arms dreamed of a revolt, and those enslaved by deeds began to exercise free will in their thoughts. And having conquered the neighbors of the barbarians, he continued on the road to the Greeks. Frist, he overturned the cities of the Greeks in Thrace, taking Amphipolis, then becoming master of Pydna and bringing Potideia in with them. He did not take Pherae without Pagasae, or the Magnesia without Pagasae, but all the cities of Thessaly were overturned and enslaved as if this were part of a national treaty.

It is also worthy to go on to the death of this man. For as he advanced, he overturned many, and, breaking treaties, reduced the pacified to slavery to himself. Because they were displeased about his treaty-breaking, the gods brought a fitting end to his life. For they did not kill him in embattled combat, or with a worthy man witness to his death, but in the midst of his disgraceful pleasures. These disgraceful pleasures made a suitable shroud to the evils of Philip, so that he would have witnesses to his incontinence in both life and death.

Comparison

Finally, who will put Echetus next to him?[a] The one cut off the tips of thumbs but left the rest on the body; but the other cut up whole bodies and destroyed them entirely. As much as it is more ill-tempered to destroy the whole rather than only a portion, so much was Philip more terrible than Echetus.

Conclusion

To say that Philip exceeded all bounds must not be doubted; but it is necessary that anyone who speaks about him must eventually stop.[56]

EXERCISE 12.2: Analyzing a Classical Invective

Directions: After reading Aphthonius' dispraise of Philip of Macedon, analyze the techniques of the Invective by answering the questions below.

1. **Introduction**

   a. Why does Aphthonius say we need to hear invectives ("reproach of wicked men")?

   b. After talking about "wicked men," in general, he gives the name of the specific man he will write about. Does that name appear in the first or second sentence? Why do you suppose that is?

---

[a] Echetus was an extremely cruel mythological king who appears in Book 18 of Homer's *Odyssey*. In the tale, Echetus blinded and dismembered his enemies.

c. What does Aphthonius state as the reason why he wishes to dispraise Philip?

2. **Background:** Aphthonius says little about Philip's family. What does he mention here instead?

3. **Influences:** What one place and two family members are named as evil influences?

   a. Place:

   b. People:

4. **Vices:** We learn that Philip introduced "barbarian incontinence" into Greek culture.

   a. What is the meaning of *incontinence*, as it is used in this context?

   b. Explain in your own words what Aphthonius is saying here.

5. **Evil Deeds:**

   a. In the first sentence of the first paragraph, Aphthonius records evil deeds against whom?

   b. In the rest of the first paragraph, Aphthonius records evil deeds against whom?

   c. In the second paragraph, who does Aphthonius say brought Philip's life to a disgraceful end?

6. **Conclusion:** This section consists of just one compound sentence.

a. What is the purpose of the first sentence?

b. What is the effect of the second sentence?

Now You Try It

**Chapter 12 Essay
Invective**

Specifications

1. The purpose of this assignment is to demonstrate your ability to write an Invective.

2. For a topic, you can choose a person deserving of dispraise:
   - a Biblical figure (e. g., Haman in the book of Esther)
   - a historical figure (e. g., Adolf Hitler)
   - a person currently in the news (e. g., a dictator, a terrorist)

3. If necessary, do some research in the library or on the Internet to find information for each category of the Invective: Background, Education/Training, Vices, Evil Deeds, and Comparison.

4. Complete the chart in the pre-writing activity or, if your teacher prefers, by writing a formal outline.

5. Follow your teacher's instructions regarding preparation of the manuscript.

Invective: Pre-Writing Activity

I have chosen to write an Invective of_____.

Approach	Details
Background	
Education and Influences	
Vices	
Evil Deeds	
Comparison	

COMPARISON

Chapter 13

Introduction

In the mid-eighteenth century, the English *intelligentsia* began to bemoan the fact that their Italian and French counterparts had beaten them to the punch, publishing dictionaries of their national languages in 1612 and 1642, respectively. Thus, in 1746, a group of London publishers approached the greatest man of letters of their time, Samuel Johnson—known everywhere in the English-speaking world by the simple sobriquet "Dr. Johnson"—with a contract to create what is now known as *A Dictionary of the English Language*. Estimating it would take him three years to complete the dictionary, they paid him £1,575 (about $368,000 in today's economy) to do so. Dr. William Adams, an Oxford don and friend of the great man, expressed amazement that his friend could do in only three years what it had taken the entire French Academy forty years to do, to which Dr. Johnson shot back, "Let me see; forty times forty is sixteen hundred. As three to sixteen hundred, so is the proportion of an Englishman to a Frenchman."

Dr. Samuel Johnson
(1709-1784)

No comparison is as loved by the English as one which compares them favorably to their ancient rival, the French—or the "frogs," as they are termed on the "scepter'd isle." So, comparison has earned a place in the lexicon of wit. Beyond wit, there are many other uses for comparison, and the purpose of this chapter is to explore those uses in both the humanities and the sciences.

Definition and Purpose of Comparison

Before going any further, it is important to indicate exactly what is meant by the word *comparison* in this chapter. Technically speaking, the term *comparison* refers to a list of similarities between two things while the term *contrast* refers to a list of differences. In the progymnasmata, the term *comparison* can refer to either a list of similarities, a list of differences, or a mixture.

Moreover, even when listing differences, a speaker or writer is to discuss the differences between two *similar* things. Good writers must always make sure that the things they are comparing are similar enough to withstand a close examination. Except in the most imaginative of writings, one wouldn't compare a cat to a lie, for example. If such an odd comparison *were* used, it would be called a *paraprosdokian* (a figure of speech in which an unexpected ending causes the audience to review the first part of the sentence in order to catch the joke, as when Mark Twain said, "One of the striking differences between a cat and a lie is that the cat has only nine lives.")

When you hear someone say, "You can't compare apples to oranges," it is this feature of basic similitude which is meant. To explain why the apple I bought today is not a good one, I must compare it to the one I bought yesterday, which *was* a good one—that is, to one that was fresher, redder, plumper, tastier, and perhaps less costly than the bad one.

Comparisons were often used in classical times to show the differences between two persons of similar achievements. In the previous chapter, we examined an Invective in which Nero was compared to Caligula. However, a comparison can actually be written about any two similar things that have some differences—a bull terrier and a pit bull, for example, or a crab and a lobster. One could also write a comparison of two great cities (e.g., London and Paris), two fast-food restaurants (e.g., McDonald's and Burger King), or two systems of government (e.g., a direct democracy and a republic). In short, any two similar things can be subjected to close examination as long as the writer does not stray from the basic principle that one must not get bogged down comparing apples to oranges, as the saying goes.

THINK IT THROUGH: When writing the proverbs, Solomon often used comparisons to teach right and wrong. Discuss the examples below with your classmates. What was Solomon trying to teach in each one?

1. **Proverbs 19:1:** Better is a poor person who walks in his integrity than one who is crooked in speech and is a fool.

2. **Proverbs 10:1:** A wise son makes a glad father, but a foolish son is a sorrow to his mother.

3. **Proverbs 25:26:** Like a muddied spring or a polluted fountain is a righteous man who gives way before the wicked.

Organization Patterns for Comparison

There are two organization patterns for comparison: point-by-point comparison and block comparison.

I. Point-by-Point Comparison

In point-by-point comparison, the writer either makes a simple list of comparisons or writes a standard ("zigzag") type of paragraph, moving back and forth between points and details. Below is an example and diagram of each.

A. Simple List Paragraph Pattern

Eastern and Western Kansas

(1) Eastern Kansas is <u>hilly</u>, but western Kansas is <u>flat</u>. (2) Eastern Kansas abounds with numerous trees, but western Kansas is nearly treeless. (3) Eastern Kansas is more urban, but western Kansas is more rural. (4) Eastern Kansas is the home to industry, but western Kansas is largely known for agriculture.

THINK IT THROUGH: Re-read the paragraph and insert the points of comparison in the diagram below. The first one serves as an example.

Sentence	Points	Eastern	Western
1	Topography	*hilly*	*flat*
2	Vegetation		
3	Population		
4	Economy		

EXERCISE 13.1: Simple List Comparison

Directions: Read the paragraph and analyze the simple list type of comparison by answering the questions that follow.

Crocodiles and Alligators

(1) Crocodiles are about <u>19 feet</u> long, but alligators are about <u>14 feet</u> long. (2) If the mouth is closed, the crocodile's teeth are visible, but the alligator's are hidden. (3) Inside the U.S., the crocodile lives in only one state, but the alligator lives in ten. (4) Outside the U.S., crocodiles are found in Africa, Australia, and the Caribbean Basin, but alligators live only in China.

1. After reading the paragraph, insert the points of comparison in the diagram below. The first one serves as an example.

Sentence	Points	Crocodile	Alligator
1	Length	19 ft.	14 ft.
2	Jaw structure		
3	Habitat inside U.S.		
4	Habitat outside U.S.		

2. The paragraph consists of four compound sentences. Each of the four connects information about crocodiles and alligators with the same conjunction. What conjunction joins them?

3. Now focus on Rows 3 and 4 on the chart. In the paragraph, underline the words that you entered in those columns. After that, read the sentences aloud. What do you find your voice doing when you reach the underlined words? What does that tell you about what words to put at the end of a sentence of comparison?

Now let us examine the second type of listing pattern.

B. Standard ("Zigzag") Paragraph Pattern

Eastern and Western Kansas

(1) Though there are many similarities between eastern and western Kansas, there are also some distinct differences. (2) First, the geography of the two areas is quite different. (3) Whereas eastern Kansas is hilly and has a variety of trees and shrubs, western Kansas is flat and nearly treeless. (4) Second, the population of the east differs from the population of the west. (5) To be specific, eastern Kansas has all the main population centers: Topeka (127,000 people), Wichita (390,600), and the metropolitan area of Kansas City (more than 767,000 on the Kansas side alone). (6) In contrast, the largest town in western Kansas is Great Bend with a population of only 15,500. (7) The last difference is the economic base. (8) The economy of eastern Kansas is based not only on agriculture, but also on manufacturing with the aircraft industry well established in Wichita. (9) The economy of western Kansas, on the other hand, is based on agriculture and the production of natural gas with little in the way of manufacturing.

THINK IT THROUGH: In order to see the point-by-point type of comparison, study and complete the chart below by inserting sentence numbers.

Controlling idea: Comparison of eastern and western Kansas (Sentence #1)

Point: Geography (Sentence(s) #____)
 Details (Sentence(s) #____)
   A. Eastern Kansas = hilly with numerous trees and shrubs
   B. Western Kansas = flat and nearly treeless

Point: Population (Sentence(s) #____)
 Details (Sentence(s) #____-____)
   A. Eastern Kansas = more populous; cities
   B. Western Kansas = less populous; towns and farming communities

Point: Economy (Sentence #____)
 Details (Sentence(s) #____-____)
   A. Eastern Kansas = agriculture and industry
   B. Western Kansas = agriculture and production of natural gas

EXERCISE 13.2: Analyzing Zigzag Organization

Directions: Read the paragraph below and analyze the standard "zigzag" type of comparison by answering the questions that follow.

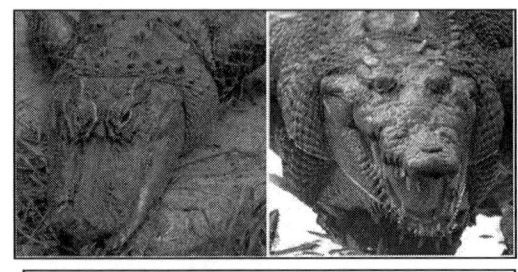

Alligators and Crocodiles

(1) Though crocodiles and alligators seem very much alike at first glance, there are some distinct differences. (2) First, there is a difference in size. (3) Whereas the crocodile is about 19 feet long, the alligator is shorter at about 14 feet. (4) Second, there is a difference in the structure of the jaw. (5) That is to say, when the crocodile has its mouth closed, its lower teeth will be visible. (6) In the closed-mouth alligator, however, the teeth are completely hidden. (7) Next, both crocodiles and alligators are found in the United States, but they are distributed differently. (8) To be specific, the U.S. crocodile can be found only in south Florida. (9) In contrast, the alligator can be found throughout Florida and Louisiana; in southern parts of Georgia, Alabama, and Mississippi; along the coast in the Carolinas; and in eastern Texas, southeast Oklahoma, and the southern tip of Arkansas. (10) Outside the U. S., the crocodile flourishes in Africa, Australia, and the entire Caribbean Basin while the alligator is found only in China.

1. Read the paragraph and, in the space below, turn it into a zigzag diagram in order to see the standard pattern on which it is based.

2. Now examine the transitions. Sentences 2, 4, and 7 list points of difference between crocodiles and alligators. What direct transitions are used to list these points?

   a. Sentence 2:

   b. Sentence 4:

   c. Sentence 7:

3. The other sentences provide the details of each point. Indicate the comparison structure used in each.

   a. Sentence 3:

   b. Sentence 5/6:

   c. Sentence 8/9:

   d. Sentence 10:

EXERCISE 13.3: Analyzing a Point-by-Point Comparison by Shakespeare (More Challenging)

<u>Directions</u>: Below is an excerpt from *Julius Caesar* by William Shakespeare in which Cassius, a villainous Roman senator, tries to persuade Brutus, an honorable senator, to join in a conspiracy against Caesar, whom they fear is becoming too powerful. After reading the excerpt, please answer the questions that follow.

CASSIUS:

> I know that virtue to be in you, Brutus,
> As well as I do know your outward favour.
> Well, honour is the subject of my story.
> I cannot tell what you and other men
> Think of this life; but, for my single self,   5
> I had as lief not be as live to be
> In awe of such a thing as I myself.

I was born free as Caesar; so were you:
We both have fed as well, and we can both
Endure the winter's cold as well as he: 10
For once, upon a raw and gusty day,
The troubled Tiber chafing with her shores,
Caesar said to me, "Darest thou, Cassius, now
Leap in with me into this angry flood,
And swim to yonder point?" Upon the word, 15
Accoutred as I was, I plunged in
And bade him follow; so indeed he did.
The torrent roar'd, and we did buffet it
With lusty sinews, throwing it aside
And stemming it with hearts of controversy; 20
But ere we could arrive the point proposed,
Caesar cried, "Help me, Cassius, or I sink!"
I, as Aeneas, our great ancestor,
Did from the flames of Troy upon his shoulder
The old Anchises bear, so from the waves of Tiber 25
Did I the tired Caesar. And this man
Is now become a god, and Cassius is
A wretched creature and must bend his body,
If Caesar carelessly but nod on him.
He had a fever when he was in Spain, 30
And when the fit[a] was on him, I did mark
How he did shake: 'tis true, this god did shake;
His coward lips did from their colour fly,
And that same eye whose bend doth awe the world
Did lose his lustre: I did hear him groan: 35
Ay, and that tongue of his that bade the Romans
Mark him and write his speeches in their books,
Alas, it cried, "Give me some drink, Titinius,"
As a sick girl. Ye gods, it doth amaze me

---

[a] This is a reference to Caesar's epilepsy.

> A man of such a feeble temper should 40
> So get the start of the majestic world
> And bear the palm alone.⁵⁷

Even though Shakespeare wrote this monologue in poetry, it consists of a topic sentence and two supporting examples. Take a few moments to dig this out by answering the questions below.

1. Which of the following would be the best re-phrasing of the topic sentence (Lines 1-10)?

    A. I am in awe of Caesar.

    B. Honour is the subject of my story.

    C. Caesar is no better than we are.

2. In the first supporting example (Lines 11-26), Cassius compares himself to and _____. Caesar to _____.

3. In the second supporting example (Lines 30-39), Cassius compares Caesar to _____.

Now You Try It

Chapter 13, Essay 1
Point-by-Point Comparison

Specifications

1. The purpose of this assignment is to demonstrate your ability to write a one-paragraph Point-by-Point Comparison.

2. For a topic, choose one of the following:
   - a book and its movie version
   - competing electronic devices (e.g., Mac and PC)
   - an athlete active today and an athlete from the past
   - two members of your family (e.g., parent and self, two siblings, etc.)
   - a Bible figure and a person who had similar behavior or experiences
   - the pandemic of 1917 and the pandemic of 2020

3. Complete the chart in the pre-writing activity, or, if your teacher prefers, prepare a formal phrase outline.

4. Follow your teacher's instructions regarding the preparation of the manuscript.

Point-by-Point Comparison: Pre-Writing Activity

In this essay I will compare _____ and _____.

Point 1: _____

Details:

A.

B.

Point 2: _____

Details:

A.

B.

Point 3: _____

Details:

A.

B.

II. Block Comparison

You will notice that in the point-by-point comparisons, all the material is handled in one paragraph. However, in block comparison, as its name suggests, you will have two *blocks* of information. The first block (or paragraph) contains all the necessary points about Topic A. The second block (or paragraph) contains all the necessary points about Topic B. The model below shows the comparison of eastern and western Kansas when re-written in block style.

Eastern and Western Kansas

(1) There are recognizable differences between the eastern and western parts of the state of Kansas. (2) Geographically, the eastern part of the state is more hilly with the Flint Hills ranging from north to south in the easternmost quarter of the state. (3) There are also numerous trees, both deciduous and evergreen. (4) In terms of population, eastern Kansas comprises the three main population centers of the state: Topeka (127,000), Wichita (390,600) and the metropolitan area of Kansas City (more than 767,000 on the Kansas side alone). (5) Last, with respect to the economic base, eastern Kansas is not only part of the Grain Belt of the United States but is also home to major industries such as airplane manufacturing in Wichita.

(6) Western Kansas is notably different. (7) Unlike eastern Kansas, which is hilly and rich in trees, western Kansas is flat and nearly treeless. (8) In addition, whereas eastern Kansas has large cities, western Kansas comprises farming communities and small towns (the largest being Great Bend with 15,500). (9) Last, unlike eastern Kansas, which has industries, western Kansas is largely agricultural supplemented by the production of natural gas. (10) In short, the motorist driving from Kansas City to Denver will notice quite a change in the scenery while moving from east to west across Kansas.

THINK IT THROUGH: In order to see the block type of comparison, study and complete the chart below by inserting sentence numbers.

> **Topic Sentence (Sentence(s) # ___)**
> There are recognizable differences between eastern and western Kansas.
>
> **A. Eastern Kansas (Sentence(s) #_____)**
>   1. Geography (hilly)
>   2. Vegetation (numerous trees)
>   3. Population (more populous; cities)
>   4. Economic base (agriculture and industry)
>
> **B. Western Kansas (Sentence(s) # _____)**
>   1. Geography (flat)
>   2. Vegetation (nearly treeless)
>   3. Population (less populous; towns and farming communities)
>   4. Economic base (agriculture and natural gas)
>
> **Conclusion (Sentence(s) # _____)**
> In short, the motorist driving from Kansas City to Denver will notice quite a change in the scenery while moving from east to west across Kansas.

EXERCISE 13.4: Analyzing Block Comparison

Directions: After reading "Alligators and Crocodiles," analyze the block type of comparison by answering the questions that follow.

Alligators and Crocodiles

(1) There are several ways to distinguish crocodiles from alligators. (2) First, crocodiles are about nineteen feet long and range in color from brown to olive green. (3) In terms of jaw structure, they have long, V-shaped snouts, and when their mouths are closed, their lower teeth are still visible. (4) Finally, the crocodile is found in Africa, Australia, and the Americas, specifically in south Florida and the entire Caribbean Basin.

(5) Alligators, on the other hand, are different in every category. (6) For one thing, they are shorter, growing only fourteen feet long, and they are limited in color to

blackish-gray. (7) They have wide, U-shaped snouts, and, unlike crocodiles, when their jaws are closed, their teeth are completely hidden. (8) Last, with respect to their location, the alligator is more widespread throughout the United States, being found throughout Florida and Louisiana; in southern parts of Georgia, Alabama, and Mississippi; along the coast in the Carolinas; and in eastern Texas, southeast Oklahoma, and the southern tip of Arkansas. (9) Outside the U. S., the alligator can only be found in China, but it is important to note that the Chinese alligator is an extremely endangered species. (10) Since the habitats of the American alligator are nurturing to its Chinese cousin, zoos and wildlife refuges in Louisiana and Florida are helping to breed and re-introduce Chinese alligators into the wild in China in an effort to increase their numbers there.

(11) All in all, crocodiles and alligators (collectively referred to as *crocodilia*) are an ancient species which deserve our respect and protection.

1. In order to see the block type of comparison, study and complete the chart by inserting sentence numbers.

Topic Sentence (Sentence(s) # ___)
There are several ways to distinguish crocodiles from alligators.
A. Crocodiles (Sentence(s) # ___)
1. Size and color (19 feet; brown and olive green)
2. Jaw structure (long, V-shaped snouts; teeth visible)
3. Habitat (Africa; Australia; Caribbean Basin, incl. Florida)
B. Alligators (Sentence(s) # ___)
1. Size and color (14 feet; blackish-gray)
2. Jaw structure (wide, U-shaped snouts; teeth hidden)
3. Habitat (Florida, Louisiana, Georgia, Alabama, Mississippi, the Carolinas, Texas, Oklahoma, Arkansas; China)
4. Threatened in China (Louisiana and Florida helping)
Conclusion (Sentence(s) # ___)
All in all, crocodiles and alligators (collectively referred to as *crocodilia*) are an ancient species which deserve our respect and protection.

2. Now examine the way transitions are handled in a block comparison. Look first at Paragraph 1. Except for the topic sentence, this paragraph contains information only about crocodiles that transitions are used to list the points and details?

    Sentence 2:

    Sentence 4:

3. Now look at Paragraph 2. What transitions are used to assist the reader in moving from point to point?

    Sentence 6:

    Sentence 8:

4. What words are used in order to draw the comparisons?

    Sentence 6:

    Sentence 7:

    Sentence 8:

    Sentence 9:

5. The block comparison affords generous space for discussion. What topics were introduced in the block comparison that were absent in the list type of comparison?

    Sentences 2 and 6:

    Sentences 3 and 7:

    Sentence 10:

Now You Try It

Chapter 13, Essay 2
Block Comparison

Specifications

1. The purpose of this assignment is to demonstrate your ability to write a Block Comparison. Your essay can show similarities and/or differences.

2. For a topic, choose one of the following or, if your teacher approves, another topic that interests you:
   - school and home school
   - rules of play in the National League and the American League in Major League Baseball (e. g., designated hitter)
   - two Biblical figures (e. g., Peter and Paul)
   - homes you have lived in

3. Complete the chart in the pre-writing activity, or, if your teacher prefers, prepare a formal phrase outline. Please identify at least three characteristics of each of the things or persons you are comparing.

4. Follow your teacher's instructions regarding preparation of the manuscript.

Block Comparison: Pre-Writing Activity

In this essay, I will compare _____ and _____.

A. _____

1.

2.

3.

4.

B. _____

1.

2.

3.

4.

SPEECH-IN-CHARACTER

Chapter 14

Introduction

In the *Argonautica* by Apollonius of Rhodes, Jason and his crew (the argonauts) have undertaken a quest for the Golden Fleece. As with Odysseus, Jason encounters many adventures and dangers along the way. One of these occurs in Book III, where the argonauts, nearing the island of Ares, are attacked by the Stymphalian birds, who attack by dropping their sharp-pointed feathers of metal, injuring one of the crew. Seeing this, one of the argonauts, Amphidamas, son of Aleus, addresses the crew, thus:

> The island of Ares is near us; you know it yourselves now that ye have seen these birds. But little will arrows avail us, I trow, for landing. But let us contrive some other device to help us, if ye intend to land. . . .
>
> For not even could Heracles,[a] when he came to Arcadia, drive away with bow and arrow the birds that swam on the Stymphalian lake. I saw it myself. But he shook in his hand a rattle of bronze and made a loud clatter as he stood upon a lofty peak; and the birds fled far off, screeching in bewildered fear.
>
> Wherefore now too let us contrive some such device, and I myself will speak, having pondered the matter beforehand. Set on your heads your helmets of lofty crest, then half row by turns, and half fence the ship about with polished spears and shields. Then all together raise a mighty shout so that the birds may be scared by the unwonted din, the nodding crests, and the uplifted spears on high. And if we reach the island itself, then make mighty noise with the clashing of shields.[58]

This speech, divided here into three paragraphs, is called a Speech-in-Character, which, as you will see in this chapter, usually has three distinct parts. We will return to

---

[a] Heracles is another name for Hercules.

this passage as we move through the chapter, but first let us look at the definition and purpose of Speech-in-Character.

Definition and Purpose of Speech-in-Character

The Speech-in-Character is usually a speech given by the main character in a poem, play, or novel. The first purpose is to reveal the character of the speaker—to look at the way he or she faces adversity, for example. However, since authors and playwrights often have an idea they wish to communicate to their audience, the Speech-in-Character may also go some way toward giving all of us the perspective that we need in order to deal with what life throws our way.

Handling Universal Themes with Speech-in-Character

The literature of western civilization started with Homer, who may have been the first to create the Speech-in-Character, which he used as his primary method of character development in both the *Iliad* and the *Odyssey*. As you probably know, these epic poems were part of an oral tradition, that is, the storyteller (or, *rhapsode*) recited the tales from memory for the entertainment of an audience. Perhaps the surviving relic from these tales in our own times would be the ghost story told around a campfire. With darkness all around and the fire flickering on the faces of the listeners, the gathered group, weary from the day's activities, sits spellbound as the storyteller stirs their fears with nothing more than words that float into the night.

The value of a Speech-in-Character is that it allows the audience to see into the hearts and minds of the characters, perhaps learning a bit about themselves along the way, because for every one of life's situations common to us all, there is a heartstring attached—longing for home (as Odysseus), railing against the Fates (as Oedipus), wailing out one's remorse (as Creon), wondering if going on is worth the cost (as Hamlet), lamenting that the one you love is hated by your family (as Juliet), or even crabbing about having to improve one's English (as the Cockney, Alfred Doolittle).

Types of Speech-in-Character

In classical and Shakespearean drama, there are basically two ways in which a speech-in-character might appear: the soliloquy and the monologue. When one considers that *sol-* is the Latin root for *alone* and *mono-* is the Greek root for *one*, it is easy to see that both of these speeches involve the speaking of just one person. To be specific, a *monologue* is a fairly long speech spoken by a single character to other characters in the scene. An example would be Odysseus' responses to Calypso and to Penelope. As the character speaks at length to another character, the audience is allowed to eavesdrop, so to speak, and to be privy to what the character is up to: Is the speaker pouring out his (or her) heart? lying? pleading? chastising someone? threatening someone?

A *soliloquy*, on the other hand, is a rather long speech spoken by one character while alone on the stage. It is a device that classical and Renaissance playwrights employed to allow the audience to hear the thoughts of the character. An example would be Juliet's famous speech that begins, "Romeo, Romeo, wherefore art thou Romeo—and a Montague? Deny thy father, and refuse thy name."[59] She speaks the lines in private on her balcony as she gazes at the night stars and the beauties of the garden. From this, the audience begins to realize what a predicament she finds herself in: the young man she has just met, with whom she has fallen in "love at first sight," is the son of her family's great enemy, the Montagues. (Of course, what Juliet doesn't realize is that Romeo has sneaked away from his friends and is hiding in the shrubbery nearby, listening to every word she says!) But, even though Romeo is overhearing her words, this speech would still be classified as a soliloquy because she is not actually addressing Romeo.

Juliet
By Philip H. Calderon, 1888

When novels developed in the eighteenth and nineteenth centuries, soliloquies and monologues were adapted for use in long passages of prose. However, while the length of a soliloquy or monologue in a play is broken up by movement on the stage, body language, facial expression, and so on, a long, unbroken passage in prose might just create boredom in a reader. Therefore, in novels, pacing is maintained—and boredom prevented—by interrupting the speech from time to time with references to the sound of the wind outside or the need to rouse the flames in the fireplace. The reader then "sees" the actions in the mind's eye as the character continues to speak, and boredom is averted.

An excellent example of this sort of thing is Alice's long monologue to her kitten—virtually a chapter in length—just before stepping through the looking glass in Lewis Carroll's *Alice through the Looking Glass and What Alice Found There* (1872). So that the reader will know what is going on in Alice's mind, Carroll decided to let her tell her thoughts to her cat. In this way, he had an opportunity to show the reader her highly imaginative nature while also hinting to the reader that what Alice finds in the world of the Red Queen is mainly a reflection (a mirror, or "looking glass") of what we see in our own world, or at least in Carroll's nineteenth-century England.

Because moviegoers and television viewers enjoy the gripping camera work, it is less common now to find soliloquies and monologues, which have largely gone out of fashion. However, the need still exists for the writer to find a way for the audience to become aware of what is going on in a character's mind, and they have found clever ways to do so. One of the best examples is to be found in the movie *Iron Man* (2008) when the main character, Tony Stark, returns from captivity in the Middle East a changed man.

To convey this change to the audience, the writer decided to employ a press conference in which the wealthy magnate of the weapons industry, scruffy from his captivity and munching on a hamburger, speaks to the press and camera crews of his intention to turn Stark Industries to more peaceful purposes. Not wanting the scene to appear long or stuffy, the writer directed the character to opt for sitting on the dais rather than standing at the microphone, which communicates to the audience that the essence of Tony's "cool" character is intact. Thus—*voilà!*—a speech-in-character is adapted to a blockbuster movie.

THINK IT THROUGH: What other techniques have you seen employed in movies or TV shows to present a Speech-in-Character?

Content of a Speech-in-Character

To write a Speech-in-Character, one creates a character, places him or her in a situation, and then writes what he or she would say in that situation, being sure to express the emotion the character is feeling.

THINK IT THROUGH: Recall briefly from Chapter 2 the plot structure of a narrative, which is diagrammed as shown below. At which stage in the plot would the speech-in-character be most likely to occur?

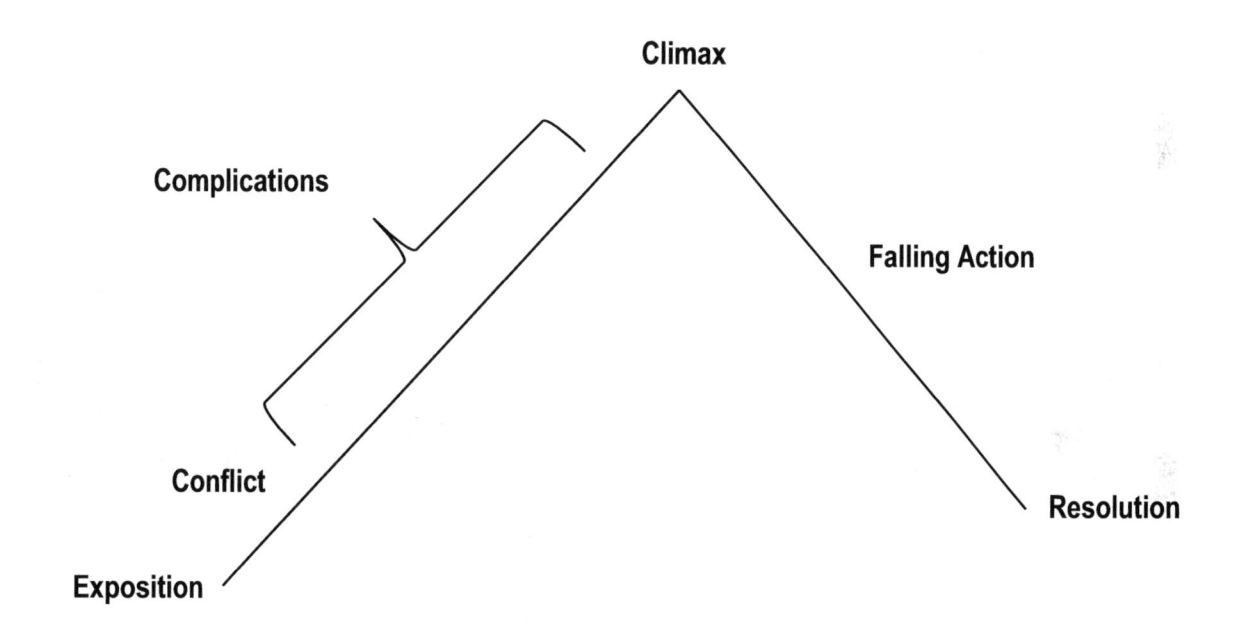

Organization of a Speech-in-Character

In the standard Speech-in-Character, there are three discernible parts, each identified with a verb tense.

1. **The present.** In this part, which is written in present tense, the speaker recounts the predicament that he or she is in.

2. **The past.** In this part, which is written in past tense and/or present perfect tense, the speaker reviews what has brought him or her to this pass.

3. **The future.** In this part, which is written in future tense, the speaker focuses on what may or will happen as a result of the action he or she is about to take.

THINK IT THROUGH: Return to the speech of Amphidamas at the beginning of the chapter. What is the present situation of the men? What had Heracles done in the same situation? What will they do to resolve the problem?

Model Speech-In-Character

THE SITUATION OF THE SPEECH: Antigone [ăn TIG ə nē] is a young lady of Thebes who is being put to death for disobeying an edict of King Creon. Her crime? She buried the body of her brother Polyneices (PŎL-ĭ-NĪ-sēz), who had been executed for rebelling against the tyrant. Creon had ordered the body to be left above ground to rot and be eaten by animals as a public warning to others, but Antigone could not abide such a heinous treatment of her brother's corpse. Arrested and tried for disobedience, Antigone is now to receive her punishment: to be sealed up in a tomb and left to die. Antigone expresses herself in this soliloquy while King Creon is in her presence. Please note that the mention of a bridal bower in line 1 refers to the fact that Antigone was engaged to be married to Creon's son.

Antigone
By Frederic
Leighton, 1882

Antigone's Speech-in-Character
By Sophocles

O grave, O bridal bower, O prison house
Hewn from the rock, my everlasting home,
Whither I go to join the mighty host
Of kinsfolk, Persephassa's guests long dead,
The last of all, of all more miserable,   5
I pass, my destined span of years cut short.
And yet good hope is mine that I shall find
A welcome from my sire, a welcome too,
From thee, my mother, and my brother dear;
From with these hands, I laved and decked your limbs   10
In death, and poured libations on your grave.

And last, my Polyneices, unto thee
I paid due rites, and this my recompense!
Yet am I justified in wisdom's eyes.
For even had it been some child of mine,   15
Or husband mouldering in death's decay,
I had not wrought this deed despite the State.
What is the law I call in aid? 'Tis thus
I argue. Had it been a husband dead
I might have wed another, and have borne   20
Another child, to take the dead child's place.

But, now my sire and mother both are dead,
No second brother can be born for me.
Thus by the law of conscience I was led
To honor thee, dear brother, and was judged   25
By Creon guilty of a heinous crime.
And now he drags me like a criminal,
A bride unwed, amerced of marriage-song
And marriage-bed and joys of motherhood,
By friends deserted to a living grave.   30
What ordinance of heaven have I transgressed?
Hereafter can I look to any god
For succor, call on any man for help?
Alas, my piety is impious deemed.
Well, if such justice is approved of heaven,   35
I shall be taught by suffering my sin;
But if the sin is theirs, O may they suffer
No worse ills than the wrongs they do to me.[60]

EXERCISE 14.1: Analysis of a Speech-in-Character

<u>Directions</u>: After reading the excerpt from Antigone, analyze the techniques of Speech-in-Character by answering the following questions.

1. Lines 1-6: What is Antigone's present situation?

2. To what past events does she refer in the following lines?

   a. Lines 10-13:

   b. Lines 24-26:

3. Lines 32-38: What does Antigone wonder (and wish) for the future?

4. Which of the following best describes the emotional tone of Antigone's speech?

   A. Repentant   B. Fearful   C. Convinced she is right

5. What lines of the text suggested your answer for Question 4?

Speech-in-Character in the Bible

Though the Jewish tradition of writing developed independently of the Greek model, it employs many of the same rhetorical types. New Testament works, on the other hand, emerged from the Hellenistic culture that developed in the Mediterranean lands after the conquests of Alexander the Great (d. 323 BC), and since Jewish education certainly had Hellenistic influence by the first century AD, we know that Paul, a Roman citizen educated by the Pharisee Gamaliel, studied the progymnasmata and classical rhetoric.

Certainly Gamaliel knew how to construct an argument based on a syllogism. This is clearly demonstrated in Acts 5:33-39 where he used an *if/then* syllogism to argue that the followers of Jesus should not be put to death. And Paul himself demonstrated familiarity with the basic syllogism that states, "All men are mortal; Socrates is a man; therefore, Socrates is mortal" by using the basic Christian syllogism, "All men are sinners; I am a man; therefore, I am a sinner," which is apparent in I Timothy 1:15.

The evangelistic variation of the syllogism—"All men are sinners; you are a man; therefore, you are a sinner"—underlies the message of Romans 3:9-23.

In the first century AD, teachers of the progymnasmata often had students adopt a *persona* and write a letter to an imaginary person. Paul, whose famous letters (or epistles) form the lion's share of the New Testament, was probably trained in this exercise and, therefore, was well-equipped for the task of communicating by means of letters to the early churches in the Roman empire.

Before beginning the imaginary letter, the student was encouraged to think his *persona* through. How different would the letter be if written by a young person as opposed to an older person? By a slave as opposed to a free person? By a woman as opposed to a man?

Similar questions would be pondered about the recipient of the letter. Important here would be the reader's age, gender, education, political persuasion, religion, social class, and occupation. One might write differently if the letter were going to a close personal friend as opposed to a political opponent.

This kind of practice with fictitious letter writers and recipients would have served Paul well as he wrote his real-life epistles to the Romans, Corinthians, Galatians, Ephesians, Philippians, Colossians, and Thessalonians as well as to the individuals Timothy, Titus, and Philemon.

THINK IT THROUGH: On his missionary journeys, Paul usually addressed the Jews in the synagogues before speaking to the Gentiles. What differences in these audiences would Paul have to take into account in order to be an effective speaker to both groups?

EXERCISE 14.2: Speech-in-Character in the Bible

Directions: Please read the Speech-in-Character which appears below and then answer the questions that follow.

THE SITUATION OF THE SPEECH: The book of Jonah tells a story of rebellion, repentance, and salvation. The Lord asked Jonah to go to Nineveh and preach, but because he was fearful, Jonah disobeyed, taking passage on a ship to Tarshish. During passage, a great storm arose, and the sailors feared a shipwreck, but Jonah convinced them to throw him overboard, saying God was angry with him, not them. Rather reluctantly they did this, and indeed the sea became calm. Then God sent a great fish to swallow Jonah whole. Saved from drowning but still in danger, Jonah began praying, as recorded in Jonah 2.

Jonah's Prayer

¹Then Jonah prayed to the LORD his God from the belly of the fish, ²saying,
  I called out to the LORD, out of my distress,
  and he answered me;
  out of the belly of Sheol I cried,
  and you heard my voice.
³ For you cast me into the deep,
  into the heart of the seas,
  and the flood surrounded me;
  all your waves and your billows
  passed over me.
⁴ Then I said, 'I am driven away
  from your sight;
  yet I shall again look
  upon your holy temple.'
⁵ The waters closed in over me to take my life;
  the deep surrounded me;
  weeds were wrapped about my head
⁶ at the roots of the mountains.
  I went down to the land
  whose bars closed upon me forever;
  yet you brought up my life from the pit,
  O LORD my God.
⁷ When my life was fainting away,
  I remembered the LORD,
  and my prayer came to you,
  into your holy temple.
⁸ Those who pay regard to vain idols
  forsake their hope of steadfast love.

Jonah Cast Forth by the Whale
By Gustave Doré, c. 1866

> ⁹ But I with the voice of thanksgiving
>   will sacrifice to you;
>   what I have vowed I will pay.
>   Salvation belongs to the LORD!
> ¹⁰And the LORD spoke to the fish, and it vomited Jonah out upon the dry land.

1. At the time of the prayer, what is Jonah's present situation?

2. Which verses use the past tense to describe what had happened to him in the moments before the fish swallowed him up?

3. Basically, what is being described in those verses?

4. Which verse indicates what Jonah will do in the future?

5. Basically, what does he promise?

Adapted Speech-in-Character

As with other progymnasmata elements, the Speech-in-Character is sometimes found in a work of literature in an adapted form. Because the speech is adapted for the unique time, place, and situation of the play, the three components—present, past, future—may not all be employed, or they may appear in a different order.

Model Adapted Speech-in-Character

THE SITUATION OF THE SPEECH: In Act I, Scene 3 of Shakespeare's play The Tragedy of Macbeth, *Macbeth, thane of Glamis [glämz] and a general in the Scottish army, encounters three "weird sisters" (normally referred to as witches) who prophesy that he will become king. He sends a letter to his wife, Lady Macbeth, whom we see in Act I, Scene 5, reading the news. The problem is that Lady Macbeth is extremely ambitious for her husband to rise, and Macbeth himself is much less ambitious. Lady Macbeth lays out the problem as she sees it in the following Speech-in-Character and hints at what action she will take (which is, we later learn, to kill the current king to make the prophecy come true). Keep in mind that this soliloquy varies from the usual pattern of "Present + Past + Future" because it is adapted to the context of the play.*

a. Lines 1-14 are in **past** tense (rather than present tense) because Lady Macbeth is reading a letter telling her what has happened.

b. Lines 15-25a make up the **present** tense segment of the speech, where Lady Macbeth explains what she considers her husband's shortcoming, his soft nature.

c. Lines 25-30 point to the **future,** what Lady Macbeth hopes to do. The imperative statement ("Hie thee hither") and the modal *may* convey the sense of future time.

Excerpt from *Macbeth* (Act I, Scene 5)
By William Shakespeare

Enter LADY MACBETH, reading a letter:

"They met me in the day of success: and I have
learned by the perfectest report, they have more in
them than mortal knowledge. When I burned in desire
to question them further, they made themselves air,
into which they vanished. Whiles I stood rapt in   5
the wonder of it, came missives from the king, who
all-hailed me 'Thane of Cawdor;' by which title,
before, these weird sisters saluted me, and referred
me to the coming on of time, with 'Hail, king that
shalt be!' This have I thought good to deliver   10
thee, my dearest partner of greatness, that thou
mightst not lose the dues of rejoicing, by being
ignorant of what greatness is promised thee. Lay it
to thy heart, and farewell."
Glamis thou art, and Cawdor; and shalt be   15
What thou art promised: yet do I fear thy nature;
It is too full o' the milk of human kindness

To catch the nearest way: thou wouldst be great;
Art not without ambition, but without
The illness should attend it: what thou wouldst highly, 20
That wouldst thou holily; wouldst not play false,
And yet wouldst wrongly win: thou'ldst have, great Glamis,
That which cries "Thus thou must do, if thou have it;
And that which rather thou dost fear to do
Than wishest should be undone." Hie thee hither,[b] 25
That I may pour my spirits in thine ear;
And chastise with the valour of my tongue
All that impedes thee from the golden round,
Which fate and metaphysical aid doth seem
To have thee crown'd withal.[61] 30

EXERCISE 14.3: Adapted Speech-in-Character

<u>Directions</u>: Please read the Speech-in-Character below and answer the questions that follow.

THE SITUATION OF THE SPEECH: Odysseus set out from the island of Calypso and came to Scheria, the island of the Phaeacians. The king, Alcinous, decided to host athletic games in honor of his guest. However, Odysseus, having been away from home for twenty years, was no longer young. Urged to compete in the games, he declined, which caused Euryalus [yū-RĪ-ə-ləs], one of the Phaeacians, to insult him, saying he must have been the skipper of "some tramp ship" and was not, according to his looks, an athlete. Odysseus responded with the following speech.

Odysseus' Speech to the Phaeacians
By Homer

1) "For shame, Sir. . . . You are an insolent fellow—so true is it that the gods do not grace all men alike in speech, person, and understanding. (2) One man may be of weak presence, but heaven has adorned this [man] with such a good conversation that he charms everyone who sees him; his honeyed moderation

---

[b] Come here.

carries his hearers with him so that he is leader in all assemblies of his fellows, and wherever he goes he is looked up to. (3) Another may be as handsome as a god, but his good looks are not crowned with discretion. (4) This is your case. (5) No god could make a finer looking fellow than you are, but you are a fool. (6) Your ill-judged remarks have made me exceedingly angry, and you are quite mistaken, for I excel in a great many athletic exercises; indeed, so long as I had youth and strength, I was among the first athletes of the age. (7) Now, however, I am worn out by labor and sorrow, for I have gone through much both on the field of battle and by the waves of the weary sea; still, in spite of all this I will compete, for your taunts have stung me to the quick."[62]

**Euryalus taunts Odysseus.
By Padraic Colum**

1. Reading through this excerpt, one sees that Odysseus does touch on (a) the *present* challenge from Euryalus, (b) his *past* experiences that have sapped his strength, and (c) his immediate *future*, Alcinous' competitive games. However, the lion's share of this excerpt (Sentences 1b, 2, 3, 4, 5, and 6) have a somewhat different focus. In your own words, summarize the main point of this speech.

2. As a reader responding to this passage, how do you feel about Odysseus' character as it is revealed in these few sentences?

Now You Try It

Chapter 14 Essay
Speech-in-Character

Specifications

1. The purpose of this assignment is to demonstrate your ability to write a Speech in Character.

2. To do this, you will create a character, place him or her in a situation, and then write the speech that the person would make about the situation.

3. Please consider all of the elements indicated on the pre-writing activity and jot down your thoughts in the space provided, or, if your teacher prefers, prepare a formal phrase outline.

4. Be sure to include all three time frames:

    a. Present tense: The character's present problem or situation

    b. Past tense: The cause of the character's present problem or situation

    c. Future tense: The character's proposed solution to the problem or situation

5. Follow your teacher's instructions regarding preparation of the manuscript.

Speech-in-Character: Pre-Writing Activity

Element	Considerations	Your Thoughts
Character	A real person from the past? An imaginary person? A type (e.g., a typical knight, a typical student, a typical soldier?)	
Situation	What situation does your character find himself/herself in? Has the character done something wrong, or has something wrong been done *to* him/her? Does he/she have a decision to make?	
Character's Age, Gender, Nationality	Too young to understand? Near death with nothing to lose? In a situation not customary for the gender? Subject to cultural expectations? At home or abroad?	
Other characteristics affecting the situation	*Physical attributes* (weak, strong, beautiful, handsome, ugly, deformed) *Mental attributes* (sane, insane)	
The character's way of thinking	Selfish? Altruistic? Clever? Confused? Logical? Illogical? Biblical? Unbiblical?	
The character's emotional state	Fearful? Determined? Nefarious? Angry? Comforting? Grateful? Ungrateful?	

I have chosen to write about _____.

THESIS

Chapter 15

Introduction

- Should people go to college?
- Does God plan everything that happens?
- Is it ever right to go to war?
- Does extraterrestrial life exist?
- Should businesses have a dress code?
- Should there be speed limits?

General questions like these are common to everyday life. People in a democracy talk about, write about, debate, and vote on issues such as these. Therefore, those who are training for life in a republic need to learn how to argue well and logically in order to help work toward the common good. In classical times, such skills have been honed in the exercise called Thesis, which you will learn and practice in this chapter.

Definition and Purpose

The exercise called Thesis is an oration or essay that presents a person's opinion about an issue of importance to a school, a religious institution, a city, a state, a nation, or the international community. Previous exercises such as Proverb, Confirmation, and Encomium have also examined the arguments for an opinion, or what is called in classical writing, a *proposition*. However, the Thesis differs from these other exercises in that before arriving at a conclusion, the speaker or writer may well examine both sides of the issue.

The questions answered by the Thesis may be *political* or *theoretical*. *Political* questions deal with human society and behavior, such as:

- Should one marry?
- Should one go to college?
- Should a city defund the police?

Theoretical questions, on the other hand, deal with ideas concerning the natural and spiritual world, such as:

- Are there forms of life on other planets?
- How old is the earth?
- Does each person have a guardian angel?

The most important thing to note is that the question answered in the Thesis must be *general*. It cannot refer to a specific person or place but must be applicable to many people, times, or places.

Approaches to Thesis

After choosing a question to answer, writers can select from among eight approaches for developing their theses. They are as follows:

- Is the proposal *necessary* or not?
- Is it *possible* or not?
- Is it *advantageous* or not?
- Is it *easy* to implement or not?
- Is it *fitting* to the culture or not?
- Is it *lawful* or not?
- Is it *customary* or not?
- Is it *just* or not?

Now let us take a more detailed look at each of these eight approaches.

1. Necessary or Unnecessary?

This approach considers whether a human action ought to be done or whether an idea ought to be true. Suppose you are considering the issue, "Should high school students be allowed to date?" Some might argue that dating is a traditional social activity among young people and is necessary in order to come to know a person before marriage. Others might argue that dating is not a necessary social activity, pointing out that if students become emotionally involved in a dating relationship, they will lose focus on their academics at a time when they need to be preparing for college and careers.

THINK IT THROUGH: In your opinion, are the answers to these questions yes—or not?

- Is it necessary for a person to have a job?
- Is it necessary for God to exist?
- Is it necessary for people to get an education?

2. Possible or Impossible?

If an action or idea is possible, then it *can* be done or it *can* exist. This question does not refer to permission, but to ability. A classical example is the question "Are there many universes?" Another way to phrase the question is this: "Is it possible that there are other universes besides our own?" The most common expression of this question in modern times, of course, is as follows: "Are there extraterrestrial forms of life?"

THINK IT THROUGH: Consider each of the following. Then put a *P* in the blank if you think it would be *Possible* or an *I* if *Impossible*.

_____ There are many gods.

_____ There are forms of life on other planets.

_____ It will someday be possible to engage in time travel.

_____ Wishing can change things.

_____ If I think, I exist.

3. Advantageous or Disadvantageous?

Another question that must be asked is whether the proposed action or idea is advantageous (beneficial). An adult might say that going to college is advantageous because a student can learn valuable skills in college and get a better job after graduation. Others might argue that going to college is disadvantageous, because one could learn practical skills on the job and not spend thousands of dollars on an education. By considering this approach to the Thesis, a writer could decide whether attending college would be good and useful for a career—or not.

THINK IT THROUGH: Discuss how the following questions could be resolved by considering whether the activity would be advantageous or disadvantageous.

- Would it be advantageous to know how to cook?
- Would it be advantageous for a business to have a dress code?
- Would it be advantageous for a person to learn how to read?

4. Easy or Difficult?

Next, one must ask whether the proposed action is easy or difficult to achieve. This argument is most persuasive when the action takes very little extra effort. A classical question was, "Should one fortify the city or not?" If there was a group of soldiers available (and there usually was when a king was thinking about fortifying a city), then there were plenty of people to work on the fortifications, making it a relatively easy task to accomplish. If it were a time of sustained peace and a standing army was not available, however, fortification would be difficult without the required work force.

THINK IT THROUGH: Discuss how easy or difficult it would be to achieve the following actions.

- Is it easy or difficult to achieve a perfect score on the SAT?
- Is it easy or difficult to train a dog to obey voice commands?

- Is it easy or difficult for God to govern the world by providence?

5. Fitting or Not Fitting?

The fifth question is whether or not the proposed idea or action is fitting. When we say that something is *fitting*, we mean that it is suitable or appropriate, like good table manners or wearing your best clothes to a party. The proverb, "It is sweet and fitting to die for one's country (*Dulce et decorum est pro patria mori*)," was the response of the poet Horace (65–8 BC) to the question, "Should one die for one's country?"

THINK IT THROUGH: Consider the various questions listed below, decide whether they are appropriate or inappropriate, and then explain why.

- Is it appropriate for schools to require uniforms?
- Is it appropriate to treat others the way you would want to be treated?
- Is it appropriate for people to eat whatever they want to?

6. Lawful or Unlawful?

This approach is concerned with the legality of an action or idea. For example, taxes are lawful in the United States because they are permitted by the Constitution. Similarly, in the United States, people can practice whatever religion they want, not one chosen by the government, because the Bill of Rights guarantees freedom of religion.

THINK IT THROUGH: Consider whether the following proposals would conflict with other laws or rules.

- There should be speed limits.
- The FCC should allow profanity on TV and radio at any time day or night.
- Immigrants to the U. S. should be allowed to have their own courts of law operating outside the American court system.

7. Customary or Uncustomary?

The question of customary action is uniquely specific to the Thesis. Because the Thesis frequently deals with questions of human society, this approach answers the questions in the context of a particular culture. Suppose you are considering the question, "Should one marry?" You might argue that marriage and family have always been integral building blocks of any stable culture. Therefore, marriage is emphatically a customary action.

THINK IT THROUGH: Consider the situations and questions below and decide whether they are customary or not.

- People should close their eyes while praying.
- Men should open doors for women (and boys, for girls).
- Children should be seen and not heard.

8. Just or Unjust?

Although approach #6 deals with the issue of human law, the last question determines whether an action is just or unjust in light of universal (and frequently unwritten) laws. For example, murder would be unlawful because it is contrary to God's law as summarized in the Ten Commandments. Preserving life, on the other hand, is a lawful endeavor. Apples falling to the ground would be lawful because they are following the natural law of gravity.

THINK IT THROUGH: Consider the issues below and decide whether you think they are fair or unfair. If unfair, to whom would they be unfair?

- Should a nation go to war?
- Is it ever right to kill someone?
- Should a judge ever reduce a prisoner's sentence?

Organization

When writing an essay arguing for or against a proposition, follow this plan of organization:

1. **Introduction:** State the proposition in a neutral tone.

2. **Background:** Provide some background so that the reader will be able to understand the question.

3. **Writer's Position:** State your position on the question.

4. **Arguments:** Choose those approaches which are relevant to your position and develop each in standard zigzag style. (In these models, all eight are provided as examples.)

5. **Conclusion:** Summarize the key points you have discussed.

Model Thesis Essays

Essay 1: In Praise of Praise Songs

Introduction + Background + Writer's Position

How should a church worship God? Should they sing hymns or contemporary praise songs? Many churches today are so divided over the question of worship styles that they have two services — a traditional service and a contemporary service. Often the divide is not just theological, but generational — older congregants tend to prefer the familiar hymns, while younger members enthusiastically belt out praise songs. Although hymns are good, praise songs are an equally acceptable way to worship God.

Necessary

To begin with, it is hardly necessary to say that we must worship God, but it is certainly necessary to do so in a Biblical way. Psalm 117:1 says, "Praise the Lord, all nations! Extol him, all peoples!" Paul writes in Philippians 2:10 that everyone will bow to worship God when Christ is exalted.

Possible

One possible way to worship God today is through contemporary praise songs. Christian recording artists produce dozens of new songs each year whose lyrics and chords are readily available online.

Easy

In contrast to hymns, which are usually accompanied by piano or organ, contemporary praise songs are really easy to accompany. The performers do not even have to read music if they can play chords. Additionally, praise songs are best accompanied by portable instruments such as a guitar, keyboard, or drums, making it easy to have a church service anywhere.

Advantageous

Praise songs are also advantageous personally and spiritually. Humans are emotional creatures as well as rational beings, and praise songs stir up the emotions and occupy the senses. It would be wrong to starve the heart by singing stolid hymns.

Fitting

After thirty minutes of vigorous singing, the Christian is in a fitting mood to worship God. Praise songs are uniquely able to prepare the congregation to listen to the sermon and have a great worship experience, which is advantageous to the worship experience.

Customary

Although hymns are considered to be "traditional" church music, contemporary praise songs are rapidly becoming customary. Praise songs are the most popular type of worship in America today, so they are widely accepted in this culture.

Lawful

Also, though people who attend traditional services object to the instruments used in contemporary services because they are too loud and flashy, Psalm 150 mentions a wide variety of instruments that were used in ancient Israel to praise God, such as the trumpet, lute, harp, tambourine, strings, pipe, and cymbals. This would seem to indicate that it is lawful to use a similar variety of instruments in worship today, such as keyboards, guitars, and drums.

Just

Finally, people may ask whether it is just to sing praise songs. What is in the heart matters the most. If the worshipper's intention is to worship God sincerely, then praise songs sincerely and devotedly sung should be an acceptable form of worship.

Conclusion

In short, while many may still prefer hymns, contemporary praise songs should also be accepted in today's churches. Besides being practically easy to implement, praise songs are Biblically permissible and encourage a proper attitude in the heart of the worshipper.

Essay 2: Hymns in Harmony

Introduction + Background + Writer's Position

How should a congregation worship God? Should they sing contemporary praise songs, hymns, or only psalms? Many churches have debated what kinds of music should be allowed in a worship service and how it should be accompanied. Although praise songs are very popular in contemporary society, hymns have long been a staple in American churches and continue to be the best option.

Necessary

All Christians should agree that it is necessary to praise God rightly. The Old Testament contains several examples of people who were punished severely because they did not worship God properly, such as Uzzah, the sons of Korah, and Nadab and Abihu. The worship of God is a serious subject and must be treated with respectful care.

Possible

It is possible to sing hymns, for many churches have hymnals already. If a church wishes to purchase hymnals, there are a wide variety of options from which to choose. For churches which cannot afford hymnals for all their members, the words to hymns can also be projected onto the wall, since many hymns are in the public domain and do not require copyright permission to use them.

Advantageous

Hymns are advantageous to use in worship because they are beautiful and inspire devotion in the congregation. Good hymns are carefully written by others to guide a congregation in praising God. The authors include a variety of reasons for praising God, so that the church "forget[s] not all his benefits" (Psalm 103:2).

Easy

Hymns are often easier to sing than praise songs, since the tunes are simple and familiar. If the tune is unfamiliar, the church will be able to learn it quickly and to participate in the singing without worrying about hitting the correct notes or getting the timing correct.

Fitting

The singing of hymns is peculiarly fitting for the church. Because the tunes are simple and often sung in unison, the congregation is united in their singing. When singing hymns, one must pay attention to those singing around oneself and sing together with them. The emphasis is on the church as the body of Christ, rather than on the Christian as an individual.

Lawful

Some question whether it is Biblically lawful to sing hymns, since they are not inspired Scripture. However, Scripture contains many different examples of songs praising God outside the Psalms, such as the "Song of Moses" (Exodus 15), the "Song of Hannah" (I Samuel 2), and the "Magnificat" (Luke 1). Paul's letters are filled with hymn-like passages as in Romans 9:33, where he repeated lines from Isaiah (28:16), and Philippians 2:5-11, which many scholars believe to have been an early Christian hymn. Such passages suggest that hymns were written and sung in the church from the earliest times.

Customary

Hymns were indeed customary in the ancient church after the New Testament was completed in the first century. One of the earliest hymns of the church is the "Gloria in Excelsis," still sung in Roman Catholic, Anglican, and Lutheran churches. Church fathers, such as Ambrose, wrote hymns for the church, and others have followed his example throughout the ages.

Just

Some may ask whether it is just to sing all hymns in church, since some hymns undoubtedly have poor doctrinal content. Although hymns are permitted by Scripture, poor doctrine is not. To worship God justly, hymns must be examined to see if they are in agreement with the Scriptures. If the doctrine contained in the hymn is proper, then it is proper to sing the hymn in church.

Conclusion

Many condemn hymns because they are either too old-fashioned or not approved by Scripture. However, when hymns contain proper doctrine, they should be permitted in the church and can provide great benefits to the congregation through their beauty, simplicity, and harmony.

Essay 3: Sola Scriptura, Soli Psalmi

Introduction + Background + Writer's Position

How should a congregation worship God? May they sing hymns or contemporary praise songs, or must they only sing psalms? Many argue that it is permissible and even beneficial to sing songs that are not found in Scripture. However, others rest on the saying, *"Sola scriptura, soli psalmi,"* (only Scripture, only the Psalms). They believe the best way to worship God through music is by singing the Psalms without the accompaniment of musical instruments.

Necessary

It is necessary to worship God in a way that honors and pleases him. Thus, worship should not be taken lightly. As Psalm 2:11 says, "Serve the Lord with fear, and rejoice with trembling." During the Reformation, theologians recognized the regulative principle of worship, which states that the church may only worship God in the way He has commanded.

Fitting

This principle is fitting because God is holy, glorious, and majestic. Humans are created beings and cannot fully understand God. Since humans are also corrupted by sin, they must be instructed how to worship a holy God properly—they cannot make up fitting praise on their own.

Lawful

The way that God has commanded the church to worship can first be found in the Old Testament law, specifically in the Ten Commandments. When the

Second Commandment forbids the making of idols, it also forbids worshipping God in ways that humans create. Psalms, however, are part of inspired Scripture, so, unlike contemporary praise songs, they are clearly lawful to use in worship. As David said, "Sing to him, sing praises to him; / tell of all his wondrous works!" (I Chronicles 16:9).

Just

Since we know that singing the Psalms is lawful, we can conclude that it is also just to obey God's law by avoiding uninspired hymns and praise songs. This worship ought to be simple and reverent, without the aid of musical instruments.

Possible

There are many metrical versions of the Psalms available in English, making it possible to sing Psalms in church. The Psalms can also be chanted by the congregation, which facilitates an understanding of the psalm.

Easy

It is easy to sing Psalms *a cappella* because all that is needed is a congregation and a pitch pipe. No money needs to be spent on a piano or organ, and no time needs to be spent setting up a worship band. Rather, the congregation sings the simple and unadorned Word of God.

Advantageous

Singing Psalms weekly is advantageous because it teaches God's Word to the congregation. Thus, the members are taught not only by the sermon but also by the singing. Later in the week, the Psalms sung in worship on Sunday spring to mind, and what could be better than to have your mind filled with Scripture?

Customary

Finally, singing the Psalms has been a customary practice of the church throughout the ages. The Psalms were the songs of the Jews; the New

Testament is filled with quotations from the Psalms; monks in the Middle Ages sang the Psalms every day; and the martyrs of the Reformation went to their graves singing the Psalms. Such a long-standing custom should not be lightly abandoned.

Conclusion

Singing the Psalms without instrumental accompaniment is approved and commanded by Scripture. Such divinely inspired worship is fitting to a holy God. It is also practical to implement, spiritually edifying, and customary in church tradition. Congregations today ought to return to the ancient practice of singing Psalms exclusively.

EXERCISE 15.1: Analyzing Thesis Models

Directions: After reading the model Thesis essays above, analyze Thesis by answer the questions below.

1. **Essay I, "In Praise of Praise Songs":**

    a. Which approach seems to you the most persuasive? Explain your choice.

    b. Which approach seems to be the least persuasive? Explain your choice.

2. **Essay II, "Hymns in Harmony":**

    a. Which approach seems to you the most persuasive? Explain your choice.

    b. Which approach seems to be the least persuasive? Explain your choice.

3. **Essay III, "Sola Scriptura, Soli Psalmi":**

   a. Which approach seems to you the most persuasive? Explain your choice.

   b. Which approach seems to be the least persuasive? Explain your choice.

EXERCISE 15.2: Analyzing Approaches to Thesis

Directions: Below are excerpts from persuasive speeches in Xenophon's *Expedition of the Persians (Anabasis)*. Please begin by reading the introduction. Then, as you read the excerpts, determine how the speakers employ the various approaches to Thesis.

INTRODUCTION: *The year is 401 BC. Having followed Cyrus the Younger into Persia in his attempt to seize the throne from his brother Artaxerxes II, the Greek mercenaries find themselves in hostile territory without their leader, for Cyrus had been killed at Cunaxa. Cheirisophus the Spartan, Xenophon the Athenian, and Cleanor the Orchomenian assemble the troops for a council of war in an effort to rally the depressed and fearful soldiers. Below are excerpts from their speeches in which the approaches to Thesis can be seen.*

1. CHEIRISOPHUS

   Fellow soldiers, painful indeed is our present situation, seeing that we are robbed of such generals and captains and soldiers, and, besides, that Ariaeus and his men, who were formerly our allies, have betrayed us. Nevertheless, we must quit ourselves like brave men as well as may be in these circumstances, and must not yield, but rather try to save ourselves by glorious victory if we can. Otherwise, let us at least die a glorious death, and never fall into the hands of our enemies alive. For in that case I think we should meet the sort of sufferings that I pray the gods may visit upon our foes (3.2.2-3.).[63]

   What did Cheirisophus believe was NECESSARY?

2. CLEANOR

Come, fellow soldiers, you see the perjury and impiety of the King. You see likewise the faithlessness of Tissaphernes. It was Tissaphernes who said that he was a neighbor of Greece and that he would do his utmost to save us, . . . and then he, Tissaphernes, the very man who had given such pledges, was the very man who deceived and seized our generals. More than that, he did not even reverence Zeus, the god of hospitality. Instead, he entertained Clearchus at his own table and then made that very act the means of deceiving and destroying the generals. Ariaeus, too, whom we were ready to make king, with whom we exchanged pledges not to betray one another . . . has now gone over to the bitterest foes of that same Cyrus, and is trying to work harm to us, the friends of Cyrus. Well, may these men be duly punished by the gods. We, however, seeing their deeds, must never again be deceived by them, but must fight as stoutly as we can and meet whatever fortune the gods may please to send (3.2.4-6).

Why does Cleanor believe that their decision to fight is JUST?

3. XENOPHON

[After Xenophon began to speak about the justice of their cause, one of the soldiers sneezed, which Xenophon interpreted as a sign that the gods were affirming his words. They took time to worship the god, after which Xenophon resumed his speech.] I was saying that we have many fair hopes of deliverance. For, in the first place, we are standing true to the oaths we took in the name of the gods, while our enemies have perjured themselves and, in violation of their oaths, have broken the truce. This being so, it is fair to assume that the gods are their foes and our allies—and the gods are able speedily to make the strong weak and, when they so will, easily to deliver the weak, even though they be in dire perils (3.2.19).

Xenophon
(431 BC – 354 BC)

The soldiers are fearful because they are weak in comparison to their enemy. In Xenophon's opinion, what will make their task relatively EASY?

4. XENOPHON

> You believe . . . that the rivers are a difficulty, and you think you were immensely deceived when you crossed them. Then consider whether this is not really a surpassingly foolish thing that the barbarians have done. For all rivers, even though they be impassable at a distance from their sources, become passable, without even wetting your knees, as you approach toward the sources (3.2.22).

The men are without horses. Why does Xenophon think it will be POSSIBLE for them to cross the rivers?

5. XENOPHON:

> My own view would be that we ought not yet to let it be seen that we have set out for home. We ought, rather, to be making our arrangements as if we intended to settle here. For I know that to the Mysians the king would not only give plenty of guides, but plenty of hostages, to guarantee a safe conduct for them out of his country. In fact, he would build a road for them, even if they wanted to take their departure in four-horse chariots. And I know that he would be thrice glad to do the same for us, if he saw that we were preparing to stay here (3.2.24).

How would it be ADVANTAGEOUS for the king to help?

Now You Try It

**Chapter 15 Essay
Thesis**

Specifications

1. The purpose of this assignment is to demonstrate your ability to write a Thesis.

2. To do this, you will select an issue of interest to others and argue for it or against it. You can choose one of these topics or, with your teacher's approval, another of interest to you:
   - Should schools require students to wear uniforms?
   - Should the words "under God" be removed from the Pledge of Allegiance?
   - Should pet owners have microchips implanted under the skin of their pets? (You may want to do a bit of research to learn the advantages of this procedure.)

3. Please consider all the approaches indicated on the pre-writing activity and jot down your thoughts in the space provided, or if your teacher prefers, in a formal phrase outline. Then choose the three that you consider the best to employ in your essay.

4. Follow your teacher's instructions regarding preparation of the manuscript.

Thesis: Pre-Writing Activity

I have chosen to write about _____.

Approach	Details
Necessary / Unnecessary	
Possible / Impossible	
Advantageous / Disadvantageous	
Easy / Difficult	
Fitting / Unfitting	
Lawful / Unlawful	
Customary / Uncustomary	
Just / Unjust	

LEGISLATION

Chapter 16

Introduction

Though animals and man have had a working and domestic relationship for centuries, laws regulating the treatment of animals are relatively new. In fact, no country in the world had laws protecting animals from cruel treatment until 1822 when Richard Martin, an Irish member of the British Parliament, introduced his "act to prevent cruelty to animals," which stated:

> That if any person or persons shall wantonly and cruelly beat, abuse, or ill-treat any Horse, Mare, Gelding, Mule, Ass, Ox, Cow, Heifer, Steer, Sheep, or other Cattle, . . . it shall be lawful for [the] Justice of the Peace or other Magistrate to issue his Summons or Warrant, at his Discretion, to bring the party or parties so complained of before him. . . . [A]nd if the party or parties accused shall be convicted of any such Offence—he, she, or they so convicted shall forfeit and pay any Sum not exceeding Five Pounds, not less than Ten Shillings, to His Majesty. . . ; and if the person or persons so convicted shall refuse or not be able forthwith to pay the Sum forfeited, every such Offender . . . shall . . . be committed to the House of Correction or some other Prison within the Jurisdiction within which the Offence shall have been committed, there to be kept without Bail. . . for any Time not exceeding Three Months.[64]

In 1824, Martin's associates, the well-known nineteenth-century evangelicals William Wilberforce and the Reverend Arthur Broome, founded the Society for the Prevention of Cruelty to Animals (SPCA). Motivated by Proverbs 12:10, which says, in part, "Whoever is righteous has regard for the life of his beast," they had brought sixty-three animal cruelty cases to the courts by the end of the year and worked tirelessly throughout the nineteenth-century to codify the teaching of Proverbs 12:10a into British law. As this story shows, one individual can make a great difference in the world, especially in nations where the voice of the individual is valued.

THINK IT THROUGH: Who are some persons in either the Old or New Testament who spoke up for or against laws or customs in order to bring human behavior more in line with the teachings of God?

Definition and Purpose

In ancient Athens, all adult males who had completed their military training were able—and expected—to participate in a direct democracy, stopping by the Assembly whenever they chose to do so. When legislation was pending, any of these 6,000 men could rise to speak for or against a proposed or existing law. The element of the progymnasmata called Legislation, which is the last and perhaps most important of the preliminary exercises, prepared young Athenians to participate in this key feature of democracy—the influence of individuals on the life of the community in which they have a stake. Now, 2,500 years later, teachers still hope to enable the next generation to take its place in this long tradition of nudging the citizenry toward the lighted path.

Approaches to Legislation

Arguing for or against a law is a sub-category of the progymnasmata exercise Thesis; therefore, the approaches are very similar, as the chart shows:

	Thesis Is the proposal….	Legislation Is the law….
1	*necessary?*	*necessary?*
2	*possible?*	*possible?*
3	*advantageous?*	*advantageous?*
4	*easy?*	*easy?*
5	*fitting?*	*fitting?*
6	*lawful?*	*lawful?*
7	**customary?**	**clear?**
8	*just?*	*just?*

THINK IT THROUGH: Seven of the eight approaches are the same for Thesis and Legislation, but the seventh is different. Why do you suppose "clear" has been substituted for "customary"? Can you envision any laws where people might want to consider whether the law fit their customary way of life?

Now let us take a more detailed look at each of the eight approaches as they apply to legislation.

1. Necessary or Unnecessary?

Laws restrict, prohibit, or enable human behavior, but not every human behavior needs a law to govern it. In Alabama, for example, there is a law on the books that prohibits anyone from driving while blindfolded. One wonders how many hours and how many taxpayer dollars were spent on debating, voting on, and publishing this rather unnecessary law. Matters do not appear to be much more sensible overseas. For example, in England, it is illegal to die in either House of Parliament!

THINK IT THROUGH: Here are some laws that are currently in force in the United States. Do you consider them necessary—or not?

- In Baldwin Park, California, one may not ride a bicycle in a swimming pool.
- In Sterling, Colorado, cats on the loose must wear taillights.
- In Illinois, people must conduct government business in the only official language of the state: "American."
- In Gary, Indiana, people are not allowed to enter a theatre or ride a public streetcar within four hours of eating garlic.
- In Natoma, Kansas, citizens are prohibited from throwing knives at men in striped suits.

2. Possible or Impossible?

Sometimes people will argue that a law should not be passed because it would not be possible to enforce it. The most famous example of an unenforceable law in the U. S. occurred between 1919 and 1930 when it was illegal to produce and/or sell alcohol. However, since the demand for alcohol remained as high as ever, organized crime stepped in to supply it. Illegal stills (devices used in the distillation of alcohol) sprang up in basements and barns around the country. The mafia made a fortune, and gangland wars plagued major cities such as Chicago, most notably the St. Valentine's Day Massacre of 1929 when Al Capone's South Side Italian gang wiped out the North Side Irish gang led by Bugs Moran. Since Prohibition did not end the manufacture and consumption of alcohol in the United States—and, in fact, increased the social ills of many communities—it was deemed an unenforceable law and, after a tumultuous eleven years, was repealed.

THINK IT THROUGH: Consider each of the following. Then put a *P* in the blank if you think it would be *Possible* to enforce or an *I* if *Impossible*.

_____ The University Interscholastic League, which sets rules for some high school football teams in Texas, states that during summer practices coaches are allowed to sit in the end zone but are not allowed to communicate coaching tips to their players.

_____ To date, twenty-five states have banned texting while driving.

_____ The United States federal government prohibits online gambling.

_____ In New South Wales, Australia, authorities have banned the use of high-powered lasers without a "prohibited weapons permit."

3. Advantageous or Disadvantageous?

Another approach one can take toward a proposed law is to argue whether its passage would be advantageous to the public or not. Though Prohibition was intended to help solve the problems of alcoholism and dysfunctional families, it actually proved disadvantageous because it introduced rampant crime, as seen above.

Another example involved the issue of slavery. In the nineteenth century, southern slaveholders believed that freeing the slaves would be disadvantageous to the economy of the South in its competition with the industrialized North. Abolitionists, however, felt that the disadvantages thrust upon people of African origin outweighed the economic disadvantage to the plantation owner. Naturally, what is advantageous to one group may be distinctly disadvantageous to another. Therefore, lawmakers and opinion makers commonly explore the disadvantages of a law when arguing for or against it.

THINK IT THROUGH: Discuss how the following policies in schools around the world might be advantageous or disadvantageous to students

   a. *United States:* Not allowing students to use electronic devices in the classroom

   b. *Uganda:* Not allowing students to talk to strangers at the school

   c. *France:* Not allowing students to wear any religious symbols: Muslim head scarves, Sikh turbans, Jewish skull caps, or Christian crosses

   d. *England:* Making lessons optional and giving each student the right to vote alongside adults regarding school policies or rules (from the boarding school Summerhill, the so-called "school without rules")

4. Easy or Difficult?

Another approach to debating a law is to examine whether it is easy or difficult to enforce. Questions to consider are the cost, the amount of time required by law enforcement to enforce the law, and the exertion required to enforce it. Many states have outlawed smoking in public buildings and have not found it difficult to enforce, but if the prohibition of smoking extended to private residences, it would be very difficult to enforce. The cost of employing police to search homes would be astronomical, and even if such searches could be afforded, the ill will generated in the general public would cause more trouble than it prevented.

THINK IT THROUGH: Discuss how easy or difficult it would be to pass laws such as those proposed below.

   a. *United States:* Persons concerned about the environment propose a limit on the amount of water one can use when taking a shower. How easy would this be to pass and then to enforce?

b. *India:* The Constitution of India establishes compulsory education for both boys and girls until the age of 14. However, there are few school buildings and many schools lack running water (hence, no bathrooms). How easy would it be in India to require communities to establish running water in all schools throughout the country?

c. *United States:* The Constitution of the United States guarantees the free exercise of religion. How easy would it be in the United States to require schools to set aside thirty minutes per day so that students could attend religious instruction in their own faith in separate classrooms: Christians in one room, Jews in another, Muslims in another, Buddhists in another, etc.?

5. Fitting or Not Fitting?

Another approach to legislation is to debate whether or not a law is fitting according to the customs and traditions of the people. These matters are often handled by city governments, which must regulate zoning. What exactly is zoning? Zoning is the process of designating land usage within city boundaries. For example, some areas are reserved for residences, others for retail shops, others for heavy manufacturing, and others for schools and houses of worship. Most people are in general agreement that zoning protects the quality of life in a community. However, disputes sometimes arise. For example, should a tavern be permitted to sit next door to a school? Should a theatre that shows X-rated movies be allowed to set up business across the street from a church?

Sometimes zoning issues unrelated to moral issues emerge as well. For example, Ladue, Missouri, which is a very wealthy suburb of St. Louis, for a time banned the use of iron gates (even costly and beautiful ones) that control access to the driveways of residential estates. One city authority said that the gates were not fitting because they "conflicted with Ladue's image as a pastoral town with open vistas." Others say it is perfectly fitting for homeowners to protect their property and families and, as long as attractive gating is used, there should be no problem. And so the debate goes on.[65]

THINK IT THROUGH: Consider the various issues listed below and decide whether they are appropriate or inappropriate for the people involved.

a. Some immigrants to the United States are accustomed to eating dogs. Currently supermarkets in the U.S. do not carry this kind of meat. Suppose the state mandated that such meat be made available.

b. Research has shown that girls do better in math classes when they are instructed in all-girl classrooms. Do you think it is appropriate for boys and girls to be separated for educational purposes?

6. Lawful or Unlawful?

When debating a law, one must also consider whether it is in harmony with the Constitution of the United States or with other federal, state, and local laws. For example, in the United States, a city cannot pass a law preventing people from attending church services because to do so would violate the first amendment to the United States Constitution, which states, "Congress shall make no law respecting [about] an establishment of religion, or prohibiting the free exercise thereof. . . ." Similarly, many Americans oppose laws which make it difficult to own guns, saying such laws violate their right under the Second Amendment to "keep and bear arms."

THINK IT THROUGH: Consider whether the following proposals would conflict with other laws or rules.

a. Many federal and state laws place restrictions on gun ownership, but South Dakota lawmakers proposed (admittedly with tongue-in-cheek) that everyone in South Dakota be required to purchase a gun upon turning twenty-one.

b. The United States has child labor laws protecting under-aged children from dangerous work places. However, the Amish in Lyndenville, New York, seek the right to provide job training for boys between the ages of fourteen and seventeen in woodworking shops where, by law, they are not allowed to work.

7. Clear or Unclear?

Legislators who write our laws have the responsibility to make sure that the meaning of the law is clear. When it is not, those who wish to get around the law find loopholes that allow them to do so. One example of this type is related to the anti-gambling laws in the state of Ohio. Ohio law does not allow the awarding of any cash or merchandise prize worth more than ten dollars. The law applies to any "mechanical, video, digital, or electronic device that rewards the player or players."[66] However, the *Dayton Daily News* reported on January 31, 2011, that a businessman in Springfield, Ohio, opened an Internet café which got around the specific wording of the law. At his establishment, "Customers sit behind rows of computer terminals playing games of chance with pre-purchased cards."[67] Since the Internet is not specifically mentioned in the law, would you say this man's business was legal or not?

THINK IT THROUGH: Consider the situations and questions below and decide whether the law is clear enough to make the answer obvious.

a. *Illinois:* The new Nurse Practice Act in Illinois states that registered nurses must not delegate any tasks to non-nurses that require nursing judgment. Does this mean that a teacher cannot offer an aspirin to a student with a headache?

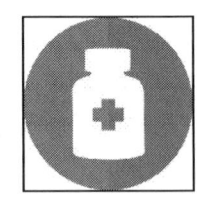

b. *California:* The Belvedere City Council passed an order which reads as follows: "No dog shall be in a public place without its master on a leash." Does this mean the master must be on a leash?

8. Just or Unjust?

The Pledge of Allegiance of the United States affirms that our nation strives to achieve "liberty and justice for all," but sometimes critics of a bill or a law will argue that it is not fair to all people. For example, the United States House of Representatives has been handling what is called the DREAM Act for over ten years now. This act, whose acronym stands for the Development, Relief and Education for Alien Minors, would provide several avenues by which young persons currently in the United States illegally could find a path to citizenship. For example, they could do so by serving in the U. S. military or graduating from a U. S. college or university.

However, opponents of the DREAM Act say that, though well intentioned, such a law could end up giving an unfair advantage to foreign-born or illegal immigrants over native-born or legally immigrated Americans. For example, former Senator Jeff Sessions (R-Ala.) has said that offering in-state tuition to illegal aliens in, say, California, would be unfair to U. S. citizens from other states, who would still have to pay the higher out-of-state tuition to attend college there. Examples like this emphasize that, in order to be fair, good intentions must be balanced with practical results.[68]

THINK IT THROUGH: Consider the issues below and decide whether you think they are fair or unfair. If unfair, to whom would they be unfair?

a. *North Carolina:* After two pit bulls killed a little girl playing in her grandmother's front yard, state legislators proposed that owners of pit bulls be required to register their dogs and take special training. Is this fair? Why or why not?

b. *Chicago, Illinois:* An automobile dealer sponsored the Chicago Bears football games. A salesman at the dealership was a Green Bay Packers fan and frequently wore a tie with the Packers' logo. Though asked not to wear the tie, he continued to do so and was fired for insubordination. Is this fair? Why or why not?

Organization

When writing an essay for or against a law, follow this plan of organization:

1. In the introduction, state the proposed law in a neutral tone.

2. Provide background in the form of a brief narrative so that the reader will be able to understand the issue.

3. State your position on the issue.

4. Choose those approaches which are relevant to your position and develop each in standard "zigzag" style. (In the model, all eight are provided as examples.)

5. Write a conclusion or clincher that briefly drives home your point.

Model Essays on Legislation

Below are two essays based on the proposal that federal trials be broadcast on television. As you read, notice the major transition at the beginning of each paragraph as well as the controlling idea which indicates what approach the paragraph is taking—for or against.

I. Yes to Broadcasting Federal Trials

Introduction

For a number of years, television cameras have been allowed in courtrooms across the United States, and television shows such as *In Session* on HLN have broadcast whole trials to the general public. However, so far, only cases tried in state courts have been allowed. Some believe the law should be changed so that federal trials can also be broadcast while others say federal cases should not be shown.

Background

Since 2005, members of the United States Senate Judiciary Committee have been trying to pass a bill called the Sunshine in the Courtroom Act, which would allow photography and broadcasting of trials in federal court. On February 28, 2013, the bill was re-introduced in the U. S. House of Representatives as H. R. 917 and was referred to committee.

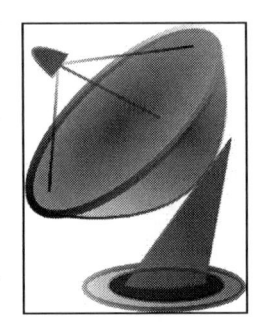

Writer's Position

There are several reasons why the Sunshine in the Courtroom Act should be passed by the Congress.

Necessary

First, the Sixth Amendment of the U. S. Constitution states that "in all criminal prosecutions, the accused shall enjoy the right to a . . . public trial." Public trials were deemed necessary by the founding fathers so that the government could not send a person to prison without following legal procedure. The more people who observe the process, the less chance there is for wrongdoing. Since only television broadcasting can ensure the widest possible public trial, it is necessary for federal trials to be broadcast.

Possible

Second, the broadcast of dozens, if not hundreds, of state trials has shown that television broadcasting is technologically possible. In addition, it is possible to broadcast trials while still preserving the rights of the defendant, as has already been shown in state trials. It is also possible to protect the identity of the jury members simply by making a rule that the cameras cannot show their faces.

Advantageous

Broadcasting federal trials would also be advantageous. It is advantageous to the accused in that it stimulates responsibility on the part of the judge and all attorneys. It is also advantageous to the general public since, unlike state trials, the cases that are tried in federal court impact all citizens of the country. Any time the government can educate the people regarding cases involving terrorism, narcotics smuggling, and violations of civil rights, the public will be well served. It also has the advantage of being educational because by observing trials, the viewing public learns how the justice system operates.

Easy

In addition, it is easy to broadcast trials. The cost is borne by the television network, so there is no cost to the taxpayer. In addition, over twenty years of experience in broadcasting state trials has paved the way for broadcasting federal trials. Procedures and policies have been worked out, making it much easier to begin broadcasting federal trials than it was when state trials were first broadcast.

Fitting

Broadcasting federal trials is also fitting for our culture. We are a free and open society. We have always had a strong commitment to the people's right to know what is happening in their government. Preventing the broadcast of federal trials goes against our usual cultural style. We would do better to broadcast them in keeping with our tradition of openness.

Lawful

In addition to being fitting, television broadcasting of federal trials would be lawful. As indicated above, the Sixth Amendment to the Constitution requires a public trial, and there is nothing in the Constitution that would prevent it.

Clear

H. R. 917 is clear in its provision. Regarding appellate courts, it states, "Except as provided under subparagraph (B), the presiding judge of an appellate court of the United States may, at the discretion of that judge, permit the photographing, electronic recording, broadcasting, or televising to the public of any court proceeding over which that judge presides."[69] Clearly authority is being given to the judge to make the decision regarding the broadcast of trials and exceptions are clearly stated. In subparagraph B, referenced in the bill, the rights of jurors are clearly protected.

Just

Broadcasting federal trials is also just. The bill also states that a judge could prevent TV broadcasting if he or she determined that such a broadcast would violate anyone's rights. Thus, no one is forcing a judge to broadcast a trial. As stated above, defendants have a stronger chance of a fair trial when the whole world is watching. Moreover, if the accused is found guilty and decides to appeal the case, the appellate court will be able to view the first trial to see if the demeanor or tone of voice of a witness or attorney was inappropriate, something a written transcript cannot reveal.

Conclusion

Since broadcasting federal trials on television is necessary to fulfill the Sixth Amendment, possible and easy to implement, advantageous to the defendant and the public, fitting to our culture, lawful, clear, and just to all concerned, the Sunshine in the Courtroom Act should be passed.

II. No to Broadcasting Federal Trials

Introduction

For many years, television cameras have been allowed in courtrooms across the United States, and television shows such as *In Session* on HLN have broadcast whole trials to the general public. However, so far, only cases tried in state courts have been allowed. Some believe the law should be changed so that federal trials can also be broadcast while others say federal cases should not be shown.

Background

Since 2005, members of the United States Senate Judiciary Committee have been trying to pass a bill called the Sunshine in the Courtroom Act, which would allow photography and broadcasting of trials in federal court. On February 28, 2013, the bill was re-introduced in the U. S. House of Representatives as H. R. 917 and was referred to committee.

Writer's Position

There are several reasons why the Sunshine in the Courtroom Act should not be passed by the Congress.

Unnecessary

It is true that the Sixth Amendment to the Constitution gives defendants the right to a public trial, but public trials have been a part of the legal system in the United States since the beginning without being broadcast. Courtrooms are still open to the public and to journalists, so it is not necessary to televise trials to make them public.

Impossible

Broadcasting trials might actually make it impossible for a defendant to get a fair trial because evening talk show hosts tend to take public stands for or against a defendant, a witness, or an attorney. Defendants are considered innocent until proven guilty, but talk-show hosts can certainly make an innocent person look guilty. If acquitted, defendants might find their reputation has been completely ruined nation-wide. How could a person ever begin to rebuild a ruined life in such a case?

Disadvantageous

When the broadcasting of trials first began, an early argument in their favor was that they would be educational for the public. However, the first trial to be broadcast was the O. J. Simpson murder trial in 1994. That trial is infamous for being a "media circus." Gerald F. Uelmen, one of the defense attorneys, stated that the TV cameras "were a mistake because they affected the behavior of all the trial participants, judge, lawyers, and, most regrettably, witnesses."[70] In addition, the trial became a source of entertainment, and many in the judicial system have said that nothing about that case was normal; therefore, broadcasting trials does not have the advantage of teaching people about our court system.

Difficult

Next, nationally broadcasting trials makes it difficult for witnesses to be protected. In 2011, the trial of Casey Anthony for the murder of her two-year-old daughter resulted in an astonishing acquittal. Without presenting any evidence at all, the defense attorneys argued that Casey's father, George Anthony, had abused his daughter when she was growing up and that, therefore, when his granddaughter drowned in the family pool, Casey was afraid of going against her father's demand that she toss the body in a swamp and lie to the police! Despite much evidence supporting the idea that Ms. Anthony did murder her daughter, she was acquitted, and Mr. Anthony will never be able to get his reputation back.

Unfitting

Though some argue that public broadcasts of trials is fitting with our open culture, it can also be said that it is distinctly unfitting for our culture to take a serious matter such as a trial and turn it into entertainment for late-night talk show hosts and every psychologist and attorney who wants to enhance his or her own name recognition. It is fitting to preserve the serious tone of a court of law and not to have satirical skits distract from the proper respect owed to a judge as happened in the satirical "dancing Itos" skit on *Saturday Night Live* when Judge Lance Ito was presiding over the O. J. Simpson case.

Unlawful

In our judicial system, the rules of procedure begin with the Supreme Court of the United States. If the justices a change is necessary, they notify Congress on May 1 so that the new rule can go into effect by December 1 of that year. Currently, Rule 53 of the Federal Rules of Criminal Procedure states, "Except as otherwise provided by a statute or these rules, the court must not permit the taking of photographs in the courtroom during judicial proceedings or the broadcasting of judicial proceedings from the courtroom."[71] And, despite pressure to make a change, there are still good reasons why the practice should remain unlawful.

Unclear

The bill before Congress would allow the broadcasting of federal courtroom trials, but it is very unclear about how these broadcasts might be handled in situations where the words of the attorneys, judges, witnesses, and defendant would need to be translated into a foreign language. If a foreign terrorist were to be on trial, his country of origin might wish to broadcast the proceedings, but there are no safeguards ensuring the qualifications of journalistic translators. This leaves open the possibility of false or misleading reporting which might generate international opposition to verdicts rendered in our courts.

Unjust

When we pledge allegiance to the flag of the United States, we acknowledge the fact that our nation strives toward "liberty and justice for all." Naturally, this applies to those accused of a crime, but the phrase "for all" means that the system should not be unjust to witnesses, attorneys, and judges. For example, in federal cases involving powerful foreign drug cartels, it would not be fair to judges or prosecutors to make their faces highly recognizable to thugs who wished to assassinate them in retaliation for their decisions. We must remain fair to *all.*

Conclusion

In conclusion, broadcasting federal trials is unnecessary, unfitting, and disadvantageous to our system of justice. It does not accord with the rules of procedure that have been in place for centuries. Broadcasting these trials would make it difficult to protect the reputations of the witnesses and nearly impossible to ensure fair treatment of the defendant in the media and could create international hostility. For these reasons, H. R. 917 should not be passed.

EXERISE 16.1: Analyzing the Model Legislation Essays

Directions: After reading the two essays based on the proposal that federal trials be broadcast on television., provide your opinion on the questions below.

1. In "Yes to Broadcasting Federal Trials":

   a. Which approach do you believe was the most persuasive? Explain why.

   b. Least persuasive? Explain why.

2. In "No to Broadcasting Federal Trials":

   a. Which approach do you believe was the most persuasive? Explain why?

   b. Least persuasive? Explain why.

Model of a Legislation Argument from the Bible

INTRODUCTION: *As the apostle Paul carried the gospel of Christ to the Gentiles, one of the issues that he had to deal with was whether the Gentiles needed to keep all of the law of the Old Testament. Large parts of his epistle to the Galatians are devoted to this question. Paul was familiar with classical rhetoric. Therefore, in order to explain his ideas on the issue of the Old Testament law, he used the approaches common to the progymnasmata exercise Legislation. Read the excerpt below and answer the questions that follow.*

Abraham Justified by Faith (Romans 4:1-8)

¹What then shall we say was gained by Abraham, our forefather according to the flesh? ²For if Abraham was justified by works, he has something to boast about, but not before God. ³For what does the Scripture say? "Abraham believed God, and it was counted to him as righteousness." ⁴Now to the one who works, his wages are not counted as a gift but as his due. ⁵And to the one who does not work but believes in him who justifies the ungodly, his faith is counted as righteousness, ⁶just as David also speaks of the blessing of the one to whom God counts righteousness apart from works:

> ⁷"Blessed are those whose lawless deeds are forgiven,
>   and whose sins are covered;
> ⁸blessed is the man against whom the Lord will not count his sin."[a]

Justified by Faith (Galatians 2:15-21)

¹⁵We ourselves are Jews by birth and not Gentile sinners; ¹⁶yet we know that a person is not justified by works of the law but through faith in Jesus Christ, so we also have believed in Christ Jesus, in order to be justified by faith in Christ and not by works of the law, because by works of the law no one will be justified.

---

[a] Psalm 32:1-2

17 But if, in our endeavor to be justified in Christ, we too were found to be sinners, is Christ then a servant of sin? Certainly not! **18** For if I rebuild what I tore down, I prove myself to be a transgressor. **19** For through the law I died to the law, so that I might live to God. **20** I have been crucified with Christ. It is no longer I who live, but Christ who lives in me. And the life I now live in the flesh I live by faith in the Son of God, who loved me and gave himself for me. **21** I do not nullify the grace of God, for if righteousness were through the law, then Christ died for no purpose.

The Righteous Shall Live by Faith (Galatians 3:10-14)

10 For all who rely on works of the law are under a curse; for it is written, "Cursed be everyone who does not abide by all things written in the Book of the Law, and do them." **11** Now it is evident that no one is justified before God by the law, for "The righteous shall live by faith" [see Romans 4:1-8 above]. **12** But the law is not of faith, rather "The one who does them shall live by them." **13** Christ redeemed us from the curse of the law by becoming a curse for us—for it is written, "Cursed is everyone who is hanged on a tree"—**14** so that in Christ Jesus the blessing of Abraham might come to the Gentiles, so that we might receive the promised Spirit through faith.

The Law and the Promise (Galatians 3:15-18)

15 To give a human example, brothers: even with a man-made covenant, no one annuls it or adds to it once it has been ratified. **16** Now the promises were made to Abraham and to his offspring. It does not say, "And to offsprings [*sic*]," referring to many, but referring to one, "And to your offspring," who is Christ. **17** This is what I mean: the law, which came 430 years afterward, does not annul a covenant previously ratified by God, so as to make the promise void. For if the inheritance comes by the law, it no longer comes by promise; but God gave it to Abraham by a promise.

Christ Has Set Us Free (Galatians 5:1-6)

1 For freedom Christ has set us free; stand firm therefore, and do not submit again to a yoke of slavery.

² Look: I, Paul, say to you that if you accept circumcision, Christ will be of no advantage to you. ³ I testify again to every man who accepts circumcision that he is obligated to keep the whole law. ⁴ You are severed from Christ, you who would be justified by the law; you have fallen away from grace. ⁵ For through the Spirit, by faith, we ourselves eagerly wait for the hope of righteousness. ⁶ For in Christ Jesus neither circumcision nor uncircumcision counts for anything, but only faith working through love.

EXERCISE 16.2: Analyzing a Legislation Argument from the Bible

<u>Directions</u>: After reading the excerpts from Paul's epistle to the Galatians, analyze Legislation by answering the questions below.

1. **Necessary:** According to Galatians 2:15-21, is it *necessary* for Gentiles to keep the Old Testament law?

2. **Possible:** According to Galatians 2:15-16, is it *possible* to be saved by keeping the Old Testament law?

3. **Advantageous:** According to Galatians 5:2-6, is it *advantageous* to cling to the law?

4. **Easy:** According to Galatians 3:10, is it *easy* to keep the Old Testament law?

5. **Fitting:** According to Galatians 5:1, is it *fitting* for those who know Christ to revert to the law?

6. **Lawful:** According to Galatians 3:16-17, does salvation through Christ conflict with the law? In other words, is it *unlawful*?

7. **Clear:** According to Romans 4:1-8 and Galatians 3:11, was it *clear* from the Old Testament narrative of Abraham and the psalm of David that righteousness came through faith, not law?

8. **Just:** According to Galatians 6:13, is it *just* for Jewish believers to tell Gentile believers to obey the Old Testament law?

Now You Try It

Chapter 16 Essay
Legislation

Specifications

1. The purpose of this assignment is to demonstrate your ability to write for or against a law.

2. To select a topic, think of an issue in the school, community, or country which you feel needs either to be regulated or de-regulated. In other words, you would like to (a) argue for or against the passage of a new rule or law or (b) argue for the repeal of a rule or law.

3. You may choose one of the following topics or, with your teacher's approval, another of interest to you:
    - Argue for or against making English the official language of the United States.
    - Argue for or against a change in a rule at your school (dress code, electronics policy, course requirements, etc.).
    - Argue for or against the re-establishment of the military draft.

4. Please consider all of the approaches indicated on the pre-writing activity and jot down your thoughts in the space provided, or, if your teacher prefers, prepare a formal outline. Then choose the three that you consider the best to employ in your essay.

5. Follow your teacher's instructions regarding preparation of the manuscript.

Legislation: Pre-Writing Activity

I will argue that _____.

Approach	Details
Necessary / Unnecessary	
Possible / Impossible	
Advantageous / Disadvantageous	
Easy / Difficult	
Fitting / Unfitting	
Lawful / Unlawful	
Clear / Unclear	
Just / Unjust	

IMAGE ATTRIBUTION

Ch. 1, Fable

Aesop. *Wikimedia Commons.* CC BY-SA 3.0.
Milo Winter. The Crow and the Pitcher. 1919. *Wikimedia Commons.* {{PD-US expired}}.
The Good Samaritan. *Wikimedia Commons.* {{US-OLD-100}}.
Hermes. *Wikimedia Commons.*CC0 1.0 Universal (CC0 1.0).
"The Wind and the Sun." *Pixabay.*

Ch. 2, Narrative

Odysseus and the Sirens. Wikimedia Commons.{{US-OLD-100}}.
Davy Crockett. *Wikimedia Commons.*{{US-Old-70}}.
Julius Caesar. *Wikimedia Commons.*{{US-PD-expired}}.
Cinderella's wedding. *Wikimedia Commons.* {{US-PD-80}}.

Ch. 3, "Description"

News reporter silhouette. *Pixabay.*
Stephen Crane. *Wikimedia Commons.* {{US-PD-old}}.
Ulysses at the Court of Alcinous. Wikimedia Commons. {{US-PD-100}}.

Ch. 4, Writing a Good Paragraph

Pencil and paper. *Pixabay.*
Polar bear. *Pixabay.*
Sunflower. *Pixabay.*
Runner. *Pixabay.*
Tornado. *Pixabay.*
Group work. *Pixabay.*
Emu. *Pixabay.*
Temple of Apollo at Delphi. Wikimedia Commons. CC BY-SA 3.0.
Hebrew square book. Wikimedia Commons. {{US-PD-expired}}.
Lioness. *Pixabay.*

Ch. 5, Outlining

Skeleton. *Public domain.*

Ch. 6, Proverb

King Solomon in Old Age. Wikimedia Commons. {{US-PD-old}}.
Benjamin Franklin. *Pixabay.*
Man at computer. P*ixabay.*

Ch. 7, Chreia

Wizard of Oz poster, 1939. Wikimedia Commons. {{PD-US-not renewed}}.
Fierce emoji. *Pixabay.*
Diogenes of Sinope. *Wikimedia Commons. CC BY-SA 3.0.*

Ch. 8, Refutation

The Capitoline she-wolf with the boys Romulus and Remus. Museo Nuovo in the Palazzo dei Conservatori, Rome. *Wikimedia Commons.* {{US-OLD-100}}.
Roman woman from a fresco in the Roman tomb of Silistra in northeastern Bulgaria. *Wikimedia Commons.* {PD-US-100}}.
Angry grandma. *Pixabay.*

Ring around the Rosie. Kate Greenaway's illustration from *Mother Goose or the Old Nursery Rhymes*, 1881. Public domain. {{PD-old-100}}.
Joseph of Arimathea. *Wikimedia Commons*. {{*PD-US-100*}}.
Caius Mucius Scaevola and Porsena by Felice Giani. *Wikimedia Commons*. {{PD-US-100}}.
Statue of Socrates in front of the National Library, Montevideo Department. Patricia Carabelli. *Wikimedia Commons*. CC BY-SA 3.0.

Ch. 9, Confirmation

Abraham Lincoln. *Pixabay*.
Heinrich Schliemann. *Wikimedia Commons*. {{PD-US-70}}.
Egyptian *baris* from Herodotus. *History*. Trans. George Rawlinson. (London, 1862). 2:131. *Internet Archive*. 11 Dec. 2007. Web. 21 Feb. 2020.<https://archive.org/details/in.ernet.dli.2015.500096/page/n151/mode/2up>.
Hatchet. *Pixabay*.
Dagon. *Wikimedia Commons*. {{PD-US-70.}}.
Plan of the walls of Nineveh. Fredarch. *Wikimedia Commons*. CC BY-SA 3.0.
Horse silhouette. *Pixabay*.

Ch. 10, Commonplace

Ladder of success. Needpix.com. CC0.
Poison. *Pixabay*.

Ch. 11, Encomium.

Hector of Troy. *Wikimedia Commons*. {{PD-US-70}}.
Saint Boniface. *Wikimedia Commons*. {{PD-US-100}}.

Ch. 12, Invective

Robert H. Jackson. Harris and Ewing Collection. Library of Congress. *Wikimedia Commons*. Public Domain.
Nero. *Wikimedia Commons*. CC BY-SA 3.0.
Nero Fiddling. *Wikimedia Commons*. {{PD-US-100}}.

Ch. 13, Comparison

Samuel Johnson by Joshua Reynolds. *Wikimedia Commons*. {{US-OLD-100}}.
Men with beards. *Pixabay*.
Alligator and crocodile. Hbk33. CC BY-SA 2.0. Modified by removing third image, gavialis gangeticus.
Businessman and farmer silhouettes. *Pixabay*.

Ch. 14, Speech-in-Character

Stymphalian bird. *Wikidot*. CC BY-SA 3.0.
Juliet. Philip H. Calderon. *Wikimedia Commons*. {{PD-US-100}}.
Alice with the cat. *Flickr*. No known copyright restrictions. <https://www.flickr.com/photos/126377022@N07/14595044538>.
Antigone. Frederick Leighton. *Wikimedia Commons*. {{PD-US-100}}.
Jonah Cast Forth by the Whale. Gustave Doré *Wikimedia Commons*. {{PD-US-70}}.
Euryalus taunts Odysseus. Padraic Colum. *The Adventures of Odysseus and The Tales of Troy*. Project Gutenberg. <http://www.gutenberg.org/files/16867/16867-h/16867-h.htm>.

Ch. 15, Thesis

Yes/No. *Pxhere*.
Space alien. *Needpix*.

Roman soldier. *Wikimedia Commons.* {{PD-US-80}}.
Lawyer. *Pixabay.*
Guitar player. *Pixabay.*
Hymnal. *Pixabay.*
Xenophon. *Wikimedia Commons.* {{PD-US-expired}}.

Ch. 16, Legislation

Law book. *Pixabay.*
Sign "prohibited." *Pixabay.*
No texting. *Pixabay.*
Voting. *Pixabay.*
Medicine. *Pixabay.*
Satellite dish. *Pixabay.*

ENDNOTES

[1] George A. Kennedy. *Progymnasmata: Greek Textbooks of Prose Composition and Rhetoric*. Atlanta: Society of Biblical Literature, 2003. xi–xii.

[2] Aesop. "The Crow and the Pitcher." *Fables of Aesop*. 14 Mar. 2019. Web. 30 July 2020. <fablesofaesop.com/the-crow-and-the-pitcher.html>.

[3] Aesop, *Aesop's and Other Fables*, 153.

[4] Aesop. "The Wind and the Sun." *Aesop's Fables*. New York: Allison, 1881. *Litscape.com*, 31 July 2013
< http://www.litscape.com/author/Aesop/The_Wind_And_The_Sun.html>.

[5] Aesop. "The Fox and the Crow." Trans. Vernon Jones. New York: Doubleday, 1912. 6. *Project Gutenberg*. 27 Feb. 2004. Web. 14 June 2020. <https://www.gutenberg.org/files/11339/11339-h/11339-h.htm#THE_FOX_AND_THE_CROW>.

[6] George A. Kennedy, ed. "The Preliminary Exercises of Aphthonius the Sophist." *Progymnasmata: Greek Textbooks of Prose Composition and Rhetoric*." Atlanta: Society of Biblical Literature, 2003. 96.

[7] Kennedy. "The Preliminary Exercises Attributed to Hermogenes." 75.

[8] The paraphrase is based on the following source: Herodotus. *The History of Herodotus*. Trans. George Rawlinson. 1.36-40. *Internet Archive*. 1994-2009. Web. 18 July 2019.
<https://archive.org/details/herodotus00herouoft/page/n55/mode/2up/search/croesus>.

[9] Kennedy. "*The Preliminary Exercises* of Nicolaus the Sophist." 136-37.

[10] "The Beautiful Athlete, Atalanta," *Buzzle*. 2000-2010, 5 July 2010 <http://www.buzzle.com/articles/greek-mythology-for-kids/>.

[11] Davy Crockett "The Tale of Sally Crockett." *Activated Storytellers*, 6 July 2010
<https://activatedstorytheatre.com/folktales/davy_crockett.html.>.

[12] Plutarch. "Julius Caesar." *Plutarch's Lives*. Trans. John Dryden. *Internet Classics Archive*, 1994–2009. Web. 6 July 2010 <http://classics.mit.edu/ Plutarch/caesar/>.

[13] Hamlin Garland. *Boy Life on the Prairie*. New York: Macmillan, 1899. 1-7. Google Books. 25 Nov. 2008. Web. 7 Aug. 2019. <https://play.google.com/books/reader?id=-9A3AAAAYAAJ&printsec=frontcover&pg=GBS.PA1>.

[14] Stephen Crane, *The Red Badge of Courage*, ed. Arthur Smith and Al Haines. 23 March 2013
<http://www.gutenberg.org/files/73/73-h/73-h.htm>.

[15] Leonard Q. Ross. "The Path through the Cemetery." *Saturday Review*. 29 November 1941. Web. 29 Apr 2014. <https://docs.google.com/viewer?url=http://64.62.200.70/PERIODICAL/PDF/SaturdayRev-1941nov29/12-13/&pli=1>.

[16] Homer. *Odyssey*. Trans. Samuel Butler. London: Longmans, 1900. 85. *Google Books*. 17 Sept. 2012. Web. 15 May 2020. <https://www.google.com/books/edition/_/LjU1AQAAMAAJ?hl=en&gbpv=1>.

[17] Thomas Bulfinch. "Pyramus and Thisbe." *Bulfinch's Mythology: The Age of Fable*. *Online Literature*. N.p. Web. 13 May 2020. <http://www.online-literature.com/bulfinch/mythology_fable/>.

[18] Plato. *The Republic*. Book 3. Trans. Benjamin Jowett. *The Internet Classics Archive*. N.d. Web. 18 May 2020. <http://classics.mit.edu/Plato/republic.4.iii.html>.

[19] Plutarch. *Life of Alexander*. Trans. John Evelyn. Dryden Series. Sections 21.1-21.6. 1683-86. *Livius*. 15 Oct. 2016. Web. 14 June 2019. <https://www.livius.org/sources/content/plutarch/plutarchs-alexander/alexander-and-the-wife-of-darius/>.

[20] Frank J. Wilstach, comp. *A Dictionary of Similes*. Boston: Little, 1916. *Bartleby.com*. 2010. Web. 19 June 2019. <www.bartleby.com/161/>.

[21] Brent Gleeson. "These Seven Motivational Navy SEAL Sayings Will Kick Your Butt into Gear." *Inc. 30 June 2015. Web. 19 June 2019.*
<https://www.inc.com/brent-gleeson/7-motivational-navy-seal-sayings-will-kick-your-butt-into-gear.html>.

[22] S. Michael Houdmann. "What Did Jesus Mean When He Said the Eye Is the Lamp of the Body? (Matthew 16:22). *GotQuestions.org*. Got Questions Ministries. N.d. Web. 17 Mar 2014. <http://www.gotquestions.org/eye-lamp-body.html#ixzz2u51Yb76U>.

[23] David P. Mikkelson. "Airport Granny." *Snopes*. 18 March 2007. Web. 5 Aug. 2020. <https://www.snopes.com/fact-check/go-granny-go/>.

[24] Mikkelson. "Mandarin Oranges Pesticide" *Snopes*. 7 Nov. 2010. Web. 5 Aug. 2020. <https://www.snopes.com/fact-check/the-mandarin-menace/>.

[25] "Does Drinking Cold Water after Meals Cause Cancer? *Snopes*. Web. 23 Aug. 2006. Web. 25 March 2013. <http://www.snopes.com>.

[26] Mikkelson. "Is 'Ring around the Rosie' about the Black Plague?" *Snopes* 17 Nov. 2000. Web. 5 Aug. 2020. <https://www.snopes.com/fact-check/ring-around-rosie/>.

[27] Livy. *From the Founding of the City*. Vol. 1. Trans. Rev. Canon Roberts [William Rasfen Roberts]. 2.12-2.13. London: Dent, 1905. *Wikisource*. 26 Aug 2915. Web. 18 Sep 2019. CC BY-SA 3.0 US. <https://en.wikisource.org/wiki/From_the_Founding_of_the_City/Book_2#12>.

[28] Plato, "Apology." Trans. Benjamin Jowett. Massachusetts Institute of Technology. 22 March 2011 <http://classics.mit.edu/Plato/apology.html >.

[29] Horatio Alger. "Honest Abe." *The Book of Virtues*. Ed. William J. Bennett (New York: Simon and Schuster, 1993) 620.

[30] Michael Newton, *Savage Girls and Wild Boys: A History of Feral Children* (New York: Thomas Dunne Books, 2003) 53-67.

[31] Herodotus. *History*. Vol. 2. Trans. George Rawlinson. London, 1862: 131-35. *Internet Archive*. 11 Dec. 2007. Web. 21 Feb. 2020. <https://archive.org/details/in.ernet.dli.2015.500096/page/n151/mode/2up>.

[32] "Nile Shipwreck Discovery Proves Herodotus Right – after 2,469 Years." *The Guardian*. 17 Mar. 2019. Web. 20 Feb. 2020. <https://www.theguardian.com/science/2019/mar/17/nile-shipwreck-herodotus-archaeologists-thonis-heraclion>.

[33] S. Michael Houdmann, ed. "Was Jonah Truly Swallowed by a Whale?" *Got Questions*. 2 Jan. 2020. Web. 18 Feb. 2020. Used with permission. <https://www.gotquestions.org/Jonah-whale.html>.

[34] Plutarch. "Life of Alexander." *Plutarch's Lives*. Trans. John Dryden. Ed. A. H. Clough, 30 July 2011. Light editing has been done for educational purposes. <http://www.gutenberg.org/cache/epub/674/pg674.html>.

[35] "Horse." *New World Encyclopedia*. 21 Sep. 2018. Web. 19 Feb. 2020. CC-by-SA 3.0. <https://www.newworldencyclopedia.org/entry/Horse> <http://creativecommons.org/licenses/by-sa/3.0/>.

[36] E. H. Plumptre. "Notes." *Lazarus and Other Poems*. London, 1884. 208-209. *Google Books*. 9 Oct. 2007. Web. 13 May 2020. <https://www.google.com/books/edition/_/qOENAAAAQAAJ?hl=en&gbpv=1>.

[37] Jeff Dixon. "Who Was the Naked Guy in the Garden of Gethsemane?" *The Church @ 434*. 8 Apr. 2010. Web. 11 May 2020. <https://touchandchange.com/who-was-the-naked-guy-in-the-garden-of-gethsemane/>.

[38] Henry Spence-Jones and Joseph Exell. "Mark 14:52 – Mark 14:53. *The Pulpit Commentary*. 7: N.p. Newark: Delmarva, 2013. *Google Books*. 14 Aug. 2015. Web. 12 May 2020. <https://books.google.com/books?id=s1VcCgAAQBAJ&pg=PT3649&lpg=PT3649&dq=#v=onepage&q&f=false>.

[39] Shakespeare. *Julius Caesar*. *Folger Shakespeare Library*. 2.1.22–28. N.d. Web. 7 Aug. 2020. <https://shakespeare.folger.edu/shakespeares-works/julius-caesar/act-2-scene-1/>.

[40] "An Homily against Gluttony and Drunkenness," *Sermons or Homilies, Appointed to be Read in Churches during the Time of Queen Elizabeth*, 3rd ed. (Oxford: Clarendon, 1814) 248, Google Books. 25 March 2013 <http://www.googlebooks.com>.

[41] Karen P. Tandy, "Speech against Drug Abuse," International Conference on Tackling Drug Abuse, Hong Kong, China S. A. R., 23 February 2003, U.S. Department of Justice, 25 March 2013 <http://www.justice.gov/dea/pr/speeches-testimony/2005/s022305p.html>.

[42] Aphthonius, *Progymnasmata*. Kennedy, *Progymnasmata*. 81, 106-108.

[43] Pliny the Elder, *The Natural History*, trans. John Bostock and H. T. Riley (London: Taylor and Francis, 1855) 29.1–27, *Perseus*, 6 May 2013 <http://www.perseus.tufts.edu>.

[44] Sirach 44:1–15. Taken from *The Catholic Edition of the Revised Standard Version of the Bible*, copyright 1965, 1966 by the Division of Christian Education of the National Council of the Churches of Christ in the United States of America. Used by permission. All rights reserved.

[45] John Foxe. *Foxe's Book of Martyrs*.49-50. *Project Gutenberg*. 25 Aug. 2>.007. Web. 6 Aug. 2020. <https://www.gutenberg.org/files/22400/22400-h/22400-h.htm>.

[46] Homer, *Odyssey*.

[47] Kennedy, *Progymnasmata*, 81.

[48] Kennedy, *Progymnasmata*, 81.

[49] Plato. The Republic. Book II. Trans. Benjamin Jowett. *Project Gutenberg.* 22 June 2016. Web. 7 Aug. 2020. <https://www.gutenberg.org/files/1497/1497-h/1497-h.htm#link2H_4_0005>.

[50] Suetonius, "Nero," *The Lives of the Twelve Caesars.* Trans. Alexander Thomson, ed. J. Eugene Reed (Philadelphia: Gebbie, 1889), *Perseus,* 30 July 2013 <http://perseus.tufts.edu>.

[51] Suetonius, "Nero."

[52] Suetonius, "Nero."

[53] Suetonius, "Nero."

[54] Cornelius Tacitus. *The Annals.* Trans. Alfred John Church, ed. William Jackson Broadribb New York: Random House, 1942), XV.44, *Perseus,* 30 July 2013 <http://perseus.tufts.edu>.

[55] See also Suetonius, *The Lives of the Twelve Caesars,* trans. by J. C. Rolfe, *Loeb Classical Library,* vol. 2. Cambridge, MA: Harvard UP, 1914. *Penelope.* University of Chicago. 15 Nov. 2010. Web. 16 Aug 2020. <http://penelope.uchicago.edu/Thayer/E/Roman/Texts/Suetonius/12Caesars/Nero*.html>.

[56] Aphthonius. *Progymnasmata, Thesaurus Linguae Graecae.* N.d. Web. 6 July 2012. <http://stephanus.tlg.uci.edu>. Excerpt translated for this volume by Amy Alexander.

[57] William Shakespeare. *Julius Caesar.* 1.2.92-133. *Play Shakespeare.* <https://www.playshakespeare.com/julius-caesar/scenes/act-i-scene-2>.

[58] Apollonius of Rhodes. *Argonautica.* Trans. R. C. Seaton. *Project Gutenberg.* 8 Nov. 2004. Web. 3 Aug. 2020. <http://www.gutenberg.org/cache/epub/13977/pg13977-images.html>.

[59] William Shakespeare, *Romeo and Juliet, Folger Shakespeare Library.* 2.2.36-52. N.d. Web. 24 May 2013. <https://shakespeare.folger.edu/shakespeares-works/romeo-and-juliet/act-2-scene-2/>.

[60] Sophocles. *Antigone.* Trans. F. Storr. Loeb Classical Library. (Cambridge, MA: Harvard University Press, 1912), 19 July 2012 <http://sophocles.thefreelibrary.com/Antigone/3-1-2>.

[61] William Shakespeare. *Macbeth.* Massachusetts Institute of Technology. N.d. Web. 29 March 2014. <http://shakespeare.mit.edu/macbeth/macbeth.1.5.html>.

[62] "Euryalus Incites Odysseus." *The Adventures of Odysseus and The Tales of Troy.* Trans. Padraic Colum New York: Macmillan, 1918. *Bartleby.* 2000. Web. 15 Jun 2013 <www.bartleby.com/75/>.

[63] Xenophon. *Anabasis.* Trans. Carleton L. Brownson. Vol. 3. (Cambridge: Harvard UP, 1922). *Perseus.* Tufts. Loeb Classics. N.d. Web. 31 Mar. 2020. <www.perseus.tufts.edu/hopper/text?doc=Xen.%20Anab.%203.2&lang=original>.

[64] Martin's Act, Parliament of the United Kingdom, 1822, 12 March 2010. *Wikisource,* 10 Jan. 2011 <http://wikisource.org>.

[65] Todd C. Frankel.. "In Wealthy Ladue, Homeowners Want the One Thing They Can't Have: Gates," 16 Jan. 2011, *St. Louis Today.* 31 Jan. 2011. <http://www.stltoday.com/news/local/ metro/ article_4e1ae6be-b084-5d06-b6a0-7fcadcf570fd.html>.

[66] Chuck Humphrey/ "Ohio Gambling Laws: Ohio Revised Code Chapter XXIX," 1 January 2011, *Gambling Law U.S.,* 31 Jan. 2011. <http://www.gambling-law-us.com/State-Laws/Ohio/>.

[67] Kristin McAllister. "Police, City Officials Frustrated with Unclear Gambling Law." *Dayton Daily News,* Online Edition. 31 Jan. 2011. Web. 13 May 2020. <https://www.daytondailynews.com/news/local/police-city-officials-frustrated-with-unclear-gambling-law/8oP0uA2gR1L2Da7M0njv7M/>.

[68] Jeff Sessions. "DREAM Act Rewards Illegal Immigration." 9 Dec. 2010, *CNN.* 30 July 2013 <http://www.cnn.com/2010/OPINION/12/08/sessions.dream.act/index.html/>.

[69] H. R. 917: Sunshine in the Courtroom Act, 113th Congress (2013–2015), 28 February 2013, *Govtrack.us,* 5 Aug. 2013 <http://www.govtrack.us/congress/bills/113/hr917/text>.

[70] Gerald F. Uelmen, "The Five Hardest Lessons from the O. J. Trial," *Issues in Ethics.* 7.1 (1996). 5 Aug. 2013 <http://www.scu.edu/ethics/publications/iie/v7n1/lessons.html>.

[71] *Federal Rules of Criminal Procedure,* Rule 53, 1 Dec. 2002, *Legal Information Institute.* 5 Aug. 2013 <http://www.law.cornell.edu/rules/frcrmp/rule_53>.

Made in the USA
Columbia, SC
03 July 2025